Free Blacks in America, 1800–1860

A Wadsworth Series:
Explorations in the Black Experience

General Editors

John H. Bracey, Jr., Northern Illinois University
August Meier, Kent State University
Elliott Rudwick, Kent State University

American Slavery: The Question of Resistance
Free Blacks in America, 1800–1860
Blacks in the Abolitionist Movement
The Rise of the Ghetto
Black Matriarchy: Myth or Reality?
Black Workers and Organized Labor
The Black Sociologists: The First Half Century
Conflict and Competition: Studies in the Recent Black Protest
Movement

The anthologies in this series present significant scholarly work on particular aspects of the black experience in the United States. The volumes are of two types. Some have a "problems" orientation, presenting varying and conflicting interpretations of a controversial subject. Others are purely "thematic," simply presenting representative examples of the best scholarship on a topic. Together they provide guidelines into significant areas of research and writing in the field of Afro-American studies. The complete contents of all the books in the series are listed at the end of this volume.

Free Blacks in America, 1800–1860

Edited by

John H. Bracey, Jr.
Northern Illinois University

August Meier
Kent State University

Elliott Rudwick
Kent State University

Wadsworth Publishing
Company, Inc.
Belmont, California

Acknowledgments

The authors wish to express their appreciation to Mrs. Barbara Hostetler, Mrs. Patricia Kufta, and Miss Eileen Petric at Kent State University, for helping in the preparation of this manuscript, and to Miss Linda Burroughs and Mrs. Helen Peoples of the Kent State University Library. They are especially indebted to James G. Coke, former Director of the Kent State University Center for Urban Regionalism.

July 1970   *JHB*
AM
ER

L. C. Cat. Card No.: 74–154817
ISBN–0–534–00022–3
Printed in the United States of America

1 2 3 4 5 6 7 8 9 10—74 73 72 71

For
Henry N. Whitney and
Lawrence S. Kaplan

AM

Contents

Free Blacks in America, 1800–1860

Introduction

The ante-bellum free people of color were a pariah group. At best, they could be described, in John Hope Franklin's words, as "quasi-free Negroes." And during the first half of the nineteenth century, the status of free Negroes actually deteriorated, except perhaps in certain New England states.

In the South, of course, free blacks had never enjoyed many rights. As time passed, legislation grew more restrictive, and their status became increasingly similar to that of the slaves. Laws required the free Negro to carry on his person a certificate of freedom; without it he might be claimed as a slave. Migration to another Southern state was severely restricted, if not completely prohibited, by the 1830s. In the courtroom, free blacks could neither serve on juries nor give testimony against whites. If convicted, they were liable to punishment more severe than that imposed on white men, and they could even be sold into slavery. Their rights of assembly were also proscribed. Evening activities were subject to a curfew in many parts of the South, and meetings of benevolent societies and churches frequently required the presence of a respectable white person, or were forbidden altogether.

Turning to the North, a distinction should be made between the original states of the Union and those subsequently established further to the West. Inequalities before the law existed in the Northeast, but they were far more pervasive in the Old Northwest, where many white Southerners had settled. The Black Laws regulating the behavior of free Negroes in the Old Northwest were in fact based upon the slave codes of the Southern states. Nowhere in the Old Northwest or in the newer states beyond the Mississippi River could blacks exercise the right to vote or serve on juries; and in many of these states they could not testify in cases involving whites. These states also attempted to discourage black settlers by requiring them to present bonds of $500 or $1,000 guaranteeing that they would not disturb the peace or become public charges. Toward the end of the ante-bellum period, Illinois, Indiana, and Oregon excluded Negro migrants entirely. Only Ohio, after a long battle, repealed its restrictive immigration legislation in 1849. Though only erratically enforced, such anti-immigration statutes intimidated Negroes.

In the Northeast, none of the states provided by law for discrimination in the courtroom, and testimony of blacks was admissible in cases involving whites. Social custom, however, barred blacks from sitting on juries, except in a few cases in Massachusetts just prior to the Civil War. Negroes enjoyed the same voting rights as whites in all the original Northern states for about thirty years after the American Revolution. Then, one by one, between 1807 and 1837, five states — New Jersey, Connecticut, New York, Rhode Island, and Pennsylvania — enacted disfranchisement provisions, though in Rhode Island the prohibition was repealed in 1842.

Besides legal restrictions on voting rights and the courts, there were other forms of proscriptions. In Northern cities, the most extreme of these was mob violence.

During the 1830s and 1840s, riots occurred in Philadelphia, New York, Pittsburgh, Cincinnati, and elsewhere. More continuous and pervasive were the patterns of segregation and employment discrimination.

The Jim Crow or segregation laws were largely a product of the late nineteenth century. In the South, segregation developed as one of the devices to control the urban free blacks and the slave population. Separation in jails and hospitals was universal. Negroes were also widely excluded from public parks and burial grounds. They were relegated to the balconies of theaters and opera houses and barred from hotels and restaurants. The New Orleans street railway maintained separate cars for the two races. Such segregation by custom and even by statute was already common during the ante-bellum period.

In the North, blacks were not segregated by law in places of public accommodation, nor, except for schools, in publicly-owned institutions. Custom, however, barred them from hotels and restaurants, and they were segregated in — if not entirely excluded from — theaters, public lyceums, hospitals, and cemeteries. Traveling by public conveyance was difficult for blacks. On stagecoaches they usually rode on the outside seat; on the early railroads they often occupied filthy accommodations in a separate car; on steamboats they were required to sleep on deck even in cold weather.

In the Southern states, education of Negroes was usually forbidden, though small private schools and classes conducted by blacks themselves were never completely eliminated. The crusade that established free public schooling thoughout the Northern states by the 1830s left blacks pretty much out of the picture. In the Western states, Negroes received no public school funds until the middle of the century or later; where schools were available to them, they were generally separate and unequal. New York and Pennsylvania also provided for separate schools by law; elsewhere in the Northeast, school segregation was established by custom, and only in Massachusetts did blacks succeed in the 1850s in securing a statute outlawing separate schools.

Because of white prejudice and discrimination, the overwhelming majority of free Negroes were unskilled laborers. Black entrepreneurs found it difficult to obtain capital from white lending institutions. White businessmen were reluctant to employ blacks in skilled or white-collar work, and where they were willing to do so, whites often refused to work with them. In fact, the Negro skilled artisan faced greater obstacles in the North than in the South. Moreover, during the course of the nineteenth century, the position of the black artisan–entrepreneur deteriorated. As the white working class grew in numbers in the Southern cities, its members made determined efforts to exclude blacks from the better-paying occupations. In 1845, for example, Georgia made it a misdemeanor for a black mechanic to contract for repair or construction work in any building. And in the Northern states, the arrival of nearly five million white immigrants shortly before the Civil War posed an alarming threat to the Negroes' already meager employment opportunities. Gradually, many blacks were displaced by immigrants, especially the Irish, as longshoremen and railroad workers, hodcarriers, waiters, barbers, and even porters and bootblacks, while Negro women began losing positions as maids, cooks, and washerwomen. On the waterfront, economic competition and hostility between the two groups was exacerbated when employers, playing one race against the other, hired black workmen as strikebreakers. In New York City this policy produced among the predominantly Irish longshoremen an intense animosity that came to a violent climax in the bloody race riots of 1863.

Yet, despite these obstacles, a minority made a comfortable living and a few founded modest fortunes. The successful free black entrepreneurs catered mainly to well-to-do whites and were concentrated in the service trades. Negroes were also engaged in the shoemaking and the building trades especially in the South. In Philadelphia, sizeable numbers of blacks were carpenters, tailors and dressmakers, brickmakers, shoemakers and bootmakers, and cabinet makers. A handful of Negroes created and dominated the fashionable catering business in the city until the end of the nineteenth century. James Forten, one of the city's principal sailmakers, employed over forty white and black workers; by the 1830s, he had acquired a fortune of $100,000. William Still, the Underground Railroad leader, was the proprietor of a successful coal and lumber yard. In Charleston, as in certain other Southern cities, blacks monopolized barbering, practically controlled the building trades, and were prominent among the shoemakers and butchers. The more outstanding carpenters or contractors employed both white men and slaves. For years, the leading hotel proprietor was a free black named Jehu Jones. In 1850 New Orleans, with its five black jewelers, four physicians, an architect, and fifty-two merchants, exhibited an even greater occupational diversity. Not only in New Orleans, but in most cities, there was enough economic differentiation to provide the basis for a social class system. While the occupational distribution among elite blacks varied from city to city, usually at the top were the successful entrepreneurs, particularly the barbers, restauranteurs, caterers, tailors, and contractors patronized by fashionable whites; the house servants of the most socially prominent white families in the Northern cities; and the handful of well-educated professional people in law, teaching, medicine, and the ministry. In the South, this elite included a tiny slave-owning Negro aristocracy. These middle and upper classes stressed home ownership, thrift, hard work, and moral respectability.

This anthology consists of selections illustrating the social and economic status of the free black community in the generation before the Civil War. While these essays are studies of selected states and cities, they are representative of conditions in other parts of the country. Many important themes are necessarily omitted, particularly the institutional life of free blacks — their churches, mutual benefit societies, lodges, and literary associations — and their protest activities and organizations. One phase of their protest activities — their participation in the abolitionist movement — is the subject of another volume in this series.

The first five articles deal with various aspects of the life of free blacks in the South. Charles S. Sydnor's article on "The Free Negro in Mississippi before the

Civil War," though written by a white Southern scholar of an older generation, nevertheless graphically shows the disabilities under which free blacks lived. E. Horace Fitchett's paper describes the origins, economic attainments, and social organization of the free blacks of Charleston and also analyzes the way they functioned as a buttress to the system of slavery. Roger A. Fischer's essay on New Orleans deals with the early evidences of segregation of free Negroes in the South's largest city. John Hope Franklin's article on North Carolina describes the economic life of free blacks in an essentially rural setting of the upper South. Finally, illuminating conditions from a different angle, is Robert Brent Toplin's extraordinary case study of Peter Still, an Alabama slave, who secured freedom for himself and his family, despite the legal and social obstacles to emancipation.

The articles in Section Two — Carter G. Woodson's essay on Cincinnati, Julian Rammelkamp's description of Providence, Dixon Ryan Fox's analysis of black disfranchisement in New York, and Rudolph M. Lapp's discussion of blacks in gold rush California — illustrate varied aspects of Afro–American life in the states of the North and West. They deal both with the oppression blacks suffered and the economic achievements they made. The selection by Robert Austin Warner is a description of the leadership ranks of Negro society in an ante-bellum Northern city.

Finally, the volume concludes with a selection by Leon Litwack, demonstrating that not only states, cities, and individual citizens, but the federal government as well, had a calculated policy of discriminating against the free black population.

Free Blacks in
the South

1

The Free Negro in Mississippi before the Civil War

Charles S. Sydnor

Between the two great social classes in ante-bellum Mississippi, the whites and the slaves, there lived a third group composed of free negroes and mulattoes. Though this group was always comparatively small in Mississippi it received much attention from the white people — attention that was usually hostile and was caused by a lively apprehension of the potential dangers that lurked in the existence of this class.

A study of the laws passed by the state legislature for the government and control of the free colored element will afford partial evidence of the hostile and fearful attitude of the white people toward the free negro. Such an examination will also form the background of our knowledge of the social and civil condition of this same group, though this background will have to be modified and supplemented by other facts before our ideas of the status of the free negro will approach reality.

Probably the key to the condition of the free negro and mulatto[1] can be found in the assumption that all colored persons were considered slaves unless the contrary could be proved. This principle was most clearly stated at various times by the Supreme Court of Mississippi. In an opinion of this court it was held that "the laws of this state presume a negro *prima facie* to be a slave."[2] A few years later a lower court was upheld in certain instructions it had given to a jury, namely, that "if the jury believed that the plaintiff was a negro, it was *prima facie* evidence that he was a slave."[3]

This theory is apparent in laws that were passed at various times requiring free colored persons to procure certificates of their unshackled condition. The general substance of these laws can be given briefly.[4] Every free negro was required to present himself at court, county or probate, and give evidence of his non-servile condition. If the proof was satisfactory the court would have the negro supplied with a certified copy of the record. This certificate would show the name, color, stature, and any distinguishing features or scars of the recipient, and this bit of parchment was all that stood between the free negro and many possible troubles. The certificate had to be renewed every three years and each time there was a fee

Charles S. Sydnor, "The Free Negro in Mississippi before the Civil War," *American Historical Review* XXXII (July 1927), 769–788. Reprinted with permission of the American Historical Association.

of one dollar — in 1831 increased to three dollars. If a white man employed a negro who claimed to be free but who could not produce his certificate, the employer was subject to a fine of ten dollars.[5] And if any captain or master of a steamboat or other river craft employed an alleged free negro who was not supplied with the required certificate, he made himself liable to the very heavy fine of a thousand dollars and in addition a possible prison sentence of from six months to a year.[6]

As for the negro who could not produce his registered bit of paper or parchment, there was the danger of being seized by some unscrupulous white person and either held or sold as a slave.[7] Any alleged free negro who did not possess a certificate might be jailed, and upon failure to establish his freedom in a certain length of time the law required his sale at public auction.[8]

Not only was the free negro's continuation of his unshackled state dependent upon his certificate, but even after he obtained it his troubles were not over. This class was decidedly hampered in its freedom of movement. For instance, a free negro could not go to another county in search of employment without running the risk of being treated as a vagrant, for any free negro found outside his own county would be so treated unless he could show that he had some honest employment at the time.[9] Furthermore, no firearms, ammunition, or military weapon could be kept by a free negro without a license which was voidable at any time.[10]

Limitations were also placed on this class in vocational and other directions. It was illegal for a free person of color to sell any goods — whether his own or as agent for another — in any place other than in the incorporated towns of the state.[11] Even in the towns there were some goods that a free negro could not sell, such as groceries and spirituous liquors. The business of keeping a house of entertainment was also closed to this class.[12] The risks that a boatmaster ran in employing a free negro, who did not have a certificate, to some extent militated against the free negro in this industry. It is probable that the interstate movements of this business required strict regulation so far as negroes were concerned, to prevent the possible escape of slaves. One more industry that was closed to all negroes, bond or free, was that of typesetting in a printing establishment. The employer was liable to a penalty of ten dollars a day for each negro he employed.[13] The idea behind this regulation can be better understood if we remember that a very heavy penalty was attached to printing or circulating any literature intended to create unrest and dissatisfaction in the slave population. Death was the penalty for a free negro or mulatto who broke this law.[14]

The civil and political status of the free negro differed from that of his slave brother chiefly in the fact that the slave could not own property while the free negro could.[15] The free negro did not have the right to vote, to serve on a jury, or to be a witness in a case in which a white person was a party. But negroes or mulattoes, whether slave or free, were competent witnesses in criminal cases against negroes or in civil pleas where free negroes or mulattoes should alone be parties.[16] An instance of the general knowledge and understanding of these limitations on the free negroes can be found in the case of Raby *et al. v.* Batiste *et ux.*[17] It was alleged that a man named Augustine was a mulatto and the settlement of this racial point was necessary in disposing of certain property. In proving that he actually was of mixed blood, witnesses were produced who testified that he did not vote, or act as a juror, and never testified against white men in court.

The Supreme Court of Mississippi experienced considerable difficulty in finding a satisfactory norm for deciding certain cases involving the property rights of free negroes.[18] If a negro were legally emancipated in the state the case offered no difficulties for as we have stated above the right of such a person to hold property was settled favorably. But it was a different matter if the free status had been attained in contravention to the laws and policy of the state. As an example of this the case of Nancy Wells may be stated. Nancy was a mulatto slave who was emancipated by her owner in Ohio in the year 1846. This was entirely legal, but her return to Mississippi a year and a half later was not. She worked as a free servant in the home of her former owner for a short time and then married a negro barber of Jackson, Mississippi, whose name was Watts. The latter was also a free negro. For some reason Nancy left her barber husband and returned to Ohio in 1851. In the meantime Nancy's master died in 1848 and left some property to her. This part of the will was contested and it finally became necessary for the highest court in the state to decide whether the bequest should be delivered to her. In a lengthy and exceedingly interesting opinion in April, 1859, the court ruled against Nancy.

The Dred Scott decision, the difference between national and state citizenship, and the application of international comity to the relation existing between the sovereign states of the Union were some of the interesting points discussed in this case. Briefly, the court held as follows. Following the line of argument presented in the Dred Scott case, an African has never been a citizen of the United States. On the other hand, any one of the sovereign states may confer state citizenship upon a negro; but a sister state has an equal right to decide what will be the effect of this act within her territories. The laws of one state having no extraterritorial operation in another state, the enforcement of these laws in the latter state depends on the comity of nations. But international comity does not require the enforcement of the act of a foreign state if this act is contrary to the laws or policy of the first state. Since the policy of Mississippi was to preserve slavery and to prevent emancipation, the action of Ohio in emancipating Nancy Wells was not binding in the state of Mississippi. Since this meant that Nancy was still considered a slave by the state of Mississippi, she could not, so far as that state was concerned, possess any property.

Part of this argument was reinforced by a different line of reasoning, which shows the venom that was creeping into the feeling of Mississippi toward the Northern states. The court practically stated that international comity no longer existed between Mississippi and Ohio, because the latter was constantly committing acts that were against the policy of Mississippi by freeing slaves from the latter state, making them citizens of Ohio, and even conniving at the escape of slaves.[19]

This interesting subject might be pursued at much greater length. Only one other instance will be given, that of a mulatto named Marcelette Marceau who was the widow of one Chatteau. She had once been a citizen of Louisiana and had been illegally brought into Mississippi from New Orleans. Though she had probably never seen Africa, the Mississippi courts held that she was a citizen of Africa. Since international law applied only between civilized nations and Africa was not in this category, the comity of nations would not operate in her behalf. As she had entered Mississippi contrary to the laws of the state she was classed as an alien enemy *prohibita* and was entitled to none of the privileges of a citizen.[20]

These cases, decided shortly before the Civil War, show the handicaps of the free colored race in their largest proportions. Earlier cases had not been decided so completely against negroes in the same class as those given above.[21] And through this whole discussion it must be remembered that the right of a free negro to acquire or hold property was never questioned, provided the free status had been attained within the state of Mississippi by some legal method. It was only where a free negro illegally entered the state or was emancipated in another state that this right was denied, and even in this latter case it was not uniformly withheld.

There were several ways by which the class of free negroes and mulattoes was increased. It was unconstitutional for a slave to be set free without the consent of the owner unless some distinguished service had been rendered by the slave to the state.[22] No case has been found where a slave was freed under this clause of the state constitution.

The basic provision concerning the emancipation of slaves occurred in a law that was passed June 18, 1822. According to this act, slaves might be manumitted by will or by a properly witnessed and recorded document, if it could be proved to the satisfaction of the state legislature that some meritorious act had been done by the slave for the owner or for the state. A special act of the legislature was necessary to validate each proposed emancipation.[23] The annoyance of getting such a special bill passed probably acted as a deterrent in some cases. It was also doubtless difficult to persuade the legislature to a belief in the meritorious act of the slave. It is interesting to note that in the year following the passage of this act, that is, in 1823, only three negroes were granted their freedom under the terms of this law. Petitions were introduced requesting the emancipation of about twice this number.[24] Generally speaking, the legislature granted such petitions very sparingly. For example, in 1826 the legislature was requested to pass bills manumitting twelve slaves. None of these passed. Similarly, five years later petitions were introduced praying the emancipation of at least ten slaves, and here again the legislature was adamant.[25]

Although only a minority of the proposed emancipations were allowed to take effect, the legislature did empower some of the petitioners to free certain specified slaves. In practically all cases security had to be given that the ex-slave would be of good behavior and would not become a public charge. Among the several instances that could be cited of slaves set free by petition of the owner and a special act of the legislature,[26] we find that Lewis and Nancy, slaves of ex-Governor David Holmes, were started on their path of freedom by the will of the ex-governor.[27]

Another case of emancipation that deserves to be remembered can be best told by quoting the act of the legislature.

An Act, to emancipate Bill, a person of color.

Whereas, William Smith, of the county of Hancock, was in his early childhood, by the dispensations of Heaven, deprived of his parents and thrown on the cold charities of the world, with no other patrimony than the negro slave hereinafter mentioned, who by his unwearied industry and fidelity, sustained his young master through this helpless season of life, and enabled him to acquire an education adequate to discharge the various duties of a free citizen, and in addition hath accumulated for his master property sufficient to enable him to obtain an easy competency: Therefore, on the petition of the said Smith,

Sec. 1. *Be it enacted by the Senate and House of Representatives of the State of Mississippi, in General Assembly convened,* That William Smith, of the county of Hancock, be, and he is hereby authorized to emancipate from the bonds of slavery, his negro man named Bill, saving the rights of creditors, and provided that the said Smith shall give bond to the state of Mississippi, with good and sufficient surety, to be approved by the county court of said county, and recorded by the clerk thereof, in the penal sum of one thousand dollars conditioned for the good behavior of the said Bill, and that he shall not become a public charge.[28]

Since we are here interested only in the free colored and mulatto population of Mississippi, it is not necessary to discuss the laws governing the emancipation of slaves who were removed from the state. Some were returned to their native land, Africa.[29] Others were removed to free states and there emancipated. Before 1842 there was very little objection and no legal obstacle to manumission under the condition that the negro stay outside the state after obtaining his freedom.[30] But though there was up to 1842 no legal objection to a slave-owner taking any number of slaves to Ohio or some other free state and there giving them their freedom, it was illegal at all times for these freedmen to return to Mississippi.[31]

Nevertheless, this law was sometimes broken, and those who were freed outside the state and then returned were examples of a second, although illegal, method of increasing the free negro population of the state. Instances of this can be given, but it is difficult to give any estimate of the total number of infractions. Those who most successfully evaded the law received the least attention. One rather notorious case was that of a slave-owner who carried with him to Ohio a negro woman and her son, there freed them and brought them back to Mississippi with him, and willed all his property to the boy. The courts held that the negress and her son were still slaves,[32] but the fact remains that to all intents and purposes they were free negroes from the time they returned from Ohio to the day their former master died. They would probably have so continued had not the property involved brought the case before the court.[33]

Rarely, a slave would be brought into Mississippi whose term of slavery was limited to a definite period of time. For instance, Mary Kenny, of Kentucky, willed that a slave by the name of Sam should be free when he became thirty-one years old.[34] If such a will had been made in Mississippi it would have had no force, unless the legislature had also passed a special act. Yet this same will, made in Kentucky and in accordance with the laws of that state, would operate to procure the freedom of Sam.[35] Cases such as these would give additional increments to the free colored population.

Still another mode of illegally adding to the size of the free colored class was simply to turn a slave loose, without either the prerequisite act of the legislature to sanction it, or the illegal ruse of first freeing the slave on free soil and then allowing the slave to return to the state. An interesting commentary on this state of affairs is to be found in a letter to a Natchez paper. The letter, which follows, was signed "Civis."

Agreeably to the provisions of the act of December 20, 1831, still in full force, no negro or slave is permitted to be manumitted or set free, and still remain in the State, without the special action of the legislature of this State. All manumissions made otherwise are null and void, unless the slave so manumitted leave the State, never to return: and as soon as he returns, by that very act, he forfeits his freedom and becomes again liable as a slave, to the creditors of the last owner, by whom, it is pretended, he is manumitted. In this condition we believe are at least fifty negroes and mulattoes now in Adams County, who affect to be free. It is a matter of notoriety, that within the last five years, a large number of slaves in this county have been thus illegally manumitted; and after having gone up the river, set foot upon the soil of Ohio or some other free or abolition State, received from them certain certificates, which are called "free papers"; forthwith they return to Mississippi, to reside as "free people of color." In many instances, we believe, the Probate Courts disregarding, or misapprehending the spirit and intention, as well as the plain letter of the law, in such cases, have granted to them certificates as required by the act of December 20, 1831, after having taken bonds and security as prescribed by the act. In this they have defeated the very object of the law, viz: the non-accumulation of free negroes in the State.

Such as do return, are liable under the law, to be taken up and sold by the sheriff as slaves.[36]

Another instance of this way of adding to the free colored population should be given at some length because of the light it throws on several phases of the free negro question. An Adams County slave, Fanny Leiper, was set free by her master some time before the year 1834. Her owner went through none of the legal requirements in this matter. He simply ceased to command her as a slave and gave her her freedom, informally, if the expression may be used, but, so far as he was concerned, completely.

Fanny was a mulatto of considerable ability, for she bought a lot in Natchez in 1834 for $175, and within two years she had built and paid for a house valued at $1500. There she resided for about ten years, until 1845, when she moved to Cincinnati, Ohio. She did not sell her property, but appointed R. S. Hammitt of Natchez to be her agent in renting the house. But Fanny was not long in her new surroundings before she had to return to Natchez because of a dispute that had arisen concerning the house and lot.

When the last payment had been made on the house in 1836, an attorney had advised Fanny to have the deed drawn jointly to herself and some white person. This advice was given, and in fact followed, because of the strong feeling in the state at that time against the free colored class. So Fanny had the deed drawn jointly to herself and to a Mr. Joseph Winscott, a river steamboat engineer who was occasionally in Natchez, but whose residence was in New Orleans. Though Fanny had the deed framed in this way, she very shrewdly took no occasion to inform Winscott of this. However, she several times discussed the whole affair with Malvina Hoffman, her next-door neighbor, who was also a free woman and colored.

After Fanny's departure to Cincinnati, Malvina took the part of the villain. She told Winscott of the joint deed to the property, and in conjunction they fraudulently secured the keys to the house from Fanny's agent, rented the house, and divided the spoils.

When Fanny returned and brought suit for her property Malvina and Winscott answered that Fanny had never been legally emancipated, and was therefore a slave and incapable of holding property. The case was appealed to the Supreme Court of the state, where Fanny was entirely upheld in her plea. In the decision of the court it was held that since Fanny's master recognized her as a free person, and since she had moved to Ohio — apparently a *bona fide* removal — she was really a free person and capable of holding property. After stating that "the conduct of the defendant Winscott, as it appears from his answer, would commend him as little to favorable consideration in a court of equity, as in good morals; and the position of the defendant Hoffman does not appear to be much more commendable," the premises were ordered returned to Fanny, together with any rents and profits that had accrued since it was out of her control.[37]

Free negroes occasionally came into Mississippi from other states, although this was against the public policy of the state as expressed in her laws. The re-enactment of any law with increased penalties implies that infractions of the law had taken place, and the law of 1822[38] which made it unlawful for free negroes or mulattoes to immigrate to Mississippi was strengthened and the penalties made more rigorous in 1842.[39] One instance of the breaking of this law we have already mentioned, namely the case of Marcelette Marceau. Certain phases of the affair should be mentioned here because of their bearing on this law and because they illustrate public opinion in this regard.

It will be remembered that Marcelette was a mulatto who had been a citizen of Louisiana and had illegally immigrated to Mississippi. Though her skin was not much darker than that of a white person, her hair was kinky and she generally kept it covered. It might be stated that if her character was at all a fair example of that of her class, the law against the immigration of free colored people into Mississippi could hardly have been too harshly enforced. But the law was not enforced at all in her case. Had it been, she should have received thirty-nine lashes and been ordered to leave the state under pain of sale into slavery. Instead she lived on terms of equality with certain white people and eventually had three or four slaves bequeathed to her. The court, however, did not allow her to possess this estate. But here is one of the remarkable facts in this affair. Although the people of Pass Christian, where Marcelette lived, seriously considered ejecting her from the community, no steps seem to have been taken to prosecute her under the law forbidding the immigration of free persons of color to Mississippi.[40]

Occasional cases can be found in which a free negro was allowed to remain in the state in spite of the fact that he could not meet the usual legal requirements. Special acts of the legislature permitted this from time to time.[41] The reason for this leniency is usually not stated, but in one case we find that permission to remain in the state was given to "a free man of color, named Alexander Reed, in consideration of services rendered by him in the war with Mexico."[42]

Since legal emancipation was difficult to consummate, and illegal manumission was beset with dangers, at least one attempt was made to provide virtual freedom but to leave the legal status of the slave unchanged. The will of Lewis Weathersby endeavored to do this for Tom and Lucy, who are mentioned in the following lines.

I give and bequeath to my son Ludovick, my servants Tom and Lucy, and their children, Matilda, Sylvester, Andrew, and Dicey, in trust and under the following conditions, viz.: I do hereby enjoin it upon my said son, to make the said slaves as comfortable in life as possible; that he furnish them and their children with a house separate from others; that he provide a horse, farming utensils, and a small tract of land for their use; that he sell their crops, furnish them with a milch cow and two hundred pounds of sugar, and one hundred pounds of coffee, yearly; and that, in consideration of these things, he shall require of them reasonable service, and should Tom and Lucy at any time be able to raise a sum of money sufficient to compensate said Ludovick, say three hundred dollars for each of their daughters, Matilda and Dicey, then he shall give up said Matilda and Dicey to said Tom and Lucy, to serve and comfort them in their old age.[43]

When this case was brought before the courts it was held that the bequest to Ludovick was valid, but that the attendant conditions were not binding.

A final mode by which the free colored class in Mississippi increased was through children of free parents. The child of a free negro or mulatto woman was of course free.

By way of summary, the free negro element in Mississippi could be legally recruited by emancipation within the state in the way provided by act of the legislature, by the birth of a child to free parents, by the lapse of the term of servitude of a slave coming from another state, or occasionally under other conditions when legalized by special act of the legislature. The class could be illegally augmented by a master freeing his slave without going through the procedure required by law, and by the immigration of free negroes into the state — whether *bona fide* free negroes, or Mississippi slaves who had been taken to a free state, there manumitted and then returned to the state.

In spite of the various ways of increasing the free negro class within the state of Mississippi, this element was never large. In the year immediately preceding the induction of Mississippi into the Union, there were 235 free persons of color within the state.[44] In 1860 the number of this same class was 773. However, the growth of this element in Mississippi's population was not gradual and regular, and the number of free persons of color at the chronological terminals of the period 1816 to 1860 can not be taken as the extreme limits of the size of this group. Reference to the table below[45] shows that the free negro class increased from 240 in the year 1810 to 458 a decade later. This increase was evidently considered alarming, for in 1822 laws were passed prohibiting emancipation except by a special act of the legislature, prohibiting the immigration of free negroes into the state, and circumscribing the life and activity of those within the commonwealth.[46] The result of these laws was to diminish the increase in this class between 1820 and 1830 to only 13.3 per cent. In the previous decade it had been 90.8 per cent.

But between 1830 and 1840 the enforcement of these laws must have been relaxed, although there was a law passed in 1831 requiring all free negroes between the ages of 16 and 50 to leave the state within ninety days on pain of being sold into slavery for five years.[47] But the force of this was largely taken away by the proviso that all who could prove to the probate court that they were good characters and not in the class of undesirables would be given a license allowing them to remain.

The number of free negroes and mulattoes reached the high-water mark of 1,366 in the year 1840, an increase of 163.2 per cent in ten years. Again it was felt necessary to enact laws to limit the increase of this class, and in 1842 these laws were forthcoming. If a free negro entered Mississippi from some other state it was required that he be whipped and ordered to depart within twenty days on pain of being sold as a slave.[48] This bit of anti-slavery legislation seems to have been efficacious for in 1850 there was evident an actual decrease of 31.9 per cent since the last census, and in 1860 the number of free negroes and mulattoes had further decreased to 773.

The comparatively small increase in the size of this group from 1800 to 1860 is an indication of the hindrances placed about their class. In this period the free negro part of the population increased only 324.72 per cent while the total population of the state grew 8,841.3 per cent.[49] A variety of reasons can be adduced to explain the slow growth of this part of Mississippi's population. On the one hand, the prohibition of the immigration of free negroes operated against any great increase of this class, and on the other hand, the difficulties incident to manumitting slaves helped to keep the number of free negroes small. Furthermore, restrictive and hostile legislation was doubtless the cause of the departure of some members of the class to other regions, and a few were probably resold into slavery because of infractions of the laws of the state.

A final cause of the slow growth of this class lay in the occasional voluntary return of a free negro into slavery. In a single session of the legislature of Mississippi bills were passed to enable three negroes to effect this change of status. Jim Wall, a negro, was empowered to become the slave of Daniel Williams, both of whom were residents of Wilkinson County. In Tallahatchie County, William Webster was authorized to attach himself as a slave to Dr. Atherald Ball. In the third instance both of the parties were women of Hinds County. Ann Mataw, a free woman of color, was given the right to become the slave of Elizabeth G. Purdom. The difference in the terminology of these acts is small. One of these we will quote because of the light it sheds on the procedure used in voluntarily assuming the rank of a slave.

An Act for the relief of James Wall, a free man of color.

Section 1. *Be it enacted by the Legislature of the State of Mississippi,* That Jim Wall, a free man of color, of the county of Wilkinson, be, and he is hereby authorized, to become the slave for life of Daniel Williams of said county, and for that purpose may appear before the police court of said county, by petition or otherwise, setting forth his desire to become such slave.

Section 2. *Be it further enacted,* That should the said Daniel Williams appear in said police court, at the time of said application by the said Jim Wall, or at any time thereafter, and signify his assent to become the master of the said Jim Wall, it shall be the duty of said police court to order and decree the said Jim Wall to be the slave for life of the said Daniel Williams, as fully to all intents and purposes as other slaves are held in fee simple, giving to the said Daniel Williams as full, and complete and absolute ownership of the said Jim Wall as if the said Jim Wall had been born the slave of the said Daniel Williams, subject to all the laws of descent and distribution in the State.

Section 3. *Be it further enacted,* That this act take effect and be in force from and after its passage.

Approved, February 11, 1860.[50]

In regard to the habitat of the free colored people of Mississippi, there are two outstanding points. In the first place, a disproportionate number of this class lived in the southwestern corner of the state, and in the second place, a rather large proportion were to be found in the cities and towns.

In 1816, one year before Mississippi became a state of the Union, there were fourteen counties in the territory that is now contained within the bounds of the state. An east and west line marking off the southern quarter of the state would include twelve of these counties. The other two, Claiborne and Warren, bordered the Mississippi River and extended a little north of this imaginary line. It is interesting to note that Adams County, in almost the extreme southwestern corner of the present State of Mississippi, contained over half of the free negroes within the territory.[51] Half of the counties did not have more than one free person of color.

In 1840, which marks the highest number of free colored persons in Mississippi at any of the census years, the problem was essentially a local one. There were at this time in the state 1,366 free negroes and mulattoes and 572 of these could be found in only four of the fifty-six counties.[52] These four counties were in the southwest and all bordered the Mississippi River. Adding a few of the adjoining counties, we find that considerably more than half of the free negroes within the state lived in the relatively small area that we have just mentioned.[53] It is thus evident that the problem created by this class was of peculiar concern to these few counties. The difficulty was further aggravated by the fact that in this section of the state the slaves were considerably more numerous than the whites.[54] Anything that might cause unrest among the slaves was a source of grave apprehension to their owners, and it was felt that free negroes did cause some trouble.

A second fact of some interest in regard to the habitat of the free colored people is the relatively large number of these people who lived in the towns and cities of the state. In 1840 the two counties in Mississippi with the largest number of this class were Adams and Warren. The total number of free persons of color in the first named county was 283, and 207 of this number were residents of the city of Natchez. In comparing this with the whites and slaves, we find that ten per cent of the slaves in Adams County lived in the city of Natchez, 57 per cent of the whites, and 73 per cent of the free colored. Almost the same state of affairs existed in Vicksburg in this year. Vicksburg contained 71 of the 104 free persons of color residing within the county.[55] Ten years later, when Adams County was the home of 258 free colored persons, only 45 of the number lived outside the bounds of Natchez. The remaining 213 were city dwellers.[56]

No data have been found on which to draw conclusions regarding the place of residence of free negroes in other counties in the state. The laws that we have mentioned[57] prohibiting free negroes from vending any goods outside the limits of towns would, however, probably have some effect in the direction of keeping this class within the urban sections of the state.

Some information has already been presented concerning the life and occupations of several members of the free colored class. It is well at this point to supplement this information. A good many members of this element of society attained a position well above that of the lowest economic plane of life. For example, in 1830 there were 519 free persons of color in Mississippi, and seventeen of this number were not only themselves free, but even owned slaves. Including the families of free negro slave-owners, 45, or about one-eleventh of all the free negroes in the state, were either slave-owners or members of a slave-owning family. From one to seven-teen was the range in the number of negroes possessed by colored masters, and the average size of these estates was about four and one-third slaves.[58]

One of those listed in the census of 1830 as a free negro slave-owner was Christopher Holly of Claiborne County. In the year just mentioned he possessed three slaves. Shortly before 1859 he died and left eight heirs, three of whom were minors who wished to sell their shares in the estate and move to another state. A special act was passed by the legislature to enable them to do this, and the proviso was attached that the shares should not be sold for less than twenty-one hundred dollars each — a figure that indicates that the estate of Christopher Holly was of considerable size.[59]

Samuel Gilson, who lived in Natchez, was another colored master in 1830. At that date his slaves were five in number. Fourteen years later Gilson carried his slaves, now increased by one addition, to Cincinnati, Ohio, and there emancipated them and settled them on free territory.[60]

In addition to farming, it is very probable that many free negroes found a means of livelihood on the various types of river craft.[61] At least two others were barbers. Watts, a colored barber of Jackson about 1848, has already been mentioned. The leading barber at Natchez in the years just before the Civil War was a free negro named McCarey. As a sideline, he taught a school, the pupils consisting of the offspring of others of his own class. His own children attended this school, and one of his sons, William, was subsequently sheriff of Adams County in the Reconstruction period.[62] Free negroes were occasionally found doing odd jobs of one sort or another such as cutting wood to be used at the capitol during the meeting of the state legislature.[63]

Numerous laws have been mentioned in this paper that show the circumscribed condition of the free negroes. Since these laws were made by the white people of the state, it is evident that the latter class did not look on the free colored people of the state with any favor. Regardless of the character of those within this class, it was felt by the whites that the mere existence of a free negro class operated as a perpetual reminder to the slaves of their own servile condition, and further suggested to them the possibility of a change from this state. We do not have to depend entirely on the laws of the state to show the feeling of the white people against the free negroes; for the same state of mind was exhibited in private letters and in newspapers. The following lines are from an unsigned letter to a Wilkinson County paper. The entire letter is rather ungrammatical. "There can be no doubt but that the sable African who has acquired his freedom in the mode sanctioned by the laws of a sovereign state, has rights which belongs not to the slave, and that they exert a most pernicious influence on the slave population wherever it can be felt, it is a fact which cannot be controverted." The free negroes are further referred to as "this useless and dangerous portion of our population."[64]

In 1831 we find Dr. John Ker, a prominent citizen of Natchez, in writing to his friend, Major Isaac Thomas, of Louisiana, stating as an incontestable proposition that "the free colored people are more injurious to society than the same number of slaves, and their removal must therefore confer a greater benefit. The number of free colored people must inevitably increase in a progressive ratio."[65]

In the 1831 session of the legislature of Mississippi there was "presented a petition from sundry citizens of Adams County, praying that a law may pass for the absolute and unconditional removal of free negroes from this state."[66] These were no uncertain words! Although the law asked for was not forthcoming, a bill was passed, which we have already mentioned,[67] that might have partially accomplished this end had it been rigidly enforced. As we have shown above it was not well enforced, but the legislature evidently expected that it would be efficient for an amendment was proposed that "it shall be the duty of the Governor, to transport all free negroes who may be banished under the provisions of this act, to the colony of Liberia, in Africa, at the expense of the county from which such free negroes may be banished."[68]

The case of Fanny Leiper has already been told and in this trial it was stated as a matter of general knowledge, that about 1836, "there was a great spirit to remove from the State all free persons of color."[69] And we have also shown that the legislature passed adversely upon most of the petitions presented to it which asked for the emancipation of slaves. At one time, when a petition of this nature was before the legislature, it was moved that it be amended, "that the said persons of color named herein, shall be removed from within the state, and not return thereto, otherwise this act to be null and void"; and it was further proposed to extend this to include "all which have heretofore been emancipated, or which may be hereafter emancipated." Neither the original bill nor the amendments passed.[70]

To give one more reference on this subject, Claiborne, in his *History of Mississippi*, states that the legislature limited the emancipation of negroes who were to remain in the state because "the residence of an intermediate class between the slave and the owner had been found incompatible."[71]

While nothing has been found to invalidate the conclusions we have reached regarding the sincere dislike and fear that the free negro class inspired in the hearts of the slave-owners of Mississippi, this subject can not be left here without giving an incomplete picture. It was the *class* that was feared and not the *individuals* that formed it. For example, we have cited the petition of certain citizens of Adams County, presented to the legislature in 1831, requesting the "absolute and unconditional removal of free negroes from this state."[72] Twelve years later, at the request of this same county and Warren County, the board of police of any county in the state was given full power to license free persons of color to reside in the county on proof of good character and on condition that a majority of the citizens desired it.[73] Furthermore, individual members of the class were sometimes the recipients of property willed to them by white people of the state.[74] The numerous petitions presented to the legislature asking for permission to emancipate slaves would have largely increased the number of the free colored class if that body had granted them all; and it is worthy of notice that many of these emanated from the very counties that were most troubled by too many free negroes.[75] Another argument to uphold the view that we have stated is to be found in the readiness with which slave-owners were willing to grant freedom to their slaves. While some of these either removed or provided for the removal of the negroes out of the state, this was doubtless caused in part by the owner's knowledge of the laws against allowing them to remain; and in other cases no provision was made for taking the slaves to other lands. And so we see that the individual negro was often treated kindly. There seems to have been no widespread feeling that this or that free negro was causing trouble to the state. But there was a decided feeling that as a class they were a real source of danger — a feeling that was inspired by the fear that the slaves might be more unruly if they realized that a state of slavery was not the necessary concomitant of a dark skin.

An historical investigator, we are told, should hold himself purely to a presentation of facts and not be concerned with questions of ethics. Sometimes considerable reading is necessary to form an opinion that can be expressed very briefly. If the material investigated is in large part sordid and by no means pleasant to read, may it not be permissible to present the conclusions, without the attendant details, even though the conclusions touch on the field of ethics?

The creation of the free colored class in Mississippi was a monument to the best and worst traits in human character. Some of these slaves were freed by their masters because of an honest interest in their welfare, and a sense of gratitude for the faithful behavior of the negro. There were some slave-holders who felt that the very system was evil. Others, not going so far, had a strong attachment — even affection and love — for some if not all of their slaves. And actuated by such feelings they sought by will or deed to free their negro slaves so that they would not fall into unkind hands. It should be remembered that such an act involved a considerable financial loss. Many of the slaves so emancipated found their free home in one of the northern states or in Africa, though some of them remained in Mississippi.[76]

On the other hand, our suspicions are sharpened when we notice the exceedingly high per cent of the free colored class who had white blood in their veins. Of the 773 free persons of color in Mississippi in the year 1860, 601 were of mixed blood, and only 172 were black. Among the slaves this condition was entirely reversed. In this same year there were 400,013 slaves who were classed as blacks, and only 36,618 who were mulattoes.[77]

The sordid side of the story is that many instances can be given in which a slave-owner emancipated a mulatto slave and in the deed or will of manumission acknowledged his own blood relationship to the slave.[78] The frequency with which cases of this kind came before the Supreme Court of the state was all too large, but some qualification should be made before this be taken as an indication of the general state of affairs. When property was bequeathed by a white man to his mulatto child, it was often difficult to predict the decision of the court.[79] It is probable that the variableness of the court in deciding such cases resulted in a large per cent of these cases being appealed to the Supreme Court of the state.

Notes

[1] Any person of one-fourth or more negro blood was a mulatto in the eyes of the law of Mississippi. Hutchinson's *Mississippi Code* (1798–1848), p. 514.

[2] Randall *v.* the State, 12 Miss. 349.

[3] Talbott *v.* Norager, 23 Miss. 572. The same principle is also to be found in Heirn *v.* Bridault and wife, 37 Miss. 209, and in Coon *v.* the State, 20 Miss. 249.

[4] Hutchinson, p. 524 (law of June 18, 1822), and p. 533 (law of Dec. 20, 1831).

[5] Hutchinson, pp. 524–525.

[6] *Ibid.,* p. 533.

[7] Randall *v.* the State, 12 Miss. 349.

[8] Hutchinson, p. 525.

[9] *Ibid.*

[10] *Ibid.,* p. 514.

[11] *Ibid.,* p. 534.

[12] *Ibid.,* p. 948; *Revised Code of Miss.* (1857), p. 255.

[13] Hutchinson, p. 948.

[14] *Ibid.,* p. 948.

[15] Compare the case of Fanny Leiper, a free negress, who owned a house and lot in Natchez, and was upheld in her ownership by the highest court in the state, with the opinion of the same tribunal in another case, where it held that a slave had "no more right to purchase, hold, or transfer property, than the mule his plough." See Leiper *v.* Hoffman *et al.,* 26 Miss. 615, and Hinds *et al. v.* Brazealle *et al.,* 3 Miss. 837.

[16] Hutchinson, p. 515.

[17] 27 Miss. 731.

[18] See the lengthy opinion of the court in Mitchell *v.* Wells, 37 Miss. 235.

[19] Mitchell *v.* Wells, 37 Miss. 235.

[20] Heirn *v.* Bridault and wife, 37 Miss. 209.

[21] Leiper *v.* Hoffman *et al.,* 26 Miss. 615; Shaw *v.* Brown, 35 Miss. 246; Harry and others *v.* Decker and Hopkins, 1 Miss. 36.

[22] Even then the master had to be paid paid a full equivalent of the slave so emancipated. See constitution of Mississippi of 1817, art. VI., sec. 1, repeated in the constitution of 1832. Hutchinson, p. 34.

[23] *Ibid.,* p. 523.

[24] *Journal of the General Assembly of Mississippi,* 1823, *passim.*

[25] *Ibid.,* 1826 and 1831, *passim.*

[26] *Laws of the State of Mississippi,* 1817, p. 205; 1828, pp. 15, 46–47; 1833, pp. 119–120.

[27] *Ibid.,* 1833, pp. 125–126.

[28] *Ibid.,* 1827, pp. 56–57.

[29] J. F. H. Claiborne, *Mississippi, as a Province, Territory, and State,* pp. 388–391.

[30] Hutchinson, p. 538 (law of Feb. 26, 1842); Leech *v.* Cooley, 14 Miss. 93; Leiper *v.* Hoffman *et al.,* 26 Miss. 615.

[31] Hutchinson, pp. 524 and 537; Hinds *et al. v.* Brazealle *et al.,* 3 Miss. 837; Leiper *v.* Hoffman *et al.,* 26 Miss. 615.

[32] Hinds *et al. v.* Brazealle *et al.,* 3 Miss. 837.

[33] For a similar instance see Mitchell *v.* Wells, 37 Miss. 235.

[34] Sam, colored, *v.* Fore, 20 Miss. 413.

[35] A similar case will be found in Roach *v.* Anderson, 28 Miss. 234.

[36] Natchez *Mississippi Free Trader,* May 13, 1841.

[37] Leiper *v.* Hoffman *et al.,* 26 Miss. 615.

[38] Hutchinson, p. 524.

[39] *Ibid.,* pp. 537–538.

[40] Heirn *v.* Bridault and wife, 37 Miss. 209. The only other case of what might be called social equality between whites and mulattoes is to be found in Shaw *v.* Brown, 35 Miss. 246.

[41] *Laws of Mississippi,* 1828, pp. 61–62; 1833, pp. 131–132; 1854, p. 295.

[42] *Ibid.,* December, 1856–February, 1857 (adjourned session), p. 104.

[43] Weathersby *et al. v.* Weathersby, 21 Miss. 685.

[44] Mississippi became a state in 1817. The number of free negroes, *i.e.,* 235, can be found in the *Mississippi Official and Statistical Register* for 1917, p. 66. It should be noted that the totals given on that page are for the entire Mississippi Territory of that time, which comprised the present states of Mississippi and Alabama. In several instances these totals have been erroneously quoted as applicable to the present boundaries of the State of Mississippi.

[45]

Year	No. of Free Colored	Percent of Change
1800	182	—
1810	240	+ 31.86
1820	458	+ 90.83
1830	519	+ 13.31
1840	1,366	+163.19
1850	930	− 31.91
1860	773	− 16.87

This table, with the exception of the last line, is from the *Census of 1850.* The number of free colored in 1860 is given in the *Census of 1860* (Population).

[46] Hutchinson, pp. 524–525.

[47] *Ibid.,* p. 533.

[48] *Ibid.,* p. 537.

[49] *Census of 1860* (Recapitulation).

[50] *Laws of Mississippi,* 1859–1860, pp. 243, 259, and 352.

[51] The number of free negroes in these counties was 129, while there were 235 in the entire state. See note 44. Also, see map of Mississippi in 1816 in the *Mississippi Official and Statistical Register* for 1908, p. 387.

[52] These four counties were Adams, Jefferson, Claiborne, and Warren.

[53] Compare the *Compendium of the Sixth Census* (1840) with a map of Mississippi.

[54] *Ibid.*

[55] These comparisons are based on statistics contained in the *Compendium of the Sixth Census* (1840).

[56] *Compendium of Census of 1850.*

[57] Hutchinson, p. 534.

[58] The following table is an excerpt from "Free Negro Owners of Slaves in the United States in 1830," in *Journal of Negro History,* IX. 65, and is the list for the State of Mississippi.

	Slaves	Total of Slaves and Family	Age Group of Owner
Adams County			
Winn, George	16	17	55–100
City of Natchez			
Carey, Robert M.	2	4	10–24
Miller, Jas	5	12	24–36
Battles, Harriet	1	3	24–36
Gilson, Sam	5	6	10–24
Claiborne County			
Willis, Mary	1	5	36–55
Bell, Henry	4	5	36–55
Butler, Hanibal	1	5	36–55
Martin, Samuel	1	7	36–55
Simpson, Gloster	2	5	36–55
Harris, Hardy	1	6	55–100
Holly, Christopher	3	5	55–100
Moore, David	5	6	24–36
Hancock County			
Asmard, Charles, Sr.	3	4	100–
Benoit, Bernard, Sr.	6	8	55–100
Perkins, William P.	17	18	10–24
Warren County			
Miller, Elisha	1	3	24–36

[59] *Laws of Mississippi,* 1859–1860, pp. 276–277.

[60] *Journal of Negro History,* IX. 42.

[61] This seems evident from the rather frequent laws, already mentioned in this paper, regulating the employment of free negroes on boats.

[62] *Journal of Negro History,* II. 356.

[63] *Laws of Mississippi,* 1846, p. 169; *ibid.,* 1854, p. 182.

[64] Woodville (Miss.) *Republican,* Aug. 4, 1827.

[65] Franklin L. Riley, "A Contribution to the History of the Colonization Movement in Mississippi," in *Publications* of the Mississippi Historical Society, IX. 348. This letter was dated June 25, 1831.

[66] *Journal of the General Assembly of Mississippi,* 1831, *House Journal,* p. 7.

[67] See note 47.

[68] *Jour. of Gen. Assem. of Miss.,* 1831, *House Jour.,* p. 252.

[69] Leiper *v.* Hoffman *et al.,* 26 Miss. 615.

[70] *Jour. of Gen. Assem. of Miss.,* 1825, *House Jour.,* pp. 102–103, 106, and 121. Another case is reported in this same *Journal,* p. 110.

[71] Claiborne, *op. cit.,* p. 388.

[72] *Jour. of Gen. Assem. of Miss.,* 1831, *House Jour.,* p. 7.

[73] Hutchinson, p. 540. It should be remembered that these two counties had the largest free negro population of any counties in the state.

[74] Hinds *et al. v.* Brazealle *et al.,* 3 Miss. 837; Luckey *et al. v.* Dykes *et al.,* 10 Miss. 60; Leech *v.* Cooley, 14 Miss. 93; Hairston *et al. v.* Hairston *et al.,* 30 Miss. 276; Barksdale *v.* Elam *et al.,* 30 Miss. 694; Shaw *v.* Brown, 35 Miss. 264; Heirn *v.* Bridault and wife, 37 Miss. 209; and Mitchell *v.* Wells, 37 Miss. 235.

[75] *Jour. of Gen. Assem. of Miss., passium.*

[76] Examples of this will be found in the cases cited in the opinion of the court in Mitchell *v.* Wells, 37 Miss. 235.

[77] *Census of 1860* (Recapitulation).

[78] Hinds *et al. v.* Brazealle *et al.,* 3 Miss. 837; Barksdale *v* Elam *et al.,* 30 Miss. 694; Shaw *v* Brown, 35 Miss. 246; Mitchell *v.* Wells, 37 Miss. 235; *Jour. of Gen. Assem. of Miss.,* 1823, *House Jour.,* p. 80; *ibid.,* 1826, *House Jour.,* p. 29. For somewhat similar cases see Heirn *v.* Bridault and wife, 37 Miss. 209; and Raby *et al. v.* Batiste *et ux.,* 27 Miss. 731.

[79] See opinion of the court in Mitchell *v.* Wells, 37 Miss. 235.

The Traditions of the Free Negro in Charleston, South Carolina[1]

E. Horace Fitchett

The free Negro in the slave system was an anomaly. The system was designed for free white men and Negro slaves. In a large measure the position of the emancipated Negro, prior to the Emancipation Proclamation, was comparable to that of the slave. Some of them preferred slavery to the type of freedom which they received.[2] They were by law deprived of education, of suffrage, and of freedom of movement; they could not testify in court against a white man, and from time to time they were prohibited from assembling in groups of more than seven without the presence of a white man.[3] However, before the slave structure was disrupted by the Civil War there were approximately one half of a million people of this class in the United States.[4] In a few communities, particularly along the seacoast, they developed into a respectable, economically independent, class-conscious group. This is notable in the case of Charleston, South Carolina.

In this discussion I shall answer briefly the following questions: (1) How did this group arise? (2) What was its economic position and how was it attained? (3) What relations did this class of people sustain with out-group members and in its own group? (4) Were there any evidences of deviations from the approved patterns of behavior? If so, what form did they take? And (5) What was the nature of the process of accommodation and social adjustment to the social system?

When the first census was taken in 1790 there were 8,089 white persons, 7,684 slaves, and 586 free Negroes in Charleston, South Carolina. Hence, the latter group constituted 3.58 per cent of the total population.[5] Many of the members of this group had no memory of a slave background or tradition. This was particularly true of the mixed bloods. Dr. Reuter advances the generalization that: "There seems to be no historical exception to the rule that when peoples come into contact and occupy the same area there is a mixture of blood that results, ultimately, in the establishment of a new modified ethnic type."[6] This condition is no less true of Charleston than of other areas. Documentary evidence may be presented to support

E. Horace Fitchett, "The Traditions of the Free Negro in Charleston, South Carolina," *Journal of Negro History* XXV (April 1940), 139–52. Permission granted by the Association for the Study of Negro Life and History.

this generalization. In 1720 one slave master, James Gilbertson, a planter, made the following provisions in his will for a mulatto woman and her children:

My will is that my mulatto woman Ruth shall be free immediately after my Decease, & also my will is that her three female children Betty, Molly, and Keatty shall be free at the age of one and Twenty years, my will is also that Ruth have the feather bed W :ch the Indians did Cutt up, also a pot and her maintenance upon my plantation during her natural life.[7]

In 1834, a prominent Charlestonian, a native of France, acknowledged in his will that the children of his housekeeper and slave were his offspring and his executors were instructed to provide for the mother and her children out of the estate. He states·

I do hereby recognize and declare that the issue of my slave and housekeeper, Celestine, are my children and I will order and direct that my executors herein named, or such person or persons that may qualify on this will, shall and do, as soon after my death as may be convenient, send the said woman Celestine and all her said issue my children, out of this State to some other State, territory or country, where they can severally be made free and their liberty secured to them respectively; and I will, order and direct that said executors or such person or persons that may qualify and act on this will shall defray the expense of transportation or conveyance of the said Celestine and her issue to said State, territory or country as expressed from the funds of my estate.[8]

In 1826 one of the wealthiest and most influential citizens of Charleston made the following stipulation in his will for his mulatto man:

In consideration of the good conduct and faithful valuable service of my mulatto man Toney by Trade a millwright I have for some years past given him to himself one half of his time say from the middle of May to the middle of November every year. It is my will and desire and I do direct that the same indulgence be given to him for six years from the time of my death during which time he may instruct other servants in his Profession to supply his place and at the expiration of six years from the time of my death I will and direct that his whole time be given up to him . . . . after the expiration of six years he may be emancipated and set free or allowed to depart from this State as (he) may . . . think proper.[9]

These wills are typical of many of those which I examined. They not only provided for the freedom of a slave but also for his economic security. In a very real sense they imply that these persons were not slaves. They were in some instances recognized as the offspring of the upper caste member; they were allowed freedom of action and movement; and they were accorded special privileges. Thus they were not treated as slaves nor did they conceive of themselves as slaves. Indeed, in some of the wills the testator indicated that the servant should not be considered a slave. Such was the desire expressed in the will of Mrs. Bonneau in 1807.[10] Moreover, some of these persons obtained their freedom so early in the history of the country that the conditions of slave status could easily have been lost to their descendants. Their emancipation was indeed coeval with that of many of the white servant class. In the *South Carolina Gazette* for January, 1738, the following advertisement was made for a white servant girl:

Runaway the 28th of December last, a white woman servant, about 16 years of age, named Anne Brown, born in London and can talk a little French, belonging to Edw. Townsend of Savannah, Georgia. Whoever brings the said Servant to Charleston shall have £5 in currency reward.[11]

There were also cases which free Negroes entered Charleston from other states. Such was the case of Richard Holloway, whose citizenship papers were dated January 21, 1794. He is designated in this document as a seaman, a native of Essex County, Maryland, and a mulatto about twenty years of age.[12]

In general it is fair to say that the free Negro arose out of: (1) Children born of free colored parents; (2) Mulatto children born of free colored mothers; (3) Children of free Negro and mixed Indian parentage; (4) Manumitted slaves.[13]

In the latter part of the eighteenth and during the first part of the nineteenth centuries there emerged in Charleston a relatively economically independent group of free Negroes. They were primarily the artisans of the system. Records show, moreover, that they engaged in business transactions which made the system a going concern. In 1819 they were listed in thirty branches of work. Among them were 11 carpenters, 10 tailors, 22 seamstresses, 6 shoemakers and one owner of a hotel.[14] Thirty years later they were listed in fifty different types of work. In 1859 there were among them 50 carpenters, 43 tailors, 9 shoemakers, and 21 butchers. In these trades some of them became wealthy. In the above mentioned year, "353 persons paid taxes on property and one-hundred-and-ninety were slave holders. The property on which they paid taxes was assessed at $724,570 and the amount paid on slaves aggregated $1,170."[15] If we divide this group of taxpayers into three approximately homogeneous classes, we find that there were 192 who paid taxes on property whose assessed value ranged from $1,000 to $5,000; this group owned 105 slaves, or an average of .54 slaves each. In the second division there were 21 persons who paid taxes on property whose assessed value ranged from $5,000 to $10,000, and they owned 68 slaves, or 3¼ slaves each. And in the third bracket, there were 9 persons who paid taxes on property whose value ranged from $10,000 to $40,075. This group owned 54 slaves, an average of 6 slaves each. In this class one individual paid taxes on $23,000 worth of real estate and 14 slaves; another $33,000 worth of real estate and 5 slaves; and a third paid taxes on $40,075 worth of real estate and 14 slaves.[16]

Moreover, the wills and deeds which they made indicate that they engaged in some of the most important business ventures of the system. In 1815, Jehu Jones bought a hotel at public auction for $13,000.[17] This hotel was located on the most important street in the city and in close proximity to the most fashionable Episcopal Church in the community.[18] It was patronized by the elite of the white society, including the governor of the state.[19]

In 1853 Joseph Dereef, another wealthy person of color, sold a piece of property to the city council for $3,600 for the extension of a street.[20] In 1870 his brother, R. E. Dereef, sold a part of his wharf to the South Carolina Rail Road Company for $17,000.[21] In 1833 Thomas Ingliss made provisions in his will for the support of a relative from the stocks which he held in the Mechanics Bank of the city.[22]

One of the characteristics of the free Negro of Charleston, which attracts the attention of the sociologists, is that it was a class-conscious group; and identified its interest, loyalties, and manners with the upper caste members of the society in so far as that behavior did not offend or disturb the *status quo*. They organized themselves into societies with high eligibility requirements. These associations were ostensibly charitable and benevolent, but in reality they were social and status organizations. In 1790 the Brown Fellowship Society was formed.[23] The preamble of this organization stated that its members were bona fide free brown men of good character. The fee of admission was $50.00 and the membership was restricted to fifty members. The society provided for the education of the children; assistance to the orphans and widows and burial grounds for their dead. They maintained a clubhouse where meetings were held monthly, and on each anniversary provisions were made for special observance. This institution had a continuous existence for more than a hundred years. In fact vestiges of it are still in evidence. There is left the cemetery, with large imposing tombstones and vaults; so is the foundation of the hall in which they met. It still has a secretary and a president. In spite of the fact that other Negro organizations, including a church were abolished during crises periods in this slave community, the Brown Fellowship Society kept alive. The members and their organizations were careful and cautious in their conduct. We only need to remember the conflicting philosophies and the revolutionary move-ments of the under-privileged groups of this period to appreciate how delicate and precarious the position of this group was. At their meetings they prohibited any discussion of local or national problems. Rule XVIII of the by-laws states: "All debates on controverted points of divinity or matters of the nation, governments, states or churches, shall be excluded from the conversation of this society, and whoever shall persist in such shall be fined . . ."[24] The secretary of the organization kept very careful minutes of the proceedings of the meetings, and on one occasion when the mayor of the city asked to inspect them, because of a recently enacted law to prohibit more than seven Negroes to assemble at a time, the group was praised highly for its records and avowed objectives. So they were informed that the law was not intended for them.[25] Among other things the minutes showed that a member had been expelled from the society on April 17, 1817, for violating its rules.[26]

Now the question may be asked, what were the attitudes of this class to other groups in the community? As I envisage it, their behavior was a replica of that class in the white society which they aspired to be like. Their attitudes towards their slaves ranged from exploitation to humanitarianism. Again the wills which they left give us some indication of their position. In 1825 William Pinceel made the following stipulation in his will:

I give and bequeath unto my Son Emanuel forever my Negro boy slave named Joe. I also give and bequeath unto Said Son for life my Negro boy slave named Tom and immediately after the death of my said Son, should the said Negro boy have conducted himself towards my Said Son as a faithful servant, then I direct that he be emancipated, but should he not have conducted himself then I give the said Negro boy to such person as my Said Son nominate and appoint in his last will and writing.[27]

The following will was made by a school teacher in 1831. He taught in Charleston between 1815 and 1830, and was one of the most active members of the Brown Fellowship Society:

I desire that soon after my decease instruction shall be given to have all my stock and other things appertaining to my plantation in the country together with the plantation itself sold and the money arising from the same shall go to defray all expenses, taxes & provided however the said plantation cannot be sold at a fair price and it can be worked by the hands now there viz. Scipio, Abram and Peggy so as to pay expenses taxes and so forth in such case the same shall not be sold but retained for the benefit of the family if at all event, the Negroes on said plantation whose names are above mentioned be disposed of there shall be an exception of Scipio whom it is my wish shall be retained together with my slaves in town viz.: Fanny and Mary to be subservient to the wishes of my beloved wife Jennet Bonneau and children.[28]

Some of these masters also left their slaves or former slaves provided for economically. In 1859 John L. Francis left $1,000 to one servant and $200 to another, together with his wardrobe.[29]

The emphasis which the free Negro of this class placed upon mixed blood, free ancestry, economic position, and a devotion to the tenets of the slave system set them apart from and above other classes in the community. Moreover, their in-group tendencies were so strong that the free black people of the city were constrained to organize themselves into a society of free blacks. The first rule of this society says that it will ". . . . consist of a number of respectable Free Dark men, as a majority may determine: not less than seven or more than thirty-five which number of seven shall be considered a quorum to transact business at any time . . ."[30]

It is fair to say that the upper caste free Negro served as a custodian of the system. He interrupted plans which the detached, discontented, underprivileged Negroes designed to overthrow or to offend the mores of the system. In 1822 the Intended Denmark Vesey Insurrection[31] was circumvented by a member of this class who instructed an informed slave to go and tell his master. The insurrection had been in the process of development for four years and was considered one of the most intricate ever undertaken in this country. It had as its model the uprising of the blacks in San Domingo. Its leader had travelled through the Islands as the slave of a slave trader. Upon receiving his freedom he settled in Charleston and assumed the position of the leader of the slaves. It is estimated that from 6,000 to 9,000 slaves were identified with this movement. Only about thirty of the leaders were executed for the plot.[32] On the other hand the slave who divulged the plans was emancipated by the State of South Carolina and paid an annual stipend for the rest of his life.[33] Meantime the free Negro received $1,000 and exemption from taxation for the rest of his life.[34]

There are other evidences of unrest, but I shall take time to mention only a few of them. Between 1832 and 1853 approximately 400 free Negroes left South Carolina for Liberia, Africa.[35] They were impelled by the claims of the American Colonization Society on the one hand and the insecurity of their positions on the other. In a mass meeting which was held by this group in 1831 in the interst of emigrating to Africa, the theme was that "in Liberia you will enjoy moral and political freedom." In December, 1832, one-hundred-forty-six persons of this class departed from Charleston for Liberia.[36] As far as I have been able to ascertain none of them were members of the Brown Fellowship Society.

The relations which the aristocratic free Negro sustained in his own family and among other members of his group deserve study and analysis. They provided for the education of their children; they married inside a restricted class; dowries were apparently provided for the daughters; and great care was taken in the protection and transmission of property and slaves.

In 1794 George Bedon indicated in his will that:

. . . . it is my particular desire and request that my two Sons . . . . should be brought up in a Christian like manner and kept to school for the benefit of an Education until they arrive at the age of fifteen years then my two sons to be bound out during the term of six years to some handicraft trade under a kind and able master and in like manner my Daughter until she arrives at the age of fourteen years to be bound to a discreet and careful Mantua-maker a person of good character who will be so kind as to take care of an orphans morals as well as to teach her the trade.[37]

In 1861 Jacob Weston, one of the wealthier members of this caste, stipulated in his will that his wife and son should live in England after his death and that the son should be educated there. It was indicated that they be maintained out of the family estate.[38] The same testator designated that the support of his wife should be revoked if she married again.[39]

As was the practice generally, so it was in this group that marriage and courtship relations were expected to have the approval of the parents of the interested parties. The following letter was written in 1832, in reply to one which a young man had sent to the parents of his friend:

Charleston, March 19th, 1832

Dear Sir:

It affords me the pleasure of giving you the approbation of Mr. Kougley and myself towards the affection you have for my daughter Cecelia. It has met her approbation for your visiting the house on her account, as to your standing in life we are perfectly acquainted with, as to objections we can have none, therefore we must join both hand and heart in wishing you all the prosperity and happiness this world can afford. I hope it is with the approbation of your family that you have addressed my daughter with respect. Dear Sir   We are yours,

Jacob and Mary Kougley [40]

The Marriage Book of St. Phillip's Church, founded in 1672, shows that 168 mulattoes were married by the rectors of that institution between 1828 and 1860.[41] There were a considerable number of marriages among the families who were either business partners or who were identified with the same social and fraternal organization; in other words by usage and expectation, selections were made from in-group members. Records show that even the slaves of business partners entered into marriage relations. On November 16, 1837, Mingo, the slave of R. E. Dereef, was married to Hatira, the slave of Robert Howard.[42] These men were partners in the wood business.

The exhibition of a feeling of class-consciousness and the effort to maintain group solidarity were best exemplified in the activities of the Brown Fellowship Society. Through this medium social relations were cultivated, a system of education fostered, provisions for caring for the sick, the orphan and widow were made; and many men of wealth acted in an advisory and legal capacity as executors of the last wills of the members of the group.[43] When the Society was one hundred years old its name was changed to the *Century Fellowship Society.* Early in the twentieth century an auxiliary organization was formed which they named the *Daughters of the Century Fellowship Society.* The object of this branch of the association ". . . the erection of a hall to the memory of the men who won a page in the social history of the eighteenth century."[44] On the 117th anniversary of the organization, the president, in his annual address, epitomized the career of his caste in the following words: "Fortunately there were the classes in society, and as our forefathers allied themselves with them, as a consequence they had their influence and protection and they had to be in accord with them and stood for what they stood for. If they stood for high incentive so did our fathers. *If they stood for slavery so did our fathers to a certain extent. But they sympathized with the oppressed,* for they had to endure some of it . . ."[45]

In conclusion, the free Negro of Charleston answers nicely to the "marginal man" concept.[46] By virtue of his biological characteristics, because of his partial accessibility to two social worlds, as a result of his feeling of superiority to one of these worlds, and his position of inferiority to the other he was either constrained to become a misfit or to carve out a positon which the community accepted and which he respected. Because of the nature of the social system he became a member of a separate caste which incorporated the interests, loyalties and usages of the upper caste members of the society in so far as this behavior did not offend or disturb the hierarchical arrangements. In this position he was able to circumvent the harsh ordinances which were designed to perpetuate the slave economy and to assuage the circumstances of his existence.

It is fair to say, however, that when the system was disrupted during the Civil War, this group provided the leadership, and the basis of organized, stable life for the Negro community.

This study has shown that (1) intimate human relations, whether between subordinates and superiors or between persons of equal rank, result in irresistible and inevitable *claims*[47] and *obligations* of each upon the other. In this case these relations gave rise to the emergence of a large group of free Negroes in the slave society. (2) City life with its heterogeneous population and its consequent conflict and fusion of cultures, with its competition and division of labor tends to secularize human relations and institutions, and to facilitate freedom of movement, action and thought. Hence, if the city economy is to move on with efficiency, even the lowest servant in it must have economic value, and this is inevitably interlaced with the process of mobility. The city offered the free Negro his best opportunity for economic success. It is further shown that (3) in a society in which a group's position is not definitely defined by the mores and traditions efforts will be made to copy the patterns of conduct of those groups which have prestige, recognition and security. Lastly, it is shown that (4) the extent to which this class of Negroes in Charleston differed from similar groups in the total slave economy marked the extent to which the modes of life and patterns of conduct in the community as a whole, differed from the rest of the slave communities. The difference, in other words, is one of degree rather than kind.

Notes

[1] Paper read before the 18th Annual Institute of the Society for Social Research, August 19, 1939, at the University of Chicago. This paper is based on an investigation the writer is making of the free Negro in Charleston, S.C. It was made possible by an award from the Julius Rosenwald Fund for the year 1938–39. The writer expresses his appreciation to Professors Robert E. Park, W. Lloyd Warner, and Herbert Blumer for many stimulating and valuable suggestions.

[2] Phillips, U.B., *American Negro Slavery* (New York, 1918), p. 446.

[3] *Ibid.*, p. 448; *A Digest of the Ordinance of Charleston, 1783–1844,* p. 377.

[4] *Negro Population in the United States, 1790–1915,* p. 53.

[5] *Census of Charleston, 1848,* p. 10.

[6] Reuter, E. B. (ed.), *Race and Culture Contacts* (New York, 1934), pp. 7–9.

[7] *Record of Wills of Charleston County,* Vol. 1, 1671–1724, p. 50. Through the courtesy and cooperation of Miss Parmelee Cheves of the Charleston Free Library, and Professor J. H. Easterby of the College of the City of Charleston, I was permitted to examine a large number of verbatim, typewritten copies of old wills of Charleston County.

[8] *Record of Wills of Charleston County,* Vol. 40, Book A, 1834–1839, p. 203.

[9] *Record of Wills,* Vol. 37, Book A, 1826–1834, pp. 184–185.

[10] *Record of Wills,* Vol. 33, Book C, 1807–1818, pp. 1180–1181.

[11] *The South Carolina Gazette,* No. 209, Jan., 1738.

[12] *Citizenship Papers of Richard Holloway.* By the courtesy of Mrs. Mae Holloway-Purcell, a descendant of the family, I was permitted to examine this document.

[13] Russell, John H., *The Free Negro in Virginia, 1619–1865,* pp. 40–41.

[14] Based on a study of the *Directory of Charleston,* 1819, pp. 21–98.

[15] *List of Taxpayers of the City of Charleston for 1860,* pp. 315–334.

[16] *Ibid.*

[17] *Register of the Mesne Conveyance Office,* Book M8, pp. 399–402.

[18] *Register of Mesne Conference Office,* pp. 21–98.

[19] Adams, F. C., *Manuel Periera* (Washington, D.C., 1853), pp. 88–89.

[20] *Conveyance Deed Book,* H13, p. 237.

[21] *Ibid., Deed Book,* P15, p. 81.

[22] *Record of Wills,* Vol. 40, Book A, 1834–1839, pp. 289–290.

[23] *Rules and Regulations of the Brown Fellowship Society.* (1st November, 1790.)

[24] *Rules and Regulations of the Brown Fellowship Society,* p. 12.

[25] Jervey, T. D., *Robert Y. Haynes and His Times,* pp. 63–69. Jervey quotes here a letter which he obtained from the minutes of the Society.

[26] *Ibid.*

[27] *Record of Wills,* Vol. 36, Book C, 1818–1826, p. 1125.

[28] *Ibid.,* Vol. 39, Book C, 1826–1834, p. 905.

[29] *Ibid.,* Vol. 51, Book B, 1862–1868, p. 588.

[30] Browning, J. B., "The Beginnings of Insurance Enterprise among Negroes," *Journal of Negro History,* Vol. XXII, No. 4, Oct., 1937, p. 424.

[31] "Denmark Vesey," *The Atlantic Monthly,* Vol. 7, 1861, pp. 728–744.

[32] *Ibid.,* p. 740.

[33] *Statutes at Large of South Carolina,* Vol. 6, p. 194. This volume was the property of Jonathan Jasper Wright, the Negro Associate Justice of the Supreme Court of South Carolina

during the Reconstruction era. He is the only Negro ever to hold such a position in the United States. His books were donated to Claflin College, Orangeburg, S.C., by the late Dr. William Francis Holmes of Florence, S.C. Dr. Holmes read law under Judge Wright and the degree was conferred upon him at Claflin University.

[14] *Ibid.*, p. 195.

[15] *The African Repository and Colonial Journal,* Vol. III (Washington, D.C., 1833), "Opinions of a Freeman of Colour in Charleston," Oct., 1832, pp. 241–242, pp. 76–77.

[16] *Ibid.,* Vol. XXXIII, May, 1857, No. 5, pp. 152–155.

[17] *Record of Wills,* Vol. 25, Book A, 1793–1800, p. 208.

[18] *Records of Wills,* Vol. 50, Book A, 1860–1868, p. 222.

[19] *Ibid.*

[40] *The Holloway Scrap Book.*

[41] By the courtesy of Rev. Merritt Williams, Rector of St. Phillip's Church, the writer was permitted to examine the *Marriage Book* for entries of free Negroes.

[42] *Marriage Book of St. Phillip's Church.*

[43] *Minute Book of the Brown Fellowship Society,* 1869–1911. This material was made accessible through the courtesy of Mr. W. S. Montgomery, the Secretary.

[44] *The Holloway Scrapbook.*

[45] *Ibid.*

[46] Stonequist, Everett V., "The Problem of the Marginal Man," *The American Journal of Sociology,* Vol. XLI, July, 1935, pp. 3–4; and Park, Robert E., "Human Migration and the Marginal Man," *The American Journal of Sociology,* Vol. XXXIII (1928), pp. 881–893.

[47] This idea was received from a lecture by Dr. R. E. Park in a class in collective behavior in the summer of 1935 at the University of Chicago. The course was offered by Dr. Herbert Blumer.

Racial Segregation in Ante-Bellum New Orleans

Roger A. Fischer

The search for the roots of racial segregation has occupied the attention of scholars since the appearance of C. Vann Woodward's *The Strange Career of Jim Crow* in 1955. Interpreting the "separate but equal" legislation enacted by the southern states after 1887 as a fundamental turning point in the region's race relations, Woodward wrote of the "relative recency" of segregation and claimed that to identify the system with the ante-bellum South was "to forget the nature of relations between races under the old regime."[1] In a new introduction to a 1957 edition, Woodward carefully qualified his thesis by admitting the antiquity of white supremacist thought, the proscriptions imposed upon free Negroes before the Civil War, and the exclusion of Negroes from many public facilities after Appomattox. But his central premise remained resolute, that "the era of genuine segregation was yet to come — the era when the principle was consciously and deliberately applied to all possible areas of contact between the races, and when the code became a hard-and-fast dogma of the white race."[2]

The theory that racial segregation had been developed during a "capitulation to racism" after 1887 won wide acceptance among historians eager to discredit the antiquity of the system. Some scholars carried the Woodward thesis to extremes, ignoring the cautious qualifications of its creator and neglecting altogether the period before the Civil War. A textbook on post-bellum southern history published in 1963 informed its readers that during the ante-bellum period "the circumstances which later gave rise to the segregation codes could not exist."[3] Another scholar, writing an interpretation of *Plessy* v. *Ferguson* in 1963, set forth the blanket assertion that "Racial segregation in the Old South had been unknown."[4] As late as 1966 a third historian stated categorically that the segregation system "did not spring directly from slavery or from the timeworn customs of many generations."[5]

The logic that lay behind this assumption was compelling. In an agricultural society composed of masters and slaves, racial segregation would have been not only

Roger A. Fischer, "Racial Segregation in Ante-Bellum New Orleans," *American Historical Review* LXXIV (February 1969), 926–37. Reprinted with permission of the American Historical Association and the author.

impossible but unnecessary, for slavery was in itself the supreme segregator. The iron discipline, rigid routine, and absolute authority that were combined to preserve plantation order were their own means of racial control, rendering any secondary reminders of the color line superfluous. Since familiarity on the plantation carried with it no possible inference of racial equality, the masters and their families often joined in such festivities among the slaves as weddings and banquets. As Ellen Betts, raised a slave in Louisiana's Teche country, fondly remembered, "When the work slight, us black folks sure have the balls and dinners and such. We git all day to barbecue meat down on the bayou, and the white folks come down and eat 'longside the colored."[6] In a rural setting where whites and Negroes lived in virtually a total state of interdependence, formal race separation would have been an absurdity, hindering daily routine and serving no possible purpose. In their assumption that rural plantation slavery and formal segregation could not have existed side by side, Woodward and his disciples were substantially correct.

The fundamental flaw in this line of reasoning was that it greatly over-simplified the role of the Negro before the Civil War. In 1860 more than 220,000 free Negroes resided in the North, beyond the pale of the slavery system altogether. Another 260,000 free people of color lived in the South, congregating in sizable communities in the major cities.[7] A substantial number of southern slaves were owned by urban masters and kept in conditions vastly different from those prevailing on the rural farms and plantations.[8] Investigating these exceptions, other scholars engaged in the search for the origins of Jim Crow sharply challenged the "relative recency" of his birth. Leon F. Litwack's seminal study of Negroes in the ante-bellum North reported that racial segregation was widespread, systematic, and rigid in the "freedom land" across the Ohio.[9] V. Jacque Voegeli found abundant evidence of similar patterns in the Old Northwest during his investigation of racial attitudes in that region during the Civil War.[10] Richard C. Wade's study of slavery in ante-bellum southern cities demonstrated that racial segregation had existed side by side with the "peculiar institution" where personal racial control had been weakened by the complexities of urban slavery.[11] These investigations offered convincing evidence that Jim Crow was not the child of the era of Pitchfork Tillman.[12]

Segregation first developed formally in the ante-bellum cities, North and South, where the complexities of urban life and the anonymous nature of the city population made a mockery of the personal supervision of racial relationships that had prevailed in the country. On the farms and plantations, where the roles of master and slave were absolute, interracial contacts did not endanger the great caste barriers on which the sovereignty of the white race rested. But in the cities, where whites and Negroes were brought together frequently as total strangers, white supremacy and black subordination were neither automatic nor implicit. Such basic functions as dining, drinking, entertainment, and travel became public and institutional with the development of restaurants, taverns, theaters, and public conveyances. In the cities interracial contact was eliminated by the whites in order to preserve the distinctions of caste among strangers. Urban segregation often developed hand in hand with the decline of personal racial control and the rise of public accommodations.

Such was the case in New Orleans, the largest and most cosmopolitan city in the lower South. Very old by western standards, the city already had highly developed public accommodations when it became a part of the United States in 1803. A great port city linking the Mississippi River Valley with the commerce of the world, New Orleans continually played host to thousands of transients from all corners of the globe. Its resident white population was a veritable potpourri of native Creoles, rural southerners, Yankees, Germans, French, Irish, and others.[13]

The Negro slaves, 23,448 of them in 1840, enjoyed conditions far different from those prevailing in the surrounding rural regions. Domestic servants were given many of the duties of household management, including marketing and other missions that allowed them to roam about the streets of the city, as the New Orleans *Bee* complained in 1835, "at liberty to purchase what they please, and where they please, without the personal inspection of any member of the family."[14] Many slaves worked as carpenters, longshoremen, draymen, factoryworkers, and mechanics. Along with the free Negroes, they monopolized the market and vending trades.[15] The complexities of these tasks brought liberties and responsibilities unknown to rural slaves. Nearly all New Orleans slaves came into contact with whites who were not masters and Negroes who were not slaves; nearly all enjoyed a generous measure of personal freedom unheard of on the farms and plantations.

The most independent of all New Orleans slaves were those whose labor was "hired-out."[16] This system, designed to meet urban demands for a fluid labor supply within the bounds of slavery, allowed a prospective employer to rent the services of another man's slave. In some cases, these slaves saw nothing of their masters except periodically to turn over a stipulated portion of their earnings. Many of them rented their own dwellings and lived virtually free from the whites. The New Orleans *Daily Picayune* was hardly exaggerating in 1859 when it bemoaned their liberty "to engage in business on their own account, to live according to the suggestions of their own fancy, to be idle or industrious, as the inclination for one or the other prevailed, provided only the monthly wages are regularly gained."[17] In many instances, all that separated these slaves from total independence was the academic matter of their legal status.

Adding to the unique diversity of ante-bellum New Orleans society was a community of free people of color that numbered nearly twenty thousand at its peak in 1840.[18] Unlike most of the free Negroes in the rural regions, who eked out pitiful existences at tne sufferance of ever-wary whites, the New Orleans *gens de couleur* exercised a wide latitude of liberties. Strikingly diverse, their community contained moneylenders and mendicants, brokers and bootblacks, poets and prostitutes.[19] Separated from the slaves by their legal status and set apart from the whites by the color of their skin, the free Negroes of New Orleans added a third dimension to the complex racial structure of the city.

Attitudes of the slaves and free Negroes reflected the unusual scope of freedom they enjoyed. As one student of ante-bellum New Orleans society observed, Negro behavior was "singularly free of that deference and circumspection which might have been expected in a slave community."[20] In 1806 the legislature of the Territory of Orleans, perhaps indulging in a little wishful thinking, adopted a statute forbidding free Negroes and slaves from presuming themselves "equal to the white."[21] Seldom has a law been more universally disregarded. To judge from complaints in the newspapers, Negro insolence toward whites was common, particularly on the banquettes in front of the numerous taverns that catered illegally but openly to the Negro trade.[22] Mourning the decline of racial discipline in 1859, the New Orleans *Daily Picayune* complained that the Negroes "have become intemperate, disorderly, and have lost the respect which the servant should entertain for the master."[23]

In crime as in demeanor, New Orleans Negroes, free and slave, made a mockery of the "Sambo" stereotype. Petty pilferage was common here as elsewhere, but the more resourceful black thieves stole horses, picked pockets, embezzled, swindled, and executed daring armed robberies.[24] Negroes assaulted whites with pistols, knives, clubs, rocks, barrel staves, brickbats, broken bottles, water buckets, horse-whips, cold chisels, and billiard cues.[25] In rare cases, free Negroes and slaves even defied the ultimate taboo of a white supremacist society by raping white women and girls.[26] These assaults on person and property constantly reminded white New Orleanians that theirs was not an order in which they commanded and the Negroes instinctively and meekly obeyed.

Control over the Negro population was, in short, virtually nonexistent in New Orleans. The personal system of race discipline that worked so well in the rural areas simply could not function in an urban amalgam of absentee owners, indifferent strangers, and unusually sophisticated free Negroes and slaves. As the system died, the burden of maintaining the social distinctions of white supremacy fell increasingly on a public color line, first practiced in the city's municipal facilities and places of public accommodation. If urban conditions had made the law of the lash obsolete, it was hoped that segregation of Negroes in public places would constantly remind them of their lowly station in society.

Theaters and public exhibitions were legally segregated by an ordinance adopted on June 8, 1816, that forbade "any white person to occupy any of the places set apart for people of color; and the latter are likewise forbidden to occupy any of those reserved for white persons."[27] This edict merely ratified a long-standing policy of the management, for most exhibition halls and theaters had for many years segregated their customers by allocating rear sections or galleries for their Negro patrons. When Bernardo Coquet remodeled his ballroom into the St. Philip Street Theatre in 1810, he included in his alterations the construction of a tier of "upper boxes for women of color."[28] These galleries soon became known as "nigger heavens," a term that survived in the common vernacular for a century and a half, until the practice itself was finally abandoned.

Of all such seating arrangements, the one that attracted the most attention from visitors was the gallery that accommodated the free Negro aristocracy in the French

Opera House. Thomas Low Nichols, the English food faddist and spiritualist, interpreted the "nigger heaven" as something of a victory for the free Negroes, referring to their gallery as "the portion of the house devoted to ladies and gentlemen of colour, . . . into which no common white trash was allowed to intrude."[29] But other visitors viewed the arrangment differently. The English geologist Sir Charles Lyell made reference to the economic and cultural attainments of the *gens de couleur* confined to the gallery and denounced their ostracism as a "tyranny of caste."[30] The Hungarian traveler Ferencz A. Pulszky agreed. Fascinated by the paradox inherent in the social position of the free Negro elite, he observed: "Some of them were pointed out to me as very wealthy, but no money can admit them to the pit, or to the boxes."[31]

The races were also segregated in the more lowly public pursuits. The city jails kept white and Negro prisoners in separate quarters and dressed them in different colored uniforms. On August 11, 1836, the city council extended the racial distinction to labor details by adopting an ordinance requiring free Negroes and slaves confined for more than three days to be put to work "cleaning and repairing the streets and public roads or levees, or on any other public work,"[32] apparently exempting the white prisoners from such duties.

Streetcar segregation, not required by city law, was practiced as company policy from the time the cars were placed in service in New Orleans in the 1820's. A few of the omnibus lines excluded Negroes altogether, but others operated special cars for colored passengers, identified by large stars painted on the front, rear, and both sides to avoid confusion.[33] This practice gave rise to local use of the term "star" to denote all varieties of segregated Negro facilities, much as the label "Jim Crow" would later be adopted throughout the United States a half century later.

White restaurants and saloons were strictly segregated by local custom and management policies, as they were throughout the ante-bellum South.[34] Hotels were also off limits to Negroes, but exceptions were made for the personal attendants of the white guests. None of the local private clubs and local chapters of national fraternal organizations admitted Negroes to membership. By the beginning of the Civil War, the free Negroes who sought club membership and could pay for the privilege had already formed a large number of lodges and benevolent societies of their own.[35]

Education for free Negroes developed in a similar way. Excluded from the white private schools in New Orleans since early in the eighteenth century, the children of the *gens de couleur* were also denied admission into the new public-school system that developed in the city in the 1840's. Forced to fall back upon their own resources, the free Negroes instituted and supported a large number of private schools, varying from exclusive academies in the best continental tradition to such charity shcools as the *École des Orphelins Indigents,* generously endowed by Aristide Marie, Thomy Lafon, and other free Negro philanthropists.[36]

The Charity Hospital of Louisiana, located in New Orleans, opened its doors to sick whites and Negroes alike, but segregated the races within the institution.

It served the medical needs of a great international seaport; in 1859 its patients were described as being "of every age and sex, of every color, from the blue-eyed, fair-browed Anglo-American, to the tawn, sun-browned child of the Tropics."[37] In the ante-bellum period, before increasing Negro admissions led to entirely separate wings for whites and Negroes, segregation was accomplished by separate wards for the two races. On the eve of the Civil War, Charity Hospital was operating three of its eleven surgical wards for the care of Negro patients.[38]

In pre-Civil War New Orleans the color line extended to the grave. On March 5, 1835, a long-standing local practice was written into law when the city council adopted an ordinance zoning the city's cemeteries into three sections, allotting one-half of the space for whites, one-fourth for slaves, and one-fourth for free Negroes.[39] Six years later segregation in cemeteries was carried a step further by an ordinance requiring separate burial registration lists for whites and Negroes.[40]

Segregation in public pursuits was applied thoroughly throughout the ante-bellum period. Free Negroes and slaves were systematically excluded from white accommodations and social activities and were relegated to separate and usually second-class quarters in the public facilities to which they were admitted. The system achieved its immediate purpose quite well, for it removed any danger that unwilling whites would be forced to surrender the social prerogatives of the master race by mingling with Negroes in public places. But it had its limitations. While the segregation system prevented Negroes from crossing the color line and participating in white activities and using white facilities, it was virtually powerless to prevent whites who so desired from mixing freely with Negroes in colored taverns, bawdyhouses, and dance halls. In these clandestine pursuits, the color line broke down completely.

The innumerable taverns or "grog shops" catering illegally but openly to Negroes frequently brought the races together in the brotherhood of John Barleycorn. According to shocked complaints in the newspapers, it was quite common for white men and boys to frequent these Negro saloons "to revel and dance . . . for whole nights with a lot of men and women of saffron color, or quite black, either slave or free."[41] According to the "city intelligence" column of the *Daily Picayune,* one such "intolerable nuisance" on the corner of Baronne and Perdido Streets nightly entertained "a mixed assemblage of slaves, free negroes, and disreputable whites of both sexes."[42] In these taverns, in private rooms, and in back alleys, whites and Negroes often congregated over a deck of cards or a pair of dice.[43]

Men and women in search of sexual pleasures commonly made a mockery of the color line. The practice of *placage,* the more or less permanent arrangements between white men and free women of color, was fairly widespread.[44] Far more common, however, were the momentary dalliances between whites and Negroes in the more tawdry brothels and "cribs." Although the majority of these interracial affairs consisted of Negro prostitutes entertaining white men, some of the bawdyhouses offered white and colored women to all customers, regardless of race.[45] One such establishment next to the home of United States Senator Pierre Soulé on Basin

Street annoyed the august lawmaker so much that he filed a complaint against the bordello "where whites and blacks meet indiscriminately" and "make the night the accomplice of their vices and the time for their hellish amusements."[46]

Liaisons between Negro men and white women beyond the pale of prostitution occasionally occurred. Many of these were thoroughly sordid affairs, like that of the white woman and free Negro man arrested in 1855 for "carrying the depravity of Dauphine street even beyond its recognized extent."[47] Others gave every indication of true and lasting affection. A white woman, arrested in 1852 for living with a runaway slave, held in her arms "a mulatto male child, about two years of age," on whom she reportedly bestowed "all the endearments of a mother."[48] Whatever the circumstances, these liaisons between white women and Negro men defied the most sensitive taboo of a white supremacist society.

Many white New Orleanians feared that the very foundations of their social order were endangered by these transgressions of the color line. The Negroes, they reasoned, would hardly stand in awe of the master race if they danced and drank and gambled with whites or even on rare occasion enjoyed the favors of a white woman. This surreptitious mixing of the races, moreover, posed a real danger to the institution of slavery. Not only would such clandestine contacts with whites "corrupt" the slaves, but they also offered ideal opportunities for white *provocateurs* to spread the insidious doctrines of abolitionism among the servile population.

The first attack upon transgressions against the color line was aimed at the quadroon balls, by all accounts the most celebrated of all interracial activities carried on in the city. Free Negro balls had attracted large numbers of eager white men since the colonial period, but the quadroon ball was born in 1805, when a dance hall proprietor named Auguste Tessier began holding balls twice a week limited to white men and free Negro women. The experiment proved enormously successful, and the quadroon ball was soon established as one of New Orleans' major attractions. White men flocked to the balls for easy sex, for an introduction that might lead to a *placage,* or simply for the pleasure of an evening of dancing.

But the quadroon balls soon collected a host of implacable enemies. Strait-laced critics mourned the decline of morality, and guardians of the color line prophesied the collapse of white supremacy. White women, enraged when their escorts neglected "the white privets to gather black grapes,"[49] clamored for the elimination of the balls. Apparently the members of the city council agreed or found it impossible to withstand the feminine fury, for they adopted an ordinance on January 4, 1828, forbidding white men, with or without masks, from attending "dressed or masked balls composed of men and women of color."[50] The decree, however, did little to dampen the enthusiasm for the balls. No serious efforts were made to enforce it, and the city council abandoned its attempts to legislate against interracial amusements for nearly thirty years.

During the 1850's the intensifying sectional controversy brought renewed efforts to curb contacts between whites and Negroes. As tensions mounted and forebodings of conspiracies against the peculiar institution became a southern fixation, white New Orleanians grew increasingly suspicious of all activities that brought whites and Negroes together. These fears found expression in a series of new segregation laws aimed directly at those pursuits that most flagrantly defied the conventions of the color line. A pair of ordinances passed in December 1856 and January 1857 tried to eliminate interracial gambling in Negro taverns. The measure enacted on December 13, 1856, prohibited proprietors of taverns and coffeehouses from letting "white persons and colored persons . . . play cards together, or any other game in their house."[51] If such activities came to the attention of the authorities, the unfortunate barkeeper could be fined as much as one hundred dollars. The companion decree, adopted three weeks later, set the punishments for the participants. Whites and free Negroes could be fined from twenty-five to one hundred dollars, and slaves were to be assessed fifteen lashes.[52] An ordinance passed on March 10, 1857, outlawed mixed bawdy-houses: it prohibited white and colored women "notoriously abandoned to lewdness" from living in the same dwelling and also prohibited free Negroes from lodging white prostitutes.[53]

After Louisiana left the Union and the hostilities began, rampant fears that slaves, free Negroes, and white strangers might be enemy agents in their midst led white New Orleanians to still greater surveillance of interracial contacts. The results occasionally assumed absurd proportions. In May 1861 Dr. Thomas Jinnings, a prominent free Negro physician and Sunday-school teacher, took his wife to a charity fair sponsored by the white Episcopal church with which his Sunday school was affiliated. Jinnings was promptly arrested and formally charged with "intrading [sic] himself among the white congregation . . . and conducting hisself [sic] in a manner unbecoming the free colored population of this city, and in a manner to create insubordination among the servile population of this State."[54] Jinnings was released and the charges dropped only after several white parishioners testified that the doctor had behaved well and that he and his wife had been invited to the affair by one of the white ladies of the congregation.

Many New Orleans Negroes bitterly resented the segregation codes and practices that defined their lowly station in virtually every aspect of their public lives. In 1833 a group of Negro men bound for Lake Pontchartrain led an armed attack on a white streetcar that had refused to carry them.[55] But expressions of their discontent were largely limited to such sporadic outbursts, for they lacked the power to do anything else.

With the collapse of the old regime, however, New Orleans Negroes expressed their resentments more forcefully. Shortly after the city fell to the Federals in 1862, free Negro leaders mounted a campaign against the color line that rocked the segregation system to its very foundations before the campaign finally collapsed fifteen years later. A massive Negro demonstration led to the desegregation of city streetcars in May 1867.[56] New Orleans Negro representatives led the successful campaigns in the constitutional convention of 1867–1868 that wrote desegregation of public accommodations and public schools into the law of Louisiana.[57] A number of Negro boys and girls studied in white New Orleans public schools from 1871 to 1877, and a few of their elders sat in white theater boxes, ate in white restaurants, and drank in white saloons during the same period.[58] The drive to destroy the New Orleans color line persisted for fifteen years and finally collapsed when the Federal soldiers were withdrawn and the state Republican regime became a casualty of national reconciliation.

The Democratic redeemers who came to power in 1877 lost no time in redefining the Negro's "place" in Louisiana life. They immediately restored the color line in the New Orleans public schools and offered silent support to *de facto* segregation practices in places of public accommodation.[59] With the assistance of two landmark decisions by the United States Supreme Court, the redeemers soon dismantled the egalitarian legal apparatus put together piece by piece under the Radicals.[60] Finally in 1890 they began to write their "final solution" into Louisiana law with a series of "separate but equal" statutes. Soon New Orleans Negroes were again segregated in virtually every public pursuit.

The new segregation code was not an exact duplicate of its predecessor, for the two systems differed in scope and origin. The newer segregation was written into law and was designed to preserve racial distances throughout Louisiana, while the code that developed in New Orleans before the Civil War had been purely local in its scope and influence. The ante-bellum "star" system had been fashioned in an era alarmed by threats to its peculiar institution, while the "Jim Crow" code of the 1890's was put together by men who carried with them the bitter memories of Radical Reconstruction. But the results were strikingly similar: both systems effected a thoroughgoing separation of the races and the visible subordination of the New Orleans Negroes in nearly every area of public activity. If the ante-bellum code proved less than a "final solution" to race relationships in its day, it provided a remarkable preview to a later segregation system put forth as the ultimate defense of white supremacy a half century later.

Notes

---

[1] C. Vann Woodward, *The Strange Career of Jim Crow* (New York, 1955), 13–14.

[2] *Ibid.* (Galaxy ed., New York, 1957), xvii.

[3] John Samuel Ezell, *The South since 1865* (New York, 1963), 184.

[4] Barton J. Bernstein, *"Plessy v. Ferguson:* Conservative Sociological Jurisprudence," *Journal of Negro History,* XLVIII (July 1963), 200.

[5] *The Age of Civil War and Reconstruction, 1830–1900: A Book of Interpretive Essays,* ed. Charles Crowe (Homewood, Ill., 1966), 439.

[6] Quoted in *Lay my Burden Down: A Folk History of Slavery,* ed. B. A. Botkin (Chicago, 1945), 128.

[7] John Hope Franklin, *From Slavery to Freedom: A History of American Negroes* (2d rev. ed., New York, 1956), 215.

[8] Nearly 77,000 Negro slaves were kept in the ten largest southern cities in 1850, according to census figures for that year.

[9] Leon F. Litwack, *North of Slavery: The Negro in the Free States, 1790–1860* (Chicago, 1961).

[10] V. Jacque Voegeli, *Free But Not Equal: The Midwest and the Negro during the Civil War* (Chicago, 1967).

[11] Richard C. Wade, *Slavery in the Cities: The South, 1820–1860* (New York, 1964), 266–77.

[12] In *The Strange Career of Jim Crow* (2d rev. ed., New York, 1966), Woodward defended his emphasis on the importance of the Jim Crow laws and reiterated his opinion that a "capitulation to racism" in the 1890's produced a segregation system much more rigid and harsh than anything that had existed before that time. But he acknowledged the contributions of Litwack, Wade, and others and gave a new importance to ante-bellum and Reconstruction segregation practices as steppingstones to the Jim Crowism of the 1890's.

[13] Robert C. Reinders, *End of an Era: New Orleans, 1850–1860* (New Orleans, 1964), 17–20.

[14] New Orleans *Bee,* Oct. 13, 1835.

[15] *Ibid.;* Werner A. Wegener, "Negro Slavery in New Orleans," master's thesis, Tulane University, 1935, 58–60.

[16] An excellent summary of this practice is found in Wade, *Slavery in the Cities,* 38–54.

[17] New Orleans *Daily Picayune,* Jan. 27, 1859.

[18] Their numbers declined from 19,226 in 1840 to 10,689 in 1860, owing primarily to emigrations provoked by a series of proscriptive laws aimed at them during the 1840's and 1850's.

[19] The best description of their attainments is found in Donald E. Everett, "Free Persons of Color in New Orleans, 1803–1865," doctoral dissertation, Tulane University, 1952, 203–25. For a highly biased account, see Charles B. Rousseve, *The Negro in Louisiana: Aspects of His History and His Literature* (New Orleans, 1937), 49–91.

[20] Joseph G. Tregle, Jr., "Early New Orleans Society: A Reappraisal," *Journal of Southern History,* XVIII (Feb. 1952), 33.

[21] Quoted in Everett, "Free Persons of Color in New Orleans," 167.

[22] New Orleans *Daily Picayune,* Dec. 24, 1849, Jan. 3, Feb. 3, 1850, Apr. 1, 1855; New Orleans *Bee,* July 2, 1836, June 22, 1855.

[23] New Orleans *Daily Picayune,* Jan. 27, 1859.

[24] New Orleans *Bee,* Sept. 30, Oct. 12, 1835, July 1, 1855; New Orleans *Daily Picayune,* Jan. 16, Mar. 1, 5, 1850, Jan. 14, 16, Feb. 13, 1855.

[25] New Orleans *Bee,* Sept. 30, 1835, July 12, 1853, July 1, 1855; New Orleans *Daily Picayune,* Feb. 6, Mar. 1, 1850, Jan. 14, 16, Mar. 8, July 19, Aug. 10, Sept. 27, Nov. 3, 1855, July 13, 1858.

[26] *Ibid.,* Nov. 11, 1854, June 2, 3, 1855.

[27] John Calhoun, *Digest of the Ordinances and Resolutions of the Second Municipality of New Orleans, in Force May 1, 1840* (New Orleans, 1840), 144; Perry S. Warfield, *Digest of the Acts of the Legislature and Decisions of the Supreme Court of Louisiana Relative to the General Council of the City of New Orleans, Together with the Ordinances and Resolutions of the Former City Council, and the General Council of the City of New Orleans, in Force on the First of August, 1848* (New Orleans, 1848), 129.

[28] Quoted in Henry A. Kmen, "The Music of New Orleans," in *The Past as Prelude: New Orleans, 1718–1968,* ed. Hodding Carter (New Orleans, 1968), 217.

[29] Thomas Low Nichols, *Forty Years of American Life, 1821–1861* (New York, 1937), 355–56.

[30] Sir Charles Lyell, *A Second Visit to the United States of North America* (2 vols., New York, 1849), II, 94.

[31] Ferencz Pulszky and Theresa Pulszky, *White, Red, Black Sketches of American Society in the United States during the Visit of Their Guests* (2 vols., New York, 1853), II, 101.

[32] Calhoun, *Digest of the Ordinances,* 253; Wade, *Slavery in the Cities,* 268.

[33] New Orleans *Daily Picayune,* Nov. 9, 1864.

[34] Wade, *Slavery in the Cities,* 266–67.

[35] Everett, "Free Persons of Color in New Orleans," 258.

[36] *Ibid.;* Betty Porter, "The History of Negro Education in Louisiana," *Louisiana Historical Quarterly,* XXV (July 1942), 731.

[37] Quoted in A. E. Fossier, *The Charity Hospital of Louisiana* (New Orleans, 1923), 30.

[38] Stella O'Connor, "The Charity Hospital at New Orleans: An Administrative and Financial History, 1736–1941," master's thesis, Tulane University, 1947, 94.

[39] Grace Elizabeth King, *New Orleans: The Place and the People* (New York, 1895), 399; Wade, *Slavery in the Cities,* 270–71.

[40] *A Digest of Ordinances and Resolutions of the General Council of the City of New Orleans* (New Orleans, 1845), 6.

[41] Quoted in Kmen, "Music of New Orleans," 214.

[42] New Orleans *Daily Picayune,* Apr. 1, 1855.

[43] *Ibid.,* June 12, 1852, Feb. 20, June 10, 1855; Reinders, *End of an Era,* 165.

[44] The intricacies of these alliances are discussed in Everett, "Free Persons of Color in New Orleans," 202–209.

[45] New Orleans *Daily Picayune,* June 30, July 1, 18, Aug. 7, 1855; New Orleans *Bee,* July 14, 1853; Reinders, *End of an Era,* 166; Herbert Asbury, *The French Quarter: An Informal History of the New Orleans Underworld* (New York, 1938), 388.

[46] New Orleans *Daily Picayune,* Aug. 7, 1855.

[47] *Ibid.,* June 30, July 1, 1855.

[48] *Ibid.,* July 24, 1852.

[49] Quoted in Kmen, "Music of New Orleans," 214.

[50] Calhoun, *Digest of the Ordinances,* 128; Warfield, *Digest of the Acts* 145.

[51] Henry J. Leovy, *The Laws and General Ordinances of the City of New Orleans, Together with the Acts of the Legislature, Decisions of the Supreme Court, and Constitutional Provisions, Relating to the City Government* (New Orleans, 1857), 46.

[52] *Ibid.,* 260–61.

[53] *Ibid.,* 378.

[54] New Orleans *Daily Picayune,* May 30, 1861.

[55] New Orleans *Argus,* Aug. 1, 1833, as quoted in *Niles Register,* Aug. 24, 1833.

[56] New Orleans *Daily Crescent,* May 7, 8, 10, 1867; New Orleans *Times,* May 5, 7, 1867; New Orleans *Tribune,* May 4, 7, 9, 1867; New Orleans *Daily Picayune,* May 7, 8, 1867.

[57] *Official Journal of the Proceedings of the Convention, for Framing a Constitution for the State of Louisiana* (New Orleans, 1867–68), 4, 17, 27, 35, 60–61, 121–22, 125, 201.

[58] For school desegregation, see Louis R. Harlan, "Desegregation in New Orleans Public Schools during Reconstruction," *American Historical Review,* LXVII (Apr. 1962), 663–75. For a discussion of efforts to desegregate the city's public accommodations, see Roger A. Fischer, "The Segregation Struggle in Louisiana, 1850–1890," doctoral dissertation, Tulane University, 1967, 63–98.

[59] New Orleans *Daily Picayune,* June 27, Dec. 6, 1877.

[60] The Democrats replaced the 1868 Constitution with a new one in 1879 that ignored altogether the color line in schools and public accommodations. The Supreme Court nullified the state Enforcement Act of 1860 in *Hall* v. *De Cuir,* 95 US 485 (1878) and struck down the federal Civil Rights Act of 1875 in the Civil Rights Cases, 109 US 3 (1883).

The Free Negro in the Economic Life of Ante-Bellum North Carolina

John Hope Franklin

In a state that was as decidedly rural as ante-bellum North Carolina, and where the majority of the free Negroes lived in the rural areas,[1] it was only natural that most of them made their living from the soil. The majority of the free Negro apprentices were bound out to learn the trade of a farmer, and upon reaching manhood they expected to pursue this occupation.[2] Since, moreover, it was extremely difficult for free Negroes to secure training in the skilled trades, many who may have had the inclination were forced into other fields. They *had* to make a living. Tradition and their meager training compelled the majority of the free Negroes to seek their living from the soil.

North Carolina was never one of the chief slaveholding states. In numbers, its slaves were fewer than those of her neighbor states of Virginia, South Carolina, and Georgia.[3] As a matter of fact, sixty-seven per cent of the slave-holding families held fewer than ten slaves in 1860, while seventy-two per cent of North Carolina's families held no slaves at all.[4] This suggests that in a state where the plantation system was only fairly well entrenched, the supply of slave labor was definitely limited. The farm labor in North Carolina was done not only by the slave but, in some areas, by the members of the white farming family, by white farm laborers, and by free Negro farm laborers.[5] In finding this work opportunity, the free Negro was extremely fortunate, and his labor was not as frequently rejected as it was in the more skilled occupations. Naturally there were objections to his presence on plantations where there were slaves, but these objections were more likely to be raised to the hiring of free Negroes on the neighbor's plantation than on one's own. Though there may have been fears that the free Negro's presence on a slave plantation might cause insolence among the slaves as well as inspire desires of freedom among them, this did not prevent the white slaveholders from hiring free Negroes to perform some of the tasks from time to time.[6]

There was, moreover, an opportunity for the free Negro to secure seasonal

John Hope Franklin, "The Free Negro in the Economic Life of Ante-Bellum North Carolina," Part II, *North Carolina Historical Review* XIX (October 1942), 359–375. Reprinted by permission.

work on the farms of North Carolinians who had no slaves at all. The yeoman frequently harbored violent antipathies for the slave system and would refuse to hire slave labor even when it was available. He was more likely to look for assistance, during rush seasons, among the poor landless whites or among the free Negroes. The large number of free Negro farm laborers in counties where there was little or no slaveholding seems to support this point of view. In Cabarrus County, for example, where the slave population was small, there were fourteen free Negro farm laborers in 1860 and only four free Negro farmers.[7]

Naturally there were more free Negro farm hands in counties where the free Negro population was large. These counties, incidentally, also had a large slave population. As field hands, drivers, and all-around laborers, free Negroes found work opportunities on the largest of plantations. It was not unusual for free Negroes to live on slave plantations and to participate in the life there. Some of them had slave wives or husbands, and the benevolent master frequently permitted them to live there together, hiring the services of the free person.[8] Thomas Newton of Craven County secured his freedom from his master, Benjamin Woods, and by continuing to work for him Newton was able to purchase his wife, who had been a slave on the same plantation.[9]

Of course the number of free Negro farm laborers varied from county to county. The number to be found in any particular county depended not only upon the scarcity or abundance of farm labor, slave or free, and the attitude of the whites toward free Negro labor, but also upon the mobility of the landless free Negro population. It was extremely difficult for free Negroes, although without the trappings which usually tie people to a particular location, to move from one place to another. The reluctance of the authorities to grant passes permitting free Negroes to move about[10] and the impecunious state of a majority of the free Negroes made it quite difficult for free Negro farm laborers to migrate even to the adjoining county. It was possible, therefore, for a newly freed Negro to live and die in an area that was least suited for his advancement.

With these facts in mind, it is interesting to observe the location of the bulk of the free Negro farm hands in ante-bellum North Carolina. Of the 1,746 free Negro farm hands in the state in 1860, more than one thousand were located in the seven eastern counties which constituted the stronghold of the slave system.[11] Halifax County alone had 384 free Negro farm hands, while Pasquotank County had 284. Thirty-one counties were without any free Negro farm hands at all, while 700 were scattered among the remaining forty-eight counties.[12]

A more interesting group of free Negroes who made their living from the soil were those who either rented or owned land and planted their own crops. They may properly be called the free Negro yeomanry. It was possible for a free Negro to obtain permission from a white landowner to live on the latter's land and to cultivate a portion of it and share in the returns from his labor. This, however, was looked upon with disfavor, and white owners of land were discouraged in the practice. A law of 1827 required each white person to list all free Negroes living on his land

and to be responsible for the taxes which might be levied on such free Negroes.[13] Free Negro tenants who showed a disposition to work and to shoulder their responsibilities could still convince landowners that they would not be a burden to them. The tax lists of various counties and the census reports bear witness to the fact that there were free Negro tenants on the lands of white persons down to the end of the period. In the tax list for Beaufort County in 1850, for example, A. Eborn, a free Negro, was listed as the tenant of John Cutter, white. One wealthy white farmer, R. H. Reddick of Lower Broad Creek, had fourteen free Negro tenants on his land and was responsible for $143.93 in taxes for them. In the same list, F. Hackey, a free Negro, was the tenant of Samuel Swan, white.[14] At the end of the period, despite the financial risks on the part of white landowners, many free Negro tenants were still living on the land of white landowners.[15]

That the number of free Negroes who owned their farms was considerable can be seen in the real property columns of the unpublished population schedules of the census returns. Many of these individuals, like John Stanly of New Bern, had started with small holdings, and by thrift and business acumen had accumulated sizable holdings. They usually engaged in tobacco and cotton farming and marketed their crops in much the same way that other farmers in the state marketed theirs. By far the majority of the property owned by free Negroes was in the rural areas and was, of course, in the possession of free Negro farmers.

The free Negro farmer was generally in better circumstances than free Negroes in the other areas of economic activity. In 1860 there were 1,047 free Negroes who gave their occupation as farmers. Of this number, approximately fifty per cent possessed some real peoperty. In some cases they did not own an amount sufficient for their purposes, but the figures seem to suggest that the free Negro was becoming a landowner. David Reynolds, a farmer of Halifax County, owned $3,000 worth of real property in 1860. J. A. Collins of Hyde County had $1,000 worth of real property at the same time. The well known Thomas Blacknall of Franklin County owned $6,000 worth of land. Of the fifty-three Negroes with property valued at more than $2,500 each in 1880, thirty-one were farmers.[16]

In North Carolina the free Negroes who made their living from the soil numbered approximately three thousand. Doubtless this number could be augmented considerably when one takes into account the number of minors and housewives who assisted their fathers, brothers, and husbands in the fields. That they constituted the most important element in the economic life of the free Negro in ante-bellum North Carolina in terms of numbers and holdings is clearly shown by the facts. For the most part they went their way unnoticed. The disproportionate part of the stage occupied by the free Negroes in other pursuits was the result of the focus of light thrown upon them in the more thickly settled communities. Meanwhile the free Negro farmer, living in the inarticulate and relatively sparsely settled countryside, steadily rose in economic independence and, consequently, in the respect — somewhat disquieted, perhaps — of his fellows.

At no time during the period before the Civil War was the free Negro's right to own real property questioned. He enjoyed all the protection in the matter of acquisition, transfer, devise, and descent that other citizens of North Carolina enjoyed. The records of the county courts indicate that free Negroes used them regularly for the purpose of recording changes in ownership of real and personal property. The following record is typical of many that were found in the minutes of the county court: "A deed from Ezra F. Holmes to Southey Kease (free Negro) was proved in open court by the oath of William T. Bryan a witness thereto ordered to be registered."[17]

Having once acquired land, the free Negro could be fairly certain that the courts would protect him during his period of possession. In 1838 Benjamin Curry, a free Negro of Guilford County, was driven off the property which he had owned for twelve years. Of the four white men charged with dispossessing Curry, one claimed that the free Negro had sold him his house, land, and five slave children, and that the transaction had been executed in a deed of trust between the two parties. At the trial the solicitor for the state objected to the deed as evidence, contending that it was a slick piece of extortion and that the free Negro did not intend to give up his land. The lower court convicted the defendants of having "riotously and routously" assembled to disturb the peace of the state and with force of arms trespassed upon the property of the free Negro.

The defendants appealed the case to the Supreme Court. After making a thorough review of the facts in the case and after listening to lengthy arguments from both sides, Judge Gaston, speaking for the Court, said:

We are of the opinion that there was no error in the conviction of which the defendant complains. In cases where the laws gives to the judges a descretion over the quantum of punishment, they may, with propriety, suspend the sentence [In this case, the principal defendant had received a fine of $100.] for the avowed purpose of affording the convicted an opportunity to make restitution to the person peculiarly aggrieved by his offense.

The judgment against the defendant is, therefore, reversed, and this opinion is to be certified to the Superior Court — for the County of Guilford, with directions to award sentence of fine or of fine and imprisonment against the defendant agreeably thereto and to the laws of the state.[18]

The leniency of Judge Gaston was inspired by the defendant's having already restored the property to the free Negro. Though there was a reversal of the conviction, the case remains significant in that the Supreme Court went on record as being vigorously opposed to the abridgment of property rights even in the case of a free Negro.[19]

Free Negroes could sell or transfer their land at will as long as it was for a legal consideration. In 1833, for example, Benjamin Neale of Craven County sold one hundred acres of land, and the following indenture makes known the transaction:

February 4, 1833
State of N.C.
County of Craven

Be it known that Benjamin Neale (coloured man) for and in consideration of the sum of fifty dollars to me paid in hand by William B. Masters of the same State and County aforesaid, have bargained sold enfeoffed and confirmed unto the same Wm. B. Masters his heirs and assigns forever a certain parcel of land. . . . [A description of the land is given.] The said Benjamin Neale purchased of Thomas Cooke dec. containing by estimation one hundred acres be the same more or less. To have and to hold the said piece or parcel of land with all the woods ways waters and every other appurtenances thereunto belonging against the lawful claims of all and every other person.

Benjamin Neale [20]

The right of a free Negro to sell his property was confirmed by the Supreme Court in a decision of 1843. A white man, Pearson, rented a small tract of land for one year to Elijah Powell, a free Negro, who promised to give him one-half of the corn crop. The Justice of the Peace gave Pearson permission to sell Powell's crop. Powell asked that the sale be postponed until after the corn was gathered. When the corn was sold, one Hare objected, saying that he had already bought half of the crop from Powell. Pearson denied that Powell could sell his share, contending that he was only a servant. The Nash Superior Court said that Powell was a tenant and could dispose of his property as he pleased. In upholding this view, the Supreme Court, through Judge Daniel, said:

Even if Powell was a servant, the division had given him a share which all would have to admit. The corn had been placed in the defendant's barn upon the naked bailment for safe-keeping. The sale of it and the demand by the purchaser put an end to the bailment. [21]

It was not at all unusual for free Negroes to direct the disposition of their property through wills. Upon the death of the testator, the will was recorded in the minutes of the county court and an executor was appointed by the court. The minutes of the Beaufort County Court for 1843 give a typical example:

State of North Carolina
Beaufort County
A paper writing purporting to the last will and testament of John Hambleton deceased (free Negro) was duly proved in open court to be the last will and testament of said John Hambleton and duly executed so as to pass seal on personal estate by the oath of John W. Latham the subscribing witness thereto and ordered to be recorded and Edward Hyman the Executor named therein was qualified as Executor. [22]

An interesting case involving the will of a free Negro woman was that of the aged Mary Green of Wilmington, who left all of her property to a white attorney. She looked to him not only for counsel, the records showed, but also for protection and occasionally small sums of money. In addition to these favors, he also collected rent on property that had been accumulated by the testator's free Negro husband. The only relative, a niece, had received a house and lot from her aunt before she died. Upon the advice of the free Negro husband, all the property was left to the white attorney. The niece went into court and contended that her aunt had been under "undue influence" and sought to have the will invalidated. Upon losing the case in the New Hanover Superior Court, the niece appealed to the Supreme Court. In upholding the decision of the lower court, Judge Manly said,

It seems that the legatee [Joshua Wright] and the decedent [Mary Green] stood in relation of client and attorney *patron* and *dependent,* and the court below — informs the jury that persons bearing these relations are to be suspected and scrutinized more closely and carefully than dealings between others. These relations, as facts pertinent to the issue — were submitted to the jury with proper instructions. That was all, we think, the court was authorized to do by the law of the land.

We concur with the court below that undue influence must be fraudulent and controlling and must be shown to the satisfaction of a jury, in a court of law, upon an issue of *devisavit vel nom.*[23]

Free Negroes, as other individuals, sometimes had difficulty in establishing their rightful claim to property left to them in a will. If, however, their freedom could be established and if the circumstances under which the will was made were valid, the free Negro could secure the necessary protection in the courts of the state. In 1851, one Benjamin Dicken of Edgecombe County died. His will directed his executor to free all of his slaves and send them to some free state and divide $12,000 among them. All except one woman, who died soon after, left the state. Her daughter, who had gone to Canada, claimed her mother's share of the estate for her and the other children. The executor claimed that the mother had not complied with the stipulation of the will since she had not left the state and therefore, that her heirs could claim no part of the money intended for her. Judge Pearson, of the Supreme Court, said that the removing of the Negroes was not a condition precedent to emancipation, but a condition subsequent, "by the non-performance of which they may forfeit their newly acquired freedom." The Judge was satisfied that the deceased free Negro woman had good intentions:

1. We are satisfied that Mariah the mother of the plaintiff at the time of her death — was to all intents and purposes, a free woman, and had the capacity to take property and transmit it by succession to her personal representative.

2. We are also satisfied that the children of Mariah were entitled to call upon

her administrator to make distribution among them, as her next of kin — and we think it clear that all of her children are to be considered distributees.[24]

In one case several technicalities arose which made it difficult for a free Negro devisee to retain the town property that had been left her by a wealthy white man of Tarboro. In his will he said: "I give and devise to Mary Ann Jones, a free colored woman of the town of Tarboro and to her heirs and assigns forever, the lot of ground and house thereon erected on which she now lives." Since two lots belonging to the testator were adjacent, the executor interpreted the will literally and proceeded to take possession of the lot next to the one on which the devisee's house stood. Before his death, the testator had fenced in both lots together, and the free Negro woman used both lots for a garden and for other purposes. In 1880 Judge Manly of the Supreme Court awarded both lots to the estate of the free Negro woman — by that time deceased. He took the point of view that the gift to the free Negro woman "is not confined to the fifty yards square called a lot in the plan of the town, but extends at least to the lands enclosed and used in connection with the house." In the will the testator used the word "lot" to mean "parcel" or "piece."[25]

Perhaps the most interesting case of the period involving the inheritance of property by free Negroes arose in 1857. While a slave, a certain Miles married another slave. Afterward he was freed and subsequently purchased his wife. They had one child; then the wife was set free, and they had several other children. After this wife died, Miles married a free Negro woman by whom he had three children. When he died intestate, in 1857, a contest arose between the two sets of children over the division of the property. The children by the first wife claimed tenancy in common with the children by the second wife. When the case came before the Supreme Court, that body denied that the children by the first wife had any valid claims:

A slave cannot make a contract. Therefore, he cannot marry legally. Marriage is based upon contract. Consequently, the relation of "man and wife" cannot exist among slaves. Neither the first nor the others of the children by the first wife were legitimate. The parties after being freed ought to have married according to law; it is the misfortune of their children that they neglected or refused to do so, for no court can avert the consequences.[26]

The possession of slaves by free Negroes was the only type of personal property holding that was ever questioned during the ante-bellum period. There may not have been much objection to the ownership of one's own family by a free Negro; but when one undertook to acquire slaves to improve his economic status, there were those who looked upon it as a dangerous trend, the legality of which was seriously questioned. If the free Negro was not a full citizen, could he enjoy the same privileges of ownership and the protection of certain types of property that other citizens enjoyed? Around this question revolved a great deal of discussion at the beginning of the militant period of the antislavery movement.[27]

When a slave was found guilty of concealing a slave on board a vessel, in violation of the act of 1825, it was contended by his owner that the prisoner, a slave, was not a person or mariner within the meaning of the act and that Green, the owner of the concealed slave, was a mulatto and hence not a citizen of the state and could not own slaves. The decision of the Supreme Court, handed down in 1833 by Judge Daniel, established once and for all the rights of the free Negro in the matter of the ownership of slaves. He said:

By the laws of this State, a free man of color may own land and hold lands and personal property including slaves. Without therefore stopping to inquire into the extent of the political rights and privileges of a free man of color, I am very well satisfied from the words of the act of the General Assembly that the Legislature meant to protect the slave property of every person who by the laws of the State are entitled to hold such property, I am, therefore, of the opinon that the owner is a citizen within the meaning of the Act of Assembly, and it appearing he was a mulatto is not a reason to grant a new trial to the person who concealed his slave.[28]

The decision of Judge Daniel in this case remained the accepted point of view until the very end of the period. When the hostility between the sections was developing into open conflict, the free Negro in the South witnessed an almost complete abrogation of his rights. One of the most significant laws passed during the momentous session of the legislature in 1860–1861 was the "Act to prevent free Negroes from having the control of slaves." While it did not affect a large number of free Negroes within the state,[29] it showed the extent to which the North Carolina solons were willing to go in order to combat the forces that were striking at the heart of their long-cherished system. Among other things, the law provided:

That no free Negro, or free person of color, shall be permitted or allowed to buy, purchase, or hire for any length of time any slave or slaves, or to have any slave or slaves bound as apprentice or apprentices to him, her or them, or in any other wise to have the control, management or services of any slave or slaves, under the penalty of one hundred dollars for each offence, and shall further be guilty of a misdemeanor, and liable to indictment for the same.

Another section of the law provided that free Negroes already in the possession of slave property would not be affected by the enactment.[30]

Despite the innumerable obstacles that stood in the way of the accumulation of property by free Negroes, several amassed a considerable amount of property during their lifetime. The life of Julius Melbourn is about as interesting as one can find in the period. Born a slave in 1790 on a plantation near Raleigh, he was bought, at five years of age, by the wealthy widow of a British army official, who lived in Raleigh. When her only son was slain in a duel — said to have been fought because of some derogatory remarks concerning his mother having reared Melbourn as a gentleman — the slave was emancipated and made the sole heir to the estate of $20,000. By the time Melbourn was twenty-five years old his estate was worth about $30,000. By careful saving and shrewd investment, he was soon worth $50,000. When he decided that he could not live and die in a country "where the laws sustained and justified such disregard to individual rights and tolerated such inhumanity," as was manifested in the treatment of free Negroes, he sailed for England, where he spent the remainder of his life. That he was still wealthy is attested by the fact that he set up his son in a $20,000 mercantile business in London.[31]

Most of the free Negroes who owned property were possessors of small estates worth a few hundred dollars or less. These individuals, moreover, comprised only a small percentage of the total free Negro population. The great majority of free Negroes in North Carolina were, during the entire period, without any property whatsoever. At the end of the period, only 3,659, or slightly more than ten per cent, owned any property. Of this number, only 1,211 owned any real estate. In few counties did more than ten per cent of the free Negroes own property. Craven County, with 1,332 free Negroes in 1860, had only 179 free Negro property owners. Cabarrus County, with 115 free Negroes, had twelve free Negro owners of property. Halifax County, with its 3,452 free Negroes, however, had 463 free Negroes who owned property.[32] In 1860 free Negroes had property valued at $2,500 or more [see Table 1].[33] While this table does not represent the average holdings of the free Negro in ante-bellum North Carolina, it suggests that there was a number of individual cases in which free Negroes rose to a position of economic independence, despite obstacles.

In six counties in 1860 free Negroes owned no real estate.[34] While each county listed some personal property held by free Negroes, eight counties listed only one such person each.[35] Perhaps nothing is a more striking commentary on the plight of the free Negro in North Carolina than his inability to acquire property, both real and personal.

A study of the value of the property which free Negroes did possess will shed further light on the economic status of the free Negro in ante-bellum North Carolina. Of course it is difficult for one living in the fifth decade of the twentieth century to appreciate the figures which reveal the value of property owned by free Negroes in, say, 1860. Land values were so much lower at the time that it was quite possible for an individual with one hundred dollars worth of real property to have an adequate amount for farming purposes, and with a few hundred dollars he could erect a house that would be about as modern as the age could provide. There was a likelihood, however, that the land of the free Negro would be the least desirable in a given area. Since the majority of free Negroes were small farmers, they faced the same difficulty that other North Carolina yeomen faced: that of trying to obtain satisfactory property in the same market where the more resourceful plantation

Table 1: Free Negroes Having Property Valued at More than $2,500

Name	Occupation	Value	Name	Occupation	Value
Alee, M.	Baker	$2,750	Knight, J.	Confection	$5,905
Alston, O.	Farmer	17,644	Lan'ton, D.	Carpenter	2.500
Bell, H.		14,000	Lewis, W.	Farmer	2,750
Bethel, J.	Barber	3,550	Locklier	Farmer	5,200
Blacknall, T.	Farmer	7,300	Mangum, L.	Farmer	20,816
Bryan, C.	Farmer	2,535	Martin, W.	Farmer	2,500
Burchett, J.	Farmer	2,500	Men'hall	Farmer	3,197
Butch, H.	Farm Hand	3,450	Michael, S.	Farmer	5,000
Collins, J.	Farmer	9,000	Miller, E.	Wheelwright	8,150
Corn, D.	Farmer	5,250	Moore, D.	Barber	4,400
Corn, N.	Farmer	2,800	Norris, A.	Carpenter	3,000
Cuff, N.	Farmer	3,475	Ox'dine, J.	Farmer	9,825
Day, T.	Cab. Maker	4,000	Picar, E.		2,500
Dial, G.	Farmer	4,900	Piles, A.	Clerk	5,000
Erwin, J.	Musician	3,100	Reed, W.	Farmer	3,300
Evans, E.	Farmer	11,830	Revel, E.	Farmer	4,826
Evans, W.	Farmer	3,932	Reynolds	Farmer	4,000
Freeman, J.	Farmer	20,300	Sampson, J.	Carpenter	36,000
Graham, J.	Farmer	2,800	Scott, A.	Farmer	3,766
Green, M.	Farmer	2,600	Silvester	Farmer	2,670
Guy, W.	Farmer	2,695	Smith, N.	Farmer	2,500
Hites, E.	Carpenter	4,000	Stanly, C.	Dress Maker	4,000
Howard, J.		2,500	Steward, W.	Farmer	3,000
Jacobs, J.	Farmer	3,712	Taboon, A.	Farm Hand	5,554
Jones, M.	Housekeeper	5,500	Webb, S.	Farmer	2,810
Jones, T.		6,700	Winn, C.	Blacksmith	2,800
Jordan, J.	Farmer	4,700			

owner was making his purchases. It is a point of interest, therefore, that some free Negroes, like John C. Stanly of New Bern and James D. Sampson of New Hanover, were able to acquire some of the most desirable land in their respective communities.

On the whole, a large number of free Negroes possessed some type of personal property, ranging from silver watches to farming tools. Thus, in the larger number of counties, the value of personal property was higher than the value of real property. But the poverty of the free Negro group can be seen clearly through this study of the value of the property of the group. They possessed an aggregate wealth of $1,045,643. (See Table 2.) When one considers that more than 30,000 people had to share in this wealth of slightly more than one million dollars, the realization of their plight is inescapable. The per capita wealth of the free Negroes of North Carolina was only $34 in 1860. Thousands of these were landless and without any kind of property. Even when one ascertains the per capita wealth of the free Negro property owners, the picture remains gloomy, for they had a per capita wealth of $287. It must be remembered that fifty-three were worth more than $2,500, while several were worth more than $15,000.[36] The following table shows the value of real and personal property of free Negroes in 1860.[37]

One area in which considerable interest has always been manifested is the ownership of slaves by free Negroes. At no time during the ante-bellum period were free Negroes in North Carolina without some slaves. The motives for such ownership were perhaps varied, as in other groups. Without a doubt there were those who possessed slaves for the purpose of advancing their economic well-being. With such

Table 2: Aggregate Value of Property Owned by Free Negroes

County	Real	Personal	County	Real	Personal
Alamance	$13,500	$7,415	Jackson		$125
Alexander	500	390	Johnston	$4,060	4,853
Alleghany		600	Jones	1,500	1,875
Anson	3,798	7,660	Lenoir	625	2,250
Ashe	2,200	2,495	Lincoln	100	270
Beaufort	12,410	6,960	Macon	4,050	5,100
Bertie	1,280	3,615	Madison		615
Bladen	6,289	5,112	Martin	5,549	1,200
Brunswick	6,487	6,239	McDowell	4,000	1,000
Buncombe	3,540	3,184	Mecklenburg	8,875	3,720
Burke	200	785	Montgomery	362	1,285
Cabarrus	1,072	2,050	Moore	550	1,975
Caldwell	1,295	1,284	Nash	8,939	10,889
Camden	1,000	768	New Hanover	37,720	35,060
Carteret	3,150	950	Northampton	12,824	15,359
Caswell	4,208	5,530	Onslow	1,735	3,475
Catawba	50	75	Orange	2,800	13,375
Chatham	1,680	2,960	Pasquotank	20,440	22,195
Cherokee	350	515	Perquimans	5,000	8,601
Chowan	3,600	2,793	Person	5,180	3,080
Cleveland	3,150	4,652	Pitt	2,100	5,560
Columbus	9,135	8,990	Polk	700	1,446
Craven	29,865	21,137	Randolph	5,290	8,745
Cumberland	11,500	7,722	Richmond	10,750	20,930
Currituck	1,270	1,745	Robeson	37,555	42,159
Davidson	1,200	1,428	Rickingham	2,750	1,900
Davie		1,040	Rowan	1,300	970
Duplin	3,360	3,777	Rutherford	225	100
Edgecombe	7,100	10,350	Sampson	10,014	4,742
Forsyth	1,530	1,665	Stanly	950	835
Franklin	6,535	6,013	Stokes	325	550
Gaston	2,700	2,300	Surry	925	1,144
Gates	5,125	18,755	Tyrrel	725	1,615
Granville	15,987	13,845	Union	300	975
Greene	2,475	2,920	Wake	22,204	45,362
Guilford	5,425	13,445	Warren	9,931	13,935
Halifax	30,948	42,778	Washington	5,843	5,077
Harnett		375	Watauga	475	595
Haywood		75	Wayne	13,380	9,900
Henderson	150	100	Wilkes	2,710	3,835
Hertford	15,482	16,624	Wilson	4,984	3,999
Hyde	1,000	8,000	Yadkin	840	2,912
Iredell	330	150	Yancey	1,525	1,803

a view in mind, these free Negro slaveholders were more interested in making their farms or carpenter shops "pay" than they were in treating their slaves humanely. The enterprising free Negro owners of slaves can usually be identified because of their extensive holdings of real and personal property and because of their inactivity in the manumission movement. For thirty years Thomas Day, the free Negro cabinet maker of Milton, used slaves to help him in his business. In 1830 he had two;[38] by 1860 he had three.[39] For thirty years Thomas Blacknall of Franklin County kept slaves, though the number fell from seven to three between 1830 and 1860.[40] It seems clear that these enterprising free Negroes were at least as deeply interested in the labor of their slaves as they were in their comfort.

It seems that by far the larger portion of free Negro owners of slaves were possessors of this human chattel for benevolent reasons. There are numerous examples of free Negroes having purchased relatives or friends to ease their lot. Many of them manumitted such slaves,[41] while others held title to slaves who were virtually free. An examination of the slaveholding by free Negroes seems to bear out this point. Slave Richard Gaston ran away from his master and remained in the woods until his free Negro wife had saved the necessary funds for his purchase.[42] Lila Abshur continued to hold title to her father when the legislature acted unfavorably on her petition to emancipate him.[43] While John S. Stanly undoubtedly held some slaves with the view to increasing his wealth,[44] he held others purely out of benevolence.[45]

The fluctuation in the number of free Negro owners of slaves during the period under observation is an interesting development. At the time of the taking of the first census in 1790, twenty-five free Negroes in eleven counties owned seventy-three slaves.[46] In 1830 the number of free Negro slaveholders had increased to 191, distributed in thirty-seven counties, while their human chattel numbered 620.[47] Interestingly enough, by 1860 there were only eight free Negro owners of slaves, the latter numbering only twenty-five.[48]

Several observations can now be made. In the first place, the number of slaves held by free Negroes was usually small. Notable exceptions are the eleven slaves held by Samuel Johnston of Bertie County in 1790;[49] the forty-four slaves each owned by Gooden Bowen of Bladen County and John Walker of New Hanover County in 1830; and the twenty-four slaves owned by John Chrichlon of Martin County in 1830.[50] Free Negroes usually held one, two, or three slaves; and the petitions of free Negroes to manumit relatives suggest that a sizable number of slaves had been acquired as a result of benevolence.

In the second place, the increase in the number of free Negroes with an accompanying increase in economic independence on the part of some caused a larger number of Negro slaves to be acquired by free Negroes. No doubt, moreover, there was some effort to conform to the pattern established by the dominant slave-holding group within the state in the effort to elevate themselves to a position of respect and privilege. Thus by 1830 more than 600 slaves were held by free Negroes. Finally, the remarkable decline both in the number of free Negro slave owners and in the number of slaves held toward the end of the period suggests the increasing economic and political difficulty that the free Negro was encountering. Many of those slaves held in 1830 had been manumitted according to the plans of the free Negro owners. Other slaves had been lost in the maze of the economic setbacks that many free Negroes were experiencing.[51] Perhaps also the fervor to acquire slave relatives and set them free was waning, as the free Negro himself began to doubt the blessings of freedom.[52] Thus even before it became illegal for free Negroes to acquire slaves — in 1861 — the group had ceased to make such acquisitions. In this case the enactment made legally impossible that which the free Negro had already ceased to do.

Surrounded on all sides by a legal system which denied them the opportunity to seek a livelihood where they could and by a hostile community that often made them as unwelcome as a contagious disease, the free Negroes tried to find their place in the economic life of ante-bellum North Carolina. If they were "idle, thievish, roguish, and indolent" — a sweeping generalization that can reasonably be doubted — they merely reflected the restraints and stigma that society had placed upon them, and their reactions were no more than natural. In view of the circumstances, it is not surprising that they were not a more powerful economic force than they were. The amazing thing is that under such adverse circumstantces they were able to acquire more than a million dollars worth of property by the end of the period and to have possessed several hundred slaves during the seventy-year period ending in 1860.

Notes

[1] Only 3,197, or scarcely ten percent, of the free Negroes lived in towns in 1860. Census Office, *The Population in 1860*, pp. 350–359.

[2] See the occupations of free Negro apprentices in the unpublished population schedules for the census of 1860. (Unless otherwise indicated, all manuscripts cited in this article are in the archives of the North Carolina Historical Commission, Raleigh.)

[3] Census Office, *Population in 1860*, pp. 214, 452, 518.

[4] Guion G. Johnson, *Ante-Bellum North Carolina*, p. 468 ff.

[5] In describing the small farmer (white) in ante-bellum North Carolina, Dr. Guion Johnson refers to this group as the largest single class of whites in the state, and continues, "Their farms were small, and they cultivated their own land with the assistance of their families and an occasional hired hand or slave." Johnson, *Ante-Bellum North Carolina*, p. 65.

[6] See the unpublished population schedules for the census of 1860. Many free Negro farm laborers were listed as living with white families. This is all the more remarkable in view of the fact that, in such instances, the white farmer was responsible for all of the debts and obligations that were incurred by the free Negro.

[7] See the unpublished population schedules for the census of 1860. It is quite likely, moreover, that many of the free Negroes who gave their occupation as "common laborer" found work on the farms and may have been, more properly, "farm hands."

[8] See, for example, the unpublished population schedules for the census of 1860 (Wake County). It seems that such a practice was quite inconsistent with the point of view that the presence of free Negroes among slaves "contributes to excite and cherish a spirit of discontent and disorder among the slaves." Petition of the citizens of New Bern to the General Assembly, December, 1831, MS. in the Legislative Papers for 1831–1832.

[9] Minutes of the Court of Pleas and Quarter Sessions for Craven County, March, 1811.

[10] After 1831 free Negroes desiring to go to other counties had to receive a license from the clerk of the Court of Pleas and Quarter Sessions of the county in which they resided. *Laws, 1830–1831*, p. 11.

[11] The seven counties were Granville, Halifax, Hertford, Northampton, Pasquotank, Perquimans, and Sampson.

[12] This information was taken from the unpublished population schedules for the census of 1860. Most of the counties with no free Negro farm hands were located in the western part of the state.

[13] *Laws, 1827–1828,* p. 21.

[14] MS. in the County Records for Beaufort County, 1850 (Beaufort County Courthouse, Washington, N.C.).

[15] See the unpublished population schedules for the census of 1860.

[16] Unpublished population schedules for the census of 1860.

[17] Minutes of the Court of Pleas and Quarter Sessions for Beaufort County, December, 1843 (Beaufort County Courthouse, Washington, N.C.).

[18] State *v.* John H. Bennett, 20 N.C., p. 135 ff.

[19] See also the case of State *v.* Emory, 51 N.C., p. 142, in which the Supreme Court held that a free Negro could not be forcibly ejected from the possession of a house.

[20] MS. in the James W. Bryan Papers (University of North Carolina Library, Chapel Hill, N.C.). See also the deed from John and Rebecca Hambleton, free Negroes, to Churchill Moore, in the Minutes of the Court of Pleas and Quarter Sessions for Beaufort County, December, 1842 (Beaufort County Courthouse, Washington, N.C.).

[21] Hare *v.* Pearson, 26 N.C., p. 62.

[22] Minutes of the Court of Pleas and Quarter Sessions of Beaufort County, June, 1843 (Beaufort County Courthouse, Washington, N.C.). Free Negroes were sometimes appointed executors, as in the case of Southey Keis, of Beaufort County, who in March, 1856, appeared in court and qualified as the executor of the estate of Mary Keis. Minutes of the Court of Pleas and Quarter Sessions of Beaufort County, March, 1856 (Beaufort County Courthouse, Washington, N.C.).

[23] Wright *v.* Howe, 20 N.C., 318.

[24] Alvany, a free woman of color, *v.* Powell, 54 N.C., p. 34.

[25] Doe on the demise of Mary Ann Jones *v.* Norfleet, 20 N.C., p. 365. A plan of the lots was included in the report of the court.

[26] Doe on the demise of Frances Howard *v.* Sarah Howard, 51 N.C., p. 238.

[27] Since the possession of slaves enhanced one's social position in the community, the whites may well have objected to the ownership of slaves by free Negroes on the grounds that it would tend to upset the social structure — or that by such possession the free Negroes might begin to feel that they had "arrived" socially.

[28] State *v.* Edmund, a slave, 15 N.C., p. 278.

[29] The number of free Negroes who owned slaves was steadily decreasing. See below, pp. 372, 373.

[30] *Laws, 1860–1861,* p. 69.

[31] Julius Melbourn, *Life and Opinions of Julius Melbourn, passim.*

[32] Unpublished population schedules for the census of 1860.

[33] These statistics were compiled from the unpublished population schedules for the census of 1860.

[34] They were Alleghany, Davie, Harnett, Haywood, Jackson, and Madison. Interestingly enough, none of these counties was in the eastern part of the state.

[35] They were Catawba, Haywood, Henderson, Hyde, Jackson, Martin, McDowell, and Rutherford.

[36] Unpublished population schedules for the census of 1860.

[37] These statistics were compiled from the unpublished population schedules for the census of 1860.

[38] C. G. Woodson, *Free Negro Owners of Slaves in 1830,* p. 24.

[39] Unpublished population schedules for the census of 1860.

[40] Woodson, *Free Negro Owners,* p. 25, and the unpublished population schedules for the census of 1860.

[41] See the Minutes of the Court of Pleas and Quarter Sessions of Craven County, March, 1811. These records show that Thomas Newton, a free Negro, liberated his slave wife.

[42] C. D. Wilson, "Negroes Who Owned Slaves," *Popular Science Monthly*, LXXXI, p. 485.

[43] MS. in the Legislative Papers for 1856.

[44] In 1830 he held eighteen slaves. Woodson, *Free Negro Owners*, p. 24.

[45] In 1815 Stanly emancipated a slave woman and her five children, as well as a slave man. Minutes of the Court of Pleas and Quarter Sessions of Craven County, March, June, 1815.

[46] Census Office, *Heads of Families in the United States in 1790, passim.*

[47] Woodson, *Free Negro Owners*, pp. 24–26, and the unpublished population schedules for the census of 1830.

[48] The list was compiled by the writer from the unpublished population schedules for the census of 1860.

[49] *State Records*, XXVI, 278.

[50] Woodson, *Free Negro Owners*, pp. 24–25.

[51] In such cases the free Negro was losing his slaves in much the same way that the white slaveholder was losing his. By 1860 the rate of increase of slaves in North Carolina was noticeably declining. Taylor, *Slaveholding, passim.*

[52] By 1858 free Negroes had begun to send petitions to the General Assembly asking to be reenslaved. See the MSS. in the Legislative Papers for 1858, 1859, and 1860.

Peter Still versus the Peculiar Institution

Robert Brent Toplin

One would have to search carefully among the accounts of slaves who found their way to freedom in the antebellum period to find a reference to Peter Still. His activities never produced the political impact or excited public attention as did those of Frederick Douglass, Dred Scott and other historic figures of slave background. Yet, Still's experiences are significant, for they encompassed a variety of approaches utilized to free a fortunate minority of slaves from bondage. Manumission, escape, philanthropy — all were involved in his efforts to secure liberty for himself and his family. And the list of individuals who aided Still in his endeavors reads like an honor roll of the leading antislavery figures of the 1850's.

An incomplete biography of Peter Still appeared in 1856 as *Peter Still: The Kidnapped and the Ransomed.* Written by Kate E. R. Pickard of Syracuse, New York, the book was presented primarily as an antislavery polemic. However, the market became flooded with similar works in the 1850's, and the Pickard book never received the attention it deserved.[1]

The experiences that Peter Still encounterd during his forty-nine years in slavery are revealing enough of the peculiar institution to deserve special attention. A full account of this aspect of Still's life can be found in the Pickard biography. Only a brief sketch is presented here as background to his activities as a freedman.

The efforts of Still's parents to break away from slavery resembled, in some ways, his own quest for freedom. His mother and father were slaves in Maryland when Peter was born in 1801. A few years later, his father purchased his own freedom and settled near Greenwich, New Jersey, to await his family's preplanned escape. Their first attempt was abortive. After a sojourn in Greenwich, the mother and four children were discovered by slave hunters and taken back to Maryland. In the second escape, Still's mother managed to take only her two daughters. After a second reunion, the family settled near Burlington, New Jersey, changing their name from Steel to Still to avoid detection.

The two boys were left in bondage. Shortly after their separation from their mother, Peter and his brother Levin, ages six and eight respectively, were sold in

Robert Brent Toplin, "Peter Still versus the Peculiar Institution," *Civil War History* XIII (December 1967), 340–349. Reprinted by permission.

Kentucky. After thirteen years in that state, they were transported to Alabama. There, in 1831, Levin died. His death was a cruel blow to Peter. The brothers had been very close through their years in slavery, and Levin apparently had been responsible for keeping alive the hope for reunion with their parents, even though the memory of their family became fainter each year.

During his years in Alabama, Peter Still lived near the towns of Florence and Tuscumbia, in the northwestern part of the state, not far from Muscle Shoals. Changes in the estate of his owners led to his being "hired out" for a variety of assignments. At times he worked on plantations where he was often appointed household servant or slave foreman — positions usually reserved for the most capable slaves. Sometimes he was hired to merchants in the neighboring towns.

When Still was twenty-five years old, he married a household slave from a nearby plantation. They each remained the property of their original owners during their years in Alabama, although Still visited his wife frequently.

He became popular with the white townspeople in the area, and they respected him for his abilities. Many years later, a woman who had known him in the South recalled that he was regarded as "faithful and industrious" and "strictly truthful, one upon whose word you may rely upon implicitly."[2] Still became friendly with many of the businessmen in Tuscumbia and Florence, and the good will he earned there was to help him in later years.

A few times he entertained thoughts of escape. Only once did this idea seem to have even a slight chance of materializing. In 1844 he was hired as a cook for the Whig Party Convention at Nashville. During the evening, he walked down to the river searching for a boat which might provide a hiding place for a trip north. Finding none, he was forced to temporarily abandon his hopes for freedom.

In 1846 Still's fortunes began to change and he began working in a different direction to achieve his goal of liberation. He was hired to a bookseller in Tuscumbia who arranged an equitable working relationship. Explaining that he had little for him to do, the merchant proposed that Still hire his own time after meeting his responsibilities. He could keep everything he earned above the basic hiring cost that the merchant had to pay for his services. As this arrangement, though practiced in some of the states in the Upper South, was illegal in Alabama, the merchant led others to believe that he was receiving all of his slave's earnings.[3]

The new opportunity proved fruitful for Still. After a year of maintenance work, servantry, and other odd jobs, he managed to save about $75.00. This encouraged him to continue saving secretly with the ultimate goal of purchasing his freedom. As he did not yet trust any person outside his family enough to reveal his long-range purposes, he told his temporary manager that he spent all his earnings.

During his year of extra work, he became acquainted with Joseph Friedman, an immigrant merchant.[4] Friedman never made a direct statement about his opinions concerning Still's status, but his occasional remarks gave the impression that he was strongly opposed to the principle of slavery. Therefore, at the termination of his work contract, Still requested that his master transfer him to Friedman. The master consented, and Still entered into a new private agreement. When he finally became confident that he could reveal his plans, he found the merchant interested and sympathetic. Together they agreed that Friedman should offer the master $500.00 to buy Still. Then Still would continue working in order to reimburse his new owner and purchase his own freedom.

Freidman immediately tried to consummate the purchase, but for two years the master refused to consider selling Still. He had long been a valuable family servant and the owner intended to keep him as long as he lived. The direct approach failing, Still began to feign a cough and suggested that his master sell him, for the good of all concerned. Perhaps Friedman would be able to cure the ailment through intensive treatment.

But the owner continued to believe that Still was worth much more than $500.00. Friedman's attempts found little reception until 1849 when a number of "choice" young slaves were auctioned in Tuscumbia from the property of a recently deceased owner. Still's anxious master now agreed to complete the sale of his older slave in order to accumulate cash to purchase two healthy boys.

Joseph Friedman was out of town at the time, but his brother Isaac, who was familiar with the secret agreement, paid the $500.00. The quietly jubilant slave gave his new master about $200.00 that he had saved and was, henceforth, permitted to work entirely for his own benefit. After paying the remaining $300.00, he was given a receipt, together with a handwritten certificate of freedom.[5]

Shortly after, Isaac Friedman prepared to travel to Cincinnati and Still decided to go with him, ostensibly as his servant. He bade farewell to his wife and three children and then joined Friedman for the journey up the Tennessee and Ohio rivers. Between Cincinnati and Pittsburgh, he was accosted by several individuals who suspected he was a fugitive slave. With characteristic caution, Still managed to evade their inquiries and finally arrived safely in Philadelphia.[6]

He now set out to find his parents, only aware that he should look for a "Levin" and a "Cidney" who had settled somewhere near Philadelphia after leaving two sons more than forty years before. He especially feared revealing his purpose to an unfriendly party; in the South Still had been warned, as strange as it may sound, that abolitionists were ever ready to entrap free Negroes and sell them back into slavery!

Still soon encountered a helpful Negro who referred him to a clergyman's boarding house. There he was advised to go to the Philadelphia Anti-Slavery Office to search for records of his parents. He was introduced to a Negro clerk in the office, and as Still related the story of his background and purposes, the young man became intensely interested. Then, the clerk revealed his own identity — that his name was William Still, that his parents' names were Levin and Cidney and, indeed, they had lost two sons more than forty years before.[7] The father had been dead for many years, but the mother lived in Burlington, New Jersey, and seven other children resided between Philadelphia and Brooklyn. It was not until Peter Still personally met almost all of these people that he fully believed he had found his own family.

Still now commenced a five-year effort to take his wife and children from slavery. After a short stay in New Jersey, he traveled to Cincinnati to see Isaac Friedman. He obtained a new freedom certificate from Friedman, this one officially registered in the state of Ohio. Then he returned to Alabama, again posing as Friedman's slave. He took odd jobs as he had done before and managed to inform his family about his experiences in the North. He told them he would work to purchase their freedom, but that they should also be prepared to leave if they were approached by a stranger, as there had been some talk of an escape. He then returned north to find a way to earn money.

Still was reluctant to consent to the escape scheme. But since raising enough money to purchase his entire family seemed almost impossible, he finally allowed the dangerous adventure to be carried through. The self-appointed abductor was Seth Concklin. Little was known about him except that he had previously approached the Philadelphia Anti-Slavery Society to offer to help slaves escape from the District of Columbia. Concklin had seen a copy of the *Pennsylvania Freeman* containing a short story about Still's achievements and volunteered to go to Alabama and bring the wife and children north for only the cost of his expenses.

A daring enterprise followed. Concklin was able to lead the fugitives to escape in a small skiff on which they slowly made their way down the Tennessee River. Whenever they encountered inquisitive citizens, Concklin posed as the family's master. In the free states they received some assistance from "friends" due to the prearranged planning of the Quaker, Levi Coffin, one of the principal organizers of the underground railroad. Just when their efforts seemed close to success they were discovered by some suspicious individuals in Vincennes, Indiana. The wife and children were returned to their owner, who had offered a reward for their capture. Concklin was placed on a boat for transportation to Alabama, where he was to be tried. The events that followed are not completely clear. Levi Coffin and N. R. Johnston, who relayed the reports to William Still, believed that Concklin tried to escape. His body was found in a river with his hands and feet in chains and his skull fractured.[8]

Still was sickened by the news of failure and the death of Concklin. He now tried to find a way to purchase his family. A friend wrote to the owner of Still's family to ask his price. In his reply, the master, B. McKiernan, reasoned:

I recovered & Brought Back said 4 negroes or as You would say coulard people under the Belief that Peter the Husband was acsessery to the offence thereby putting me to much Expense & Truble to the amt $1000 which if he gets them he or his Friends must refund These 4 negroes here are worth in the market about for tha are Extraordenary fine & likely & but for the fact of Elopement I would not take 8000 Dollars for them but as the thing now stands you can say to Peter & his new discovered relations in Philadelphi I will take 5000 for the 4 culerd people. . . .[9]

William Still replied to McKiernan, asking if the price for the family could be reduced, as it seemed impossible for Peter Still or his relatives to raise the money. Parenthetically, he asked: "If the entire family cannot be purchased or freed, what can Vina and her daughter be purchased for?"[10] McKiernan gave a clearly negative answer. His price remained at $5,000, and he would not separate the family.[11]

Despite this setback, Still was undaunted. He decided to seek financial aid from friends in the North, but first he attempted to obtain certificates of character in order to make his case more effective. With the help of the Philadelphia Anti-Slavery Society, he searched for two women who had taught in the Tuscumbia Seminary in 1847 and had befriended him when he was a maintenance worker in the school. A communication with Reverend Samuel J. May in Syracuse proved helpful. May was an influential Unitarian abolitionist whose home was a station in the underground railroad.[12] He referred the case to Mrs. Kate E. R. Pickard, one of the women for whom Still had been searching. May and Mrs. Pickard soon became deeply interested in Still's progress and counseled him in his efforts. Mrs. Pickard later wrote Still's biography, while May penned the introduction.

In 1852 Still prepared to begin his journeys in search of financial support. His brother William was sympathetic to his hopes, "But what can your Brothers do!", he asked. William was skeptical about the possibility of Peter obtaining $5,000 to purchase his own family when so many others, equally deserving, were living under similar conditions of slavery.[13] Shortly after Peter left on his tour to solicit aid, his brother wrote: "I must confess to you, that I am some times led almost to despair, in reference to your accomplishing the object sought. But you must not be discouraged. persevere. hope on. and the difficulties may yet be overcome."[14]

Even Mrs. Pickard, who probably encouraged him more than anyone else to seek assistance, at first felt his chances of success were slight. In March, 1853, she told Still that a physician in Tuscumbia had informed her that there seemed very little hope that the purchase could be accomplished. "(I) ought not to flatter you with unreasonable hopes" she cautioned Still, reminding him of "poor Uncle Tom."[15]

For two years (from November, 1852 to October, 1854) Peter Still was engaged in a traveling appeal for financial assistance. He began his journey with letters of recommendation from J. Miller McKim, Secretary of the Philadelphia Anti-Slavery Office, and some of the principal citizens of Burlington, New Jersey.[16] In Syracuse he met May and renewed his old friendship with Mrs. Pickard. Then he moved on to Auburn, New York, where he addressed a church group for the first time. As Mrs. Pickard describes Still's reaction in the biography: "I was mighty skeered when Mr. Millard took me with him into the pulpit, and told me I must stand up myself, and tell my story to the people. 'Peared like I couldn't stand no how, but I said a few words, and Mr. Millard, he helped me out; so I got along mighty well."[17]

His journeys now took him to meet some of the leading antislavery spokesmen in the country. In Andover, Massachusetts, Still was received by Harriet Beecher Stowe, who gave him a letter which enhanced his appeal considerably:

Having examined the claims of this unfortunate man, I am satisfied that his is a case that calls for compassion and aid.

Though the sum demanded is so large as to look hopeless, yet if every man who is so happy as to be free, and have his own wife and children for his own, woud give even a small amount, the sum might soon be raised.

As ye would that men should do for you — do ye even so for them.[18]

Then he moved on to Boston where he presented his papers to William Lloyd Garrison, Theodore Parker and others. Garrison, the most influential figure among the radical abolitionists, temporarily held some of the money Still collected in the Boston area. Garrison was especially interested in the exploits of Seth Concklin. A short narrative of Concklin's life, which formed the appendix of *Peter Still: The Kidnapped and the Ransomed,* was sent to him before its publication.[19]

Still then continued traveling through the Northeast. In New York he met Horace Greeley, the eccentric editor of the *Tribune,* and in Albany, Thurlow Weed, the New York Whig party leader, made a contribution and gave him a letter of recommendation.[20] He stayed at the home of Gerrit Smith, the wealthy citizen of Petersboro, New York, who worked closely with Reverend May in the underground railroad.[21] In New Haven he was received by Leonard Bacon, an influential Congregationalist minister who, though previously opposed to anti-slavery agitation, was becoming increasingly abolitionist in sentiment at this time.[22]

By October, 1854, Still reached his goal of collecting $5,000. Before returning home, he visited Toronto because, as he explained to a minister in that city:

his only object in visiting Canada was not for the purpose of asking aid or to make an effort to raise money from among friends here, but for the pleasure of treading upon the "free soil of this part of her Majesty's minions" of which he had heard so much; and to see how his breathren (the fugitives from slavery) prospered. He is highly gratified with what he saw and heard. . . .[23]

During the two years that Still was soliciting aid, several of his friends were attempting to arrange the purchase of the family. At times their efforts seemed almost hopeless. After the Concklin incident, McKiernan was extremely angry with Still. Once he even told an inquirer that the family could not be bought on any terms.[24]

Besides William Still and Reverend May, three individuals were especially active in guiding the efforts to purchase the family. They were Joseph Parish, a respected physician in Burlington, New Jersey; Hamilton Willis, a Boston businessman; and Morris Hollowell, a wealthy Philadelphia merchant.

They had to exercise caution in approaching McKiernan. If he became aware of the number of people involved in the effort to purchase the family's freedom, he might raise his price. Still, himself, had to take cognizance of this possibility.

Consequently, he did not try to advertise his travels. A few notices appeared in the local newspapers, but usually he relied on letters of introduction that were passed on from one minister or antislavery leader to another.[25]

Still's friends tried to find ways to buy the family through independent agents in order to free them at a lower price. They believed that a person passing as a slave merchant and not showing any connection with Still might be able to acquire them for $3,000 to $4,000, an amount which they estimated to be closer to their market value. One of these attempts involved D. B. Birney, son of James Birney, the political abolitionist and twice presidential candidate of the Liberty party. The younger Birney, who was working in the South as an agent for a Philadelphia mercantile company, was asked to approach McKiernan to bargain for the family. But it appears that Birney gave very little effort to the project, and William Still noted that the money to be used for the purchase was carefully watched, to Birney's apparent consternation.[26]

The sale was finally negotiated late in 1854. The preliminary arrangements were made by John Simpson, a Florence, Alabama, businessman and long-time friend of Still. An agent of Hallowell's company completed the sale and escorted the family north. However, there was not sufficient money available to purchase a recently-born grandson. Still had not prepared for this contingency and the agent had no choice but to leave the child in Alabama.

Still's joyous reunion with his family brought new pressure from his friends to plan his future. What was he to do with his success story? Mrs. Pickard believed that Still and his family could become a model for the antislavery crusade. She wanted his children to "show the world that freedom is better than slavery."[27] "Everybody is watching them," she explained, "to see if it pays to buy people out of slavery."[28] She was also optimistic about the potential political and moral impact of the biography of Still that she was writing. She suggested that he meet with her in Syracuse to plan their use of the moeny from the book sales.

Still was apparently reluctant to participate in Mrs. Pickard's projects. He did not go to Syracuse despite her continued requests, and his brother William was uncooperative in sending information about the family to her — facts which would have facilitated completion of the book.[29] The most important reason for this attitude was the Still family's fear for their safety. When Peter Still made his appeals in the North, he continually told a minor lie. He described his separation from his mother as due to kidnapping. He portrayed his mother as a free woman, not a slave, as she technically was. The true history of his mother's background could not be revealed until after the Civil War. As the children's status would be determined by the previous condition of the mother, Still's mother and his relations in the North could still be legally considered slaves. Consequently, the biography that Mrs. Pickard published in 1856 told the same story that Still had doctored during his travels.[30]

Peter Still: The Kidnapped and the Ransomed never became as popular as Mrs. Pickard had imagined it would be. Soon after the first edition was completed, the publisher closed his business. The book, a moral appeal as well as a biography, faced a market glutted with an abundance of polemical works on slavery.[31]

Still lived his remaining years in relative obscurity. He purchased a ten-acre truck-farm near Burlington, New Jersey, and died there in 1868 after seeing the destruction of the institution against which he had so long held a personal grievance.[12]

It required nine years of labor for Still to take himself and his family out of slavery. To overcome the extremely difficult barriers to his success he had to employ a variety of subtle, informal and sometimes illegal methods. He could share the secret of his effort to purchase himself with only a few others. From the positon of his own freedom, the purchase of his entire family at first seemed impossible. Reluctantly, he consented to an extreme measure and the escape attempt ended tragically with the return of the fugitives and the violent death of the organizer. Then Still endeavored to solicit financial support for his cause. This approach, too, had to be carried out quietly to succeed. A public campaign would only have jeopardized his efforts to purchase his family's freedom.

At a time when the peculiar institution was becoming increasingly inflexible, the achievements of Peter Still were truly extraordinary.

Notes

[1] In the category of Pickard's book, the slave narrative, see, for example, Solomon Northrup, *Twelve Years as a Slave* (Auburn and Buffalo, 1854); J. W. Loguen, *The Reverend J. W. Loguen as a Slave and as a Freeman* (Syracuse, 1859); Josiah Henson, *Father Henson's Story of His Own Life* (1849 and 1858).

[2] Julia E. R. Marvin to Dr. Lord, Oct. 11, 1854, in the Peter Still Papers, Rutgers University Library. The Still Papers, concerning Still's activities from 1850–1861, were a gift to the Rutgers Library from Philip D. Sang, Lake Forest, Illinois.

[3] Kenneth M. Stampp, *The Peculiar Institution: Slavery in the Ante-Bellum South* (New York, 1956), p. 72.

[4] Sections of *The Kidnapped and the Ransomed* pertaining to Joseph Friedman have been reprinted with an introduction and editorial notes by Maxwell Whiteman in *The American Jewish Archives*, IX (Apr., 1957), 3–31.

[5] By completing his own purchase, Still became the fortunate member of a minority group. As Stampp notes: "Only a small number of bondsmen ever had the chance to show their desire for freedom by embracing an opportunity to gain legal emancipation. The handful who were permitted to buy themselves . . . left little doubt about how much they valued liberty." *The Peculiar Institution*, p. 97.

[6] The danger of encountering professional slave hunters was especially great at this time, shortly after the passage of the Fugitive Slave Act of 1850.

[7] William Still was active in helping to coordinate the work of the underground railroad. His well-known book, *The Underground Railroad* (Philadelphia, 1886) includes many accounts based on his experiences and the records of the Philadelphia Anti-Slavery Society.

[8] William Still, *The Underground Railroad,* pp. 27–34.

[9] *Ibid.*, pp. 34–35.

[10] William Still to B. McKiernan, Aug. 16, 1851, *Journal of Negro History,* XI (1926), 107–109.

[11] William Still, *The Underground Railroad,* p. 36.

[12] Samuel J. May, *Some Recollections of Our Anti-Slavery Conflict* (Boston, 1869); *Memoirs of Samuel Joseph May* (Boston, 1873).

[13] William Still to Peter Still, May 10, 1852, Peter Still Papers; Kate E. R. Pickard, *Peter Still: The Kidnapped and the Ransomed* (Syracuse, 1856), p. 319.

[14] William Still to Peter Still, Dec. 18, 1852, Peter Still Papers.

[15] Kate E. R. Pickard to Peter Still, Mar. 21, 1853, *ibid.*

[16] J. Miller McKim, a leading Pennsylvania abolitionist, was also active in freedmen relief work in the 1860's. James M. McPherson, *The Struggle for Equality: Abolitionists and the Negro in the Civil War and Reconstruction* (Princeton, 1964), pp. 4, 76, 127.

[17] Pickard, *Peter Still,* pp. 321–322.

[18] Undated ms.; Pickard, *Peter Still,* p. 322.

[19] The Concklin narrative was written by William Henry Furness, a Pennsylvania abolitionist. Elizabeth M. Geffen, "William Henry Furness, Philadelphia Anti-Slavery Preacher," *The Pennsylvania Magazine of History and Biography,* LXXXII (1958), 259–292. Samuel J. May to Peter Still, Aug. 9, 1853, Peter Still Papers.

[20] Letter from Horace Greeley, May 10, 1844, *ibid.* Pickard, *Peter Still,* p. 332.

[21] *Ibid.*, p. 323.

[22] *Ibid.*, p. 332; Louis Filler, *The Crusade Against Slavery: 1830–1860* (New York, 1960), pp. 261–262.

[23] Ms. In Peter Still's "Memo Book," a record of funds collected in New England, Peter Still Papers.

[24] Morris L. Hollowell to Peter Still, Sept. 19, 1854, *ibid.*

[25] Letter from Morris L. Hollowell, Sept. 19, 1854, *ibid.*

[26] William Still to Peter Still, Nov. 9, 1853, *ibid.*

[27] Kate E. R. Pickard to Peter Still, June 24, 1855, *ibid.*

[28] Kate E. R. Pickard to Peter Still, Aug. 26, 1855, *ibid.*

[29] Kate E. R. Pickard to Peter Still, June 24, 1855, *ibid.*

[30] The fabricated story about kidnapping in Maryland sounded plausible, as this state was overrun by kidnappers in the early 1800's. Dwight Lowell Dumond, *Antislavery: The Crusade for Freedom in America* (New York, 1966), p. 46.

[31] An edition of *The Kidnapped and the Ransomed* was published by the Negro Publication Society of America, Inc. in 1941.

[32] James Still, *Early Recollections and Life of Dr. James Still* (Philadelphia, 1877), pp. 153–156.

Free Blacks in the North and West

2

The Negroes of Cincinnati Prior to the Civil War

Carter G. Woodson

The study of the history of the Negroes of Cincinnati is unusually important for the reason that from no other annals do we get such striking evidence that the colored people generally thrive when encouraged by their white neighbors. This story is otherwise significant when we consider the fact that about a fourth of the persons of color settling in the State of Ohio during the first half of the last century made their homes in this city. Situated on a north bend of the Ohio where commerce breaks bulk, Cincinnati rapidly developed, attracting both foreigners and Americans, among whom were not a few Negroes. Exactly how many persons of color were in this city during the first decade of the nineteenth century is not yet known. It has been said that there were no Negroes in Hamilton County in 1800.[1] It is evident, too, that the real exodus of free Negroes and fugitives from the South to the Northwest Territory did not begin prior to 1815, although their attention had been earlier directed to this section as a more desirable place for colonization than the shores of Africa.[2] As the reaction following the era of good feeling toward the Negroes during the revolutionary period had not reached its climax free persons of color had been content to remain in the South.[3] The unexpected immigration of these Negroes into this section and the last bold effort made to drive them out marked epochs in their history in this city. The history of these people prior to the Civil War, therefore, falls into three periods, one of toleration from 1800 to 1826, one of persecution from 1826 to 1841, and one of amelioration from 1841 to 1861.

In the beginning the Negroes were not a live issue in Cincinnati. The question of their settlement in that community was debated but resulted in great diversity of opinion rather than a fixedness of judgment among the citizens. The question came up in the Constitutional Convention of 1802 and provoked some discussion, but reaching no decision, the convention simply left the Negroes out of the pale of the newly organized body politic, discriminating against them together with Indians and foreigners, by incorporating the word white into the fundamental law.[4] The legislature to which the disposition of this question was left, however, took it

Carter G. Woodson, "The Negroes of Cincinnati Prior to the Civil War," *Journal of Negro History* I (January 1916), 1'22. Permission granted by the Association for the Study of Negro Life and History.

up in 1804 to calm the fears of those who had more seriously considered the so-called menace of Negro immigration. This body enacted a law, providing that no Negro or mulatto should be allowed to remain permanently in that State, unless he could furnish a certificate of freedom issued by some court in the United States. Negroes then living there had to be registered before the following June, giving the names of their children. No man could employ a Negro who could not show such a certificate. Hiring a delinquent black or harboring or hindering the capture of a runaway was punishable by a fine of $50 and the owner of a fugitive thus illegally employed could recover fifty cents a day for the services of his slave.[5]

As the fear of Negro immigration increased the law of 1804 was found to be inadequate. In 1807, therefore, the legislature enacted another measure providing that no Negro should be permitted to settle in Ohio unless he could within twenty days give a bond to the amount of $500, guaranteeing his good behavior and support. The fine for concealing a fugitive was raised from $50 to $100, one half of which should go to the informer. Negro evidence against the white man was prohibited.[6] This law together with that of 1830 making the Negro ineligible for service in the State militia, that of 1831 depriving persons of color of the privilege of serving upon juries, and that of 1838 prohibiting the education of colored children at the expense of the State, constituted what were known as the "Black Laws."[7]

Up to 1826, however, the Negroes of Cincinnati had not become a cause of much trouble. Very little mention of them is made in the records of this period. They were not wanted in this city but were tolerated as a negligible factor. D. B. Warden, a traveler through the West in 1819, observed that the blacks of Cincinnati were "good-humoured, garrulous, and profligate, generally disinclined to laborious occupations, and prone to the performance of light and menial drudgery." Here the traveler was taking effect for cause. "Some few," said he, "exercise the humbler trades, and some appear to have formed a correct conception of the objects and value of property, and are both industrious and economical. A large proportion of them are reputed, and perhaps correctly, to be habituated to petit larceny." But this had not become a grave offence, for he said that not more than one individual had been corporally punished by the courts since the settlement of the town.[8]

When, however, the South reached the conclusion that free Negroes were an evil, and Quakers and philanthropists began to direct these unfortunates to the Northwest Territory for colonization, a great commotion arose in Southern Ohio and especially in Cincinnati.[9] How rapid this movement was, may be best observed by noticing the statistics of this period. There were 337 Negroes in Ohio in 1800; 1,890 in 1810; 4,723 in 1820; 9,586 in 1830; 17,342 in 1840; and 25,279 in 1850.[10] Now Cincinnati had 410 Negroes in 1819;[11] 690 in 1826;[12] 2,255 in 1840;[13] and 3,237 in 1850.[14]

It was during the period between 1826 and 1840 that Cincinnati had to grapple with the problem of the immigrating Negroes and the poor whites from the uplands of Virginia and Kentucky. With some ill-informed persons the question was whether that section should be settled by white men or Negroes. The situation became more alarming when the Southern philanthropic minority sometimes afforded a man like a master of Pittsylvania County, Virginia, who settled 70 freedmen in Lawrence County, Ohio, in one day.[15] It became unusually acute in Cincinnati because of the close social and commercial relations between that city and the slave States. Early in the nineteenth century Cincinnati became a manufacturing center to which the South learned to look for supplies of machinery, implements, furniture, and food.[16] The business men prospering thereby were not advocates of slavery but rather than lose trade by acquiring the reputation of harboring fugitive slaves or frightening away whites by encouraging the immigration of Negroes, they began to assume the attitude of driving the latter from those parts.

From this time until the forties the Negroes were a real issue in Cincinnati. During the late twenties they not only had to suffer from the legal disabilities provided in the "Black Laws," but had to withstand the humiliation of a rigid social ostracism.[17] They were regarded as intruders and denounced as an idle, profligate and criminal class with whom a self-respecting white man could not afford to associate. Their children were not permitted to attend the public schools and few persons braved the inconveniences of living under the stigma of teaching a "nigger school." Negroes were not welcome in the white churches and when they secured admission thereto they had to go to the "black pew." Colored ministers were treated with very little consideration by the white clergy as they feared that they might lose caste and be compelled to give up their churches. The colored people made little or no effort to go to white theaters or hotels and did not attempt to ride in public conveyances on equal footing with members of the other race. Not even white and colored children dared to play together to the extent that such was permitted in the South.[18]

This situation became more serious when it extended to pursuits of labor. White laborers there, as in other Northern cities during this period, easily reached the position of thinking that it was a disgrace to work with Negroes. This prejudice was so much more inconvenient to the Negroes of Cincinnati than elsewhere because of the fact that most of the menial labor in that city was done by Germans and Irishmen. Now, since the Negroes could not follow ordinary menial occupations there was nothing left them but the lowest form of "drudgery," for which employers often preferred colored women. It was, therefore, necessary in some cases for the mother to earn the living for the family because the father could get nothing to do. A colored man could not serve as an ordinary drayman or porter without subjecting his employer to a heavy penalty.[19]

The trades unions were then proscribing the employment of colored mechanics. Many who had worked at skilled labor were by this prejudice forced to do drudgery or find employment in other cities. The president of a "mechanical association" was publicly tried in 1830 by that organization for the crime of assisting a colored youth to learn a trade.[20] A young man of high character, who had at the cabinet-making trade in Kentucky saved enough to purchase his freedom, came to Cincinnati about this time, seeking employment. He finally found a position in a shop conducted by an Englishman. On entering the establishment, however, the workmen threw down their tools, declaring that the Negro had to leave or that they would. The unfortunate "intruder" was accordingly dismissed. He then entered the employ of a slaveholder, who at the close of the Negro's two years of service at common labor discovered that the black was a mechanic. The employer then procured work for him as a rough carpenter. By dint of perseverance and industry this Negro within a few years became a master workman, employing at times six or eight men, but he never received a single job of work from a native-born citizen from a free State.[21]

The hardships of the Negroes of this city, however, had just begun. The growth of a prejudiced public opinion led not only to legal proscription and social ostracism but also to open persecution. With the cries of the Southerners for the return of fugitives and the request of white immigrants for the exclusion of Negroes from that section, came the demand to solve the problem by enforcing the "Black Laws." Among certain indulgent officials these enactments had been allowed to fall into desuetude. These very demands, however, brought forward friends as well as enemies of the colored people. Their first clash was testing the constitutionality of the law of 1807. When the question came up before the Supreme Court, this measure was upheld.[22] Encouraged by such support, the foes of the Negroes forced an execution of the law. The courts at first hesitated but finally took the position that the will of the people should be obeyed. The Negroes asked for ninety days to comply with the law and were given sixty. When the allotted time had expired, however, many of them had not given bonds as required. The only thing to do then was to force them to leave the city. The officials again hesitated but a mob quickly formed to relieve them of the work. This was the riot of 1829. Bands of ruffians held sway in the city for three days, as the police were unable or unwilling to restore order. Negroes were insulted on the streets, attacked in their homes, and even killed. About a thousand or twelve hundred of them found it advisable to leave for Canada West where they established the settlement known as Wilberforce.[23]

This upheaval, though unusually alarming, was not altogether a bad omen. It was due not only to the demands which the South was making upon the North and the fear of the loss of Southern trade, but also to the rise of the Abolition Societies, the growth of which such a riotous condition as this had materially fostered. In a word, it was the sequel of the struggle between the proslavery and the antislavery elements of the city. This was the time when the friends of the Negroes were doing most for them. Instead of frightening them away a group of respectable white men in that community were beginning to think that they should be trained to live there as useful citizens. Several schools and churches for them were established. The Negroes themselves provided for their own first school about 1820; but one Mr. Wing had sufficient courage to admit persons of color to his evening classes after their first efforts had failed. By 1834 many of the colored people were receiving systematic instruction.[24] To some enemies of these dependents it seemed that the tide was about to turn in favor of the despised cause. Negroes began to raise sums adequate to their elementary education and the students of Lane Seminary supplemented these efforts by establishing a colored mission school which offered more advanced courses and lectures on scientific subjects twice a week. These students, however, soon found themselves far in advance of public opinion.[25] They were censured by the faculty and to find a more congenial center for their operations they had to go to Oberlin in the Western Reserve where a large number of persons had become interested in the cause of the despised and rejected of men.

During the years from 1833 to 1836 the situation in Cincinnati grew worse because of the still larger influx of Negroes driven from the South by intolerable conditions incident to the reaction against the race. To solve this problem various schemes were brought forth. Augustus Wattles tells us that he appeared in Cincinnati about this time and induced numbers of the Negroes to go to Mercer County, Ohio, where they took up 30,000 acres of land.[26] Others went to Indiana and purchased large tracts on the public domain.[27] Such a method, however, seemed rather slow to the militant proslavery leaders who had learned not only to treat the Negroes as an evil but to denounce in the same manner the increasing number of abolitionists by whom it was said the Negroes were encouraged to immigrate into the State.

The spirit of the proslavery sympathizers was well exhibited in the upheaval which soon followed. This was the riot of July 30, 1836. It was an effort to destroy the abolition organ, *The Philanthropist,* edited by James G. Birney, a Southerner who had brought his slaves from Huntsville, Alabama, to Kentucky and freed them. The mob formed in the morning, went to the office of *The Philanthropist,* destroyed what printed matter they could find, threw the type into the street, and broke up the press. They then proceeded to the home of the printer, Mr. Pugh, but finding no questionable matter there, they left it undisturbed. The homes of James G. Birney, Mr. Donaldson and Dr. Colby were also threatened. The next homes to be attacked were those of Church Alley, the Negro quarter, but when two guns were fired upon the assailants they withdrew. It was reported that one man was shot but this has never been proved. The mob hesitated some time before attacking these houses again, several of the rioters declaring that they did not care to endanger their lives. A second onset was made, but it was discovered that the Negroes had deserted the quarter. On finding the houses empty the assailants destroyed their contents.[28]

Yet undaunted by this persistent opposition the Negroes of Cincinnati achieved so much during the years between 1835 and 1840 that they deserved to be ranked among the most progressive people of the world.[29] Their friends endeavored to enable them through schools, churches and industries to embrace every opportunity to rise. These 2,255 Negroes accumulated, largely during this period, $209,000 worth of property, exclusive of personal effects and three churches valued at $19,000. Some of this wealth consisted of land purchased in Ohio and Indiana. Furthermore, in 1839 certain colored men of the city organized "The Iron Chest Company," a real estate firm, which built three brick buildings and rented them to white men. One man, who a few years prior to 1840 had thought it useless to accumulate wealth from which he might be driven away, had changed his mind and purchased $6,000 worth of real estate. Another Negro, who had paid $5,000 for himself and family, had bought a home worth $800 or $1,000. A freedman, who was a slave until he was twenty-four years old, then had two lots worth $10,000, paid a tax of $40 and had 320 acres of land in Mercer County. Another, who was worth only $3,000 in 1836, had seven houses in Cincinnati, 400 acres of land in Indiana, and another tract in the same county. He was worth $12,000 or $15,000. A woman who was a slave until she was thirty was then worth $2,000. She had also come into potential possession of two houses on which a white lawyer had given her a mortgage to secure the payment of $2,000 borrowed from this thrifty woman. Another Negro, who was on the auction block in 1832, had spent $2,600 purchasing himself and family and had bought two brick houses worth $6,000 and 560 acres of land in Mercer County, said to be worth $2,500.[30]

This unusual progress had been promoted by two forces, the development of the steamboat as a factor in transportation and the rise of the Negro mechanic. Negroes employed on vessels as servants to the travelling public amassed large sums received in the form of "tips." Furthermore, the fortunate few, constituting the stewards of these vessels, could by placing contracts for supplies and using business methods realize handsome incomes. Many Negroes thus enriched purchased real estate and went into business in Cincinnati.[31] The other force, the rise of the Negro mechanic, was made possible by overcoming much of the prejudice which had at first been encountered. A great change in this respect had taken place in Cincinnati by 1840. Many who had been forced to work as menial laborers then had the opportunity to show their usefulness to their families and to the community. Colored mechanics were then getting as much skilled labor as they could do. It was not uncommon for white artisans to solicit employment of colored men because they had the reputation of being better paymasters than master workmen of the more favored race.[32] White mechanics not only worked with colored men but often associated with them, patronized the same barber shop, and went to the same places of amusement.[33]

In this prosperous condition the Negroes could help themselves. Prior to this period they had been unable to make any sacrifices for charity and education. Only $150 of the $1,000 raised for Negro education in 1835 was contributed by persons of color. In 1839, however, the colored people raised $889.30 for this purpose, and thanks to their economic progress, this task was not so difficult as that of raising the $150 in 1835. They were then spending considerable amounts for evening and writing schools, attended by seventy-five persons, chiefly adults. In 1840 Reverend Mr. Denham and Mr. Goodwin had in their schools sixty-five pupils each paying $3 per quarter, and Miss Merrill a school of forty-seven pupils paying the same tuition. In all, the colored people were paying these teachers about $1,300 a year. The only help the Negroes were then receiving was that from the Ladies' Anti-Slavery Society, which employed one Miss Seymour at a salary of $300 a year to instruct fifty-four pupils. Moreover, the colored people were giving liberally to objects of charity. Some Negroes burned out in 1839 were promptly relieved by members of their own race. A white family in distress was befriended by a colored woman. The Negroes contributed also to the support of missionaries in Jamaica and during the years from 1836 to 1840 assisted twenty-five emancipated slaves on their way from Cincinnati to Mercer County, Ohio.[34]

During this period they had made progress in other than material things. Their improvement in religion and morals was remarkable. They then had four flourishing Sabbath Schools with 310 regular attendants, one Baptist and two Methodist churches with a membership of 800, a "Total Abstinence Temperance Society" for adults numbering 450, and a "Sabbath School or Youth's Society" of 180 members. A few of these violated their pledges, but when we consider the fact that one fourth of the entire colored population belonged to temperance organizations while less than one tenth of the whites were thus connected, we must admit that this was no mean achievement. Among the Negroes public sentiment was then such that no colored man could openly sell intoxicating drinks. This growing temperance was exhibited, too, in the decreasing fondness for dress and finery. There was less tendency to strive merely to get a fine suit of clothes and exhibit one's self on the streets. Places of vice were not so much frequented and barber shops which on Sundays formerly became a rendezvous for the idle and the garrulous were with few exceptions closed by 1840. This influence of the religious organizations reached also beyond the limits of Cincinnati. A theological student from the State of New York said after spending some time in New Orleans, that the influence of the elevation of the colored people of Cincinnati was felt all the way down the river. Travelers often spoke of the difference in the appearance of barbers and waiters on the boats.[35]

It was in fact a brighter day for the colored people. In 1840 an observer said that they had improved faster than any other people in the city. The *Cincinnati Gazette* after characterizing certain Negroes as being imprudent and vicious, said of others: "Many of these are peaceable and industrious, raising respectable families and acquiring property."[36] Mr. James H. Perkins, a respectable citizen of the city, asserted that the day school which the colored children attended had shown by examination that it was as good as any other in the city. He said further: "There is no question, I presume, that the colored population of Cincinnati, oppressed as it has been by our state laws as well as by prejudice, has risen more rapidly than almost any other people in any part of the world."[37] Within three or four years their property had more than doubled; their schools had become firmly established, and their churches and Sunday Schools had grown as rapidly as any other religious institutions in the city. Trusting to good conduct and character, they had risen to a prosperous position in the eyes of those whose prejudices would "allow them to look through the skin to the soul."[38]

The colored people had had too many enemies in Cincinnati, however, to expect that they had overcome all opposition. The prejudice of certain labor groups against the Negroes increased in proportion to the prosperity of the latter. That they had been able to do as well as they had was due to the lack of strength on the part of the labor organizations then forming to counteract the sentiment of fair play for the Negroes. Their labor competed directly with that of the whites and began again to excite "jealousy and heart burning."[39] The Germans, who were generally toiling up from poverty, seemed to exhibit less prejudice; but the unfortunate Irish bore it grievously that even a few Negroes should outstrip some of their race in the economic struggle.

In 1841 there followed several clashes which aggravated the situation. In the month of June one Burnett referred to as "a mischievous and swaggering Englishman running a cake shop," had harbored a runaway slave. When a man named McCalla, his reputed master, came with an officer to reclaim the fugitive, Burnett and his family resisted them. The Burnetts were committed to answer for this infraction of the law and finally were adequately punished. The proslavery mob which had gathered undertook to destroy their home but the officials prevented them. Besides, early in August according to a report, a German citizen defending his blackberry patch near the city was attacked by two Negroes and stabbed so severely that he died. Then about three weeks thereafter, according to another rumor, a very respectable lady was insultingly accosted by two colored men, and when she began to flee two others rudely thrust themselves before her on the sidewalk. But in this case, as in most others growing out of rumors, no one could ever say who the lady or her so-called assailants were. At the same time, too, the situation was further aggravated by an almost sudden influx of irresponsible Negroes from various parts, increasing the number of those engaged in noisy frolics which had become a nuisance to certain white neighbors.[40]

Accordingly, on Tuesday, the twenty-ninth of August, there broke out on the corner of Sixth and Broadway a quarrel in which two or three persons were wounded. On the following night the fracas was renewed. A group of ruffians attacked the Dumas Hotel, a colored establishment, on McCallister Street, demanding the surrender of a Negro, who, they believed, was concealed there. As the Negroes of the neighborhood came to the assistance of their friends in the hotel the mob had to withdraw. On Thursday night there took place another clash between a group of young men and boys and a few Negroes who seriously wounded one or two of the former. On Friday evening the mob incited to riotous acts by an influx of white ruffians, seemingly from the steamboats and the Kentucky side of the river, openly assembled in Fifth Street Market without being molested by the police, armed themselves and marched to Broadway and Sixth Street, shouting and swearing. They attacked a colored confectionery store near by, demolishing its doors and windows. James W. Piatt, an influential citizen, and the mayor then addressed the disorderly persons, vainly exhorting them to peace and obedience to the law. Moved by passionate entreaties to execute their poorly prepared plan, the assailants advanced and attacked the Negroes with stones. The blacks, however, had not been idle. They had secured sufficient guns and ammunition to fire into the mob such a volley that it had to fall back. The aggressors rallied again, however, only to be in like manner repulsed. Men were wounded on both sides and carried off and reported dead. The Negroes advanced courageously, and according to a reporter, fired down the street into the mass of ruffians, causing a hasty retreat. This mêlée continued until about one o'clock when a part of the mob secured an iron six pounder, hauled it to the place of combat against the exhortations of the powerless mayor, and fired on the Negroes. With this unusual advantage the blacks were forced to retreat, many of them going to the hills. About two o'clock the mayor of the city brought out a portion of the "military" which succeeded in holding the mob at bay.[41]

On the next day the colored people in the district under fire were surrounded by sentinels and put under martial law. Indignation meetings of law-abiding citizens were held on Saturday to pass resolutions, denouncing abolitionists and mobs and making an appeal to the people and the civil authorities to uphold the law. The Negroes also held a meeting and respectfully assured the mayor and citizens that they would use every effort to conduct themselves orderly and expressed their readiness to give bond according to the law of 1807 or leave the city quietly within a specified time. But these steps availed little when the police winked at this violence. The rioters boldly occupied the streets without arrest and continued their work until Sunday. The mayor, sheriff and marshal went to the battle ground about three o'clock but the mob still had control. The officers could not even remove those Negroes who complied with the law of leaving. The authorities finally hit upon the scheme of decreasing the excitement by inducing about 300 colored men to go to jail for security after they had been assured that their wives and children would be protected. The Negroes consented and were accordingly committed, but the cowardly element again attacked these helpless dependents like savages. At the same time other rioters stormed the office of *The Philanthropist* and broke up the press. The mob continued its work until it dispersed from mere exhaustion. The Governor finally came to the city and issued a proclamation setting forth the gravity of the situation. The citizens and civil authorities rallied to his support and strong patrols prevented further disorder.[42]

It is impossible to say exacly how many were killed and wounded on either side. It is probable that several were killed and twenty or thirty variously wounded, though but few dangerously. Forty of the mob were arrested and imprisoned. Exactly what was done with all of them is not yet known. It seems that few, if any of them, however, were severely punished. The Negroes who had been committed for safe keeping were thereafter disposed of in various ways. Some were discharged on certificates of nativity, others gave bond for their support and good behavior, a few were dismissed as non-residents, a number of them were discharged by a justice of the Court of Common Pleas, and the rest were held indefinitely.[43]

This upheaval had two important results. The enemies of the Negroes were convinced that there were sufficient law-abiding citizens to secure to the refugees protection from mob violence; and because of these riots their sympathizers became more attached to the objects of their philanthropy. Abolitionists, Free Soilers and Whigs fearlessly attacked the laws which kept the Negroes under legal and economic disabilites. Petitions praying that these measures be repealed were sent to the legislature. The proslavery element of the State, however, was equally militant. The legislators, therefore, had to consider such questions as extradition and immigration, State aid and colonization, the employment of colored men in the militia service, the extension of the elective franchise, and the admission of colored children to the public schools.[44] Most of these "Black Laws" remained until after the war, but in 1848 they were so modified as to give the Negroes legal standing in courts and to provide for their children such education as a school tax on the property of colored persons would allow[45] and further changed in 1849[46] so as to make the provision for education more effective.

The question of repealing the other oppressive laws came up in the Convention of 1850. It seemed that the cause of the Negroes had made much progress in that a larger number had begun to speak for them. But practically all of the members of the convention who stood for the Negroes were from the Western Reserve. After much heated discussion the colored people were by a large majority of votes still left under the disabilites of being disqualified to sit on juries, unable to obtain a legal residence so as to enter a charitable institution supported by the State, and denied admission to public schools established for white children.[47]

The greatest problem of the Negroes, however, was one of education. There were more persons interested in furnishing them facilities of education than in repealing the prohibitive measures, feeling that the other matters would adjust themselves after giving them adequate training. But it required some time and effort yet before much could be effected in Cincinnati because of the sympathizers with the South. The mere passing of the law of 1849 did not prove to be altogether a victory. Complying with the provisions of this act the Negroes elected trustees, organized a system, and employed teachers, relying on the money allotted them by the law on the basis of a per capita division of the school fund received by the board of education. So great was the prejudice of people of the city that the school officials refused to turn over the required funds on the grounds that the colored trustees were not electors and, therefore, could not be office-holders, qualified to receive and disburse funds. Uunder the leadership of John I. Gaines, therefore, the trustees called an indignation meeting and raised sufficient money to employ Flamen Ball, an attorney, to secure a writ of mandamus. The case was contested by the city officials, even in the Supreme Court, which decided against the officious whites.[48]

This decision did not solve the whole problem in Cincinnati. The amount raised was small and even had it been adequate to employ teachers, they were handicapped by another decision that no portion of it could be used for building schoolhouses. After a short period of accomplishing practically nothing the law was amended in 1853[49] so as to transfer the control of such schools to the managers of the white system. This was taken as a reflection on the blacks of the city and tended to make them refuse to cooperate with the white board. On account of the failure of this body to act effectively prior to 1856, the people of color were again given power to elect their own trustees.[50]

During this contest certain Negroes of Cincinnati were endeavoring to make good their claim to equal rights in the public schools. Acting upon this contention a colored man sent his son to a public school which, on account of his presence, became a center of unusual excitement. Isabella Newhall, the teacher, to whom he went, immediately complained to the board of education, requesting that he be expelled because of his color. After "due deliberation" the board of education decided by a vote of 15 to 10 that the colored pupil would have to withdraw. Thereupon two members of that body, residing in the district of the timorous teacher, resigned.[51]

Many Negroes belonging to the mulatto class, however, were more successful in getting into the white schools. In 1849 certain parents complained that children of color were being admitted to the public schools, and in fact there were in one of them two daughters of a white father and a mulatto mother. On complaining about this to the principal of the school in question, the indignant patrons were asked to point out the undesirable pupils. "They could not; for," says Sir Charles Lyell, "the two girls were not only among the best pupils, but better looking and less dark than many of the other pupils."[52]

Thereafter, however, much progress in the education of the colored people among themselves was noted. By 1844 they had six schools of their own and before the war two well-supported public schools.[53] Among their teachers were such useful persons as Mrs. M. J. Corbin, Miss Lucy Blackburn, Miss Anne Ryall, Miss Virginia C. Tilley, Miss Martha E. Anderson, William H. Parham, William R. Casey, John G. Mitchell and Peter H. Clark.[54] The pupils were showing their appreciation by regular attendance, excellent deportment, and progress in the acquisition of knowledge. Speaking of these Negroes in 1855, John P. Foote said that they shared with the white citizens that respect for education and the diffusion of knowledge, which has been one of their "characteristics," and that they had, therefore, been more generally intelligent than free persons of color not only in other parts of this country but in all other parts of the world.[55] It was in appreciation of the worth of this class to the community that in 1844[56] Nicholas Longworth helped them to establish an orphan asylum and in 1858 built for them a comfortable school building, leasing it with a privilege of purchasing it within four years.[57] They met these requirements within the stipulated time and in 1859 secured through other agencies the construction of another building in the western portion of the city.

The most successful of these schools, however, was the Gilmore High School, a private institution founded by an English clergyman. This institution offered instruction in the fundamentals and in some vocational studies. It was supported liberally by the benevolent element of the white people and patronized and appreciated by the Negroes as the first and only institution offering them the opportunity for thorough training. It became popular throughout the country, attracting Negroes from as far South as New Orleans.[58] Rich Southern planters found it convenient to have their mulatto children educated in this high school.[59]

The work of these schools was substantially supplemented by that of the colored churches. They directed their attention not only to moral and religious welfare of the colored people but also to their mental development. Through their well-attended Sunday-schools these institutions furnished many Negroes of all classes the facilities of elementary education. Such opportunities were offered at the Baker Street Baptist Church, the Third Street Baptist Church, the Colored Christian Church, the New Street Methodist Church, and the African Methodist Church. Among the preachers then promoting this cause were John Warren, Rufus Conrad, Henry Simpson, and Wallace Shelton. Many of the old citizens of Cincinnati often refer with pride to the valuable services rendered by these leaders.

In things economic the Negroes were exceptionally prosperous after the forties. Cincinnati had then become a noted pork-packing and manufacturing center. The increasing canal and river traffic and finally the rise of the railroad system tended to make it thrive more than ever. Many colored men grew up with the city. A Negro had in the East End on Calvert Street a large cooperage establishment which made barrels for the packers. Knight and Bell were successful contractors noted for their skill and integrity and employed by the best white people of the city. Robert Harlan made considerable money buying and selling race horses. Thompson Cooley had a successful pickling establishment. On Broadway A. V. Thompson, a colored tailor, conducted a thriving business. J. Pressley and Thomas Ball were the well-known photographers of the city, established in a handsomely furnished modern gallery which was patronized by some of the wealthiest people. Samuel T. Wilcox, who owed his success to his positon as a steward on an Ohio River line, thereafter went into the grocery business and built up such a large trade among the aristocratic families that he accumulated $59,000 worth of property by 1859.[60]

A more useful Negro had for years been toiling upward in this city. This man was Henry Boyd, a Kentucky freedman, who had helped to overcome the prejudice against colored mechanics in that city by exhibiting the highest efficiency. He patented a corded bed which became very popular, especially in the Southwest. With this article he built up a creditable manufacturing business, employing from 18 to 25 white and colored men.[61] He was, therefore, known as one of the desirable men of the city. Two things, however, seemingly interfered with his business. In the first place, certain white men, who became jealous of his success, burned him out and the insurance companies refused to carry him any longer. Moreover, having to do chiefly with white men he was charged by his people with favoring the miscegenation of races. Whether or not this was well founded is not yet known, but his children and grandchildren did marry whites and were lost in the so-called superior race.

A much more interesting Negro appeared in Cincinnati, however, in 1847. This was Robert Gordon, formerly the slave of a rich yachtsman of Richmond, Virginia. His master turned over to him a coal yard which he handled so faithfully that his owner gave him all of the slack resulting from the handling of the coal. This he sold to the local manufacturers and blacksmiths of the city, accumulating thereby in the course of time thousands of dollars. He purchased himself in 1846 and set out for free soil. He went first to Philadelphia and then to Newburyport, but finding that these places did not suit him, he proceeded to Cincinnati. He arrived there with $15,000, some of which he immediately invested in the coal business in which he had already achieved marked success. He employed bookkeepers, had his own wagons, built his own docks on the river, and bought coal by barges.[62]

Unwilling to see this Negro do so well, the white coal dealers endeavored to force him out of the business by lowering the price to the extent that he could not afford to sell. They did not know of his acumen and the large amount of capital at his disposal. He sent to the coal yards of his competitors mulattoes who could pass for white, using them to fill his current orders from his foes' supplies that he might save his own coal for the convenient day. In the course of a few months the river and all the canals by which coal was brought to Cincinnati froze up and remained so until spring. Gordon was then able to dispose of his coal at a higher price than it had ever been sold in that city. This so increased his wealth and added to his reputation that no one thereafter thought of opposing him.

Gordon continued in the coal business until 1865 when he retired. During the Civil War he invested his money in United States bonds. When these bonds were called in, he invested in real estate on Walnut Hills, which he held until his death in 1884. This estate descended to his daughter Virginia Ann Gordon who married George H. Jackson, a descendant of slaves in the Custis family of Arlington, Virginia. Mr. Jackson is now a resident of Chicago and is managing this estate.[63] Having lived through the ante-bellum and subsequent periods, Mr. Jackson has been made to wonder whether the Negroes of Cincinnati are doing as well to-day as Gordon and his colaborers were. This question requires some attention, but an inquiry as to exactly what forces have operated to impede the progress of a work so auspiciously begun would lead us beyond the limits set for this dissertation.

Notes

[1] Quillin, "The Color Line in Ohio," 18.

[2] "Tyrannical Libertymen," 10–11; Locke, "Antislavery," 31–32; Branagan, "Serious Remonstrance," 18.

[3] Woodson, "The Education of the Negro Prior to 1861," 230–231.

[4] Constitution, Article I, Sections 2, 6.

[5] Laws of Ohio, II, 63.

[6] Laws of Ohio, V, 53.

[7] Hickok, "The Negro in Ohio," 41, 42.

[8] Warden, "Statistical, Political and Historical Account of the United States of North America," 264.

[9] Quillin, "The Color Line in Ohio," 32.

[10] The Census of the United States, from 1800 to 1850.

[11] Flint's Letters in Thwaite's "Early Western Travels," IX, 239.

[12] Cist, "Cincinnati in 1841," 37; *Cincinnati Daily Gazette*, Sept. 14, 1841.

[13] *Ibid.*

[14] United States Census, 1850.

[15] *Ohio State Journal*, May 3, 1827; *African Repository*, III, 254.

[16] Abdy, "Journal of a Tour in the United States," III, 62.

[17] Jay, "Miscellaneous Writings on Slavery," 27, 373, 385, 387; Minutes of the Convention of the Colored People of Ohio, 1849.

[18] Barber, "A Report on the Condition of the Colored People of Ohio," 1840.

[19] Proceedings of the Ohio Antislavery Convention, 1835, 19.

[20] *Ibid.*

[21] Proceedings of the Ohio Antislavery Convention, 1835, 19.

[22] *African Repository*, V, 185.

[23] *African Repository*, V, 185.

[24] For a lengthy account of these efforts see Woodson's "The Education of the Negro Prior to 1861," 245, 328, 329; and Hickok, "The Negro in Ohio," 83, 88.

[25] Fairchild, "Oberlin: Its Origin, Progress and Results."

[26] Howe, "Historical Collections of Ohio," 356.

[27] *The Southern Workman*, XXXVII, 169.

[28] For a full account see Howe, "Historical Collections of Ohio," 225–226.

[29] Barber, "Report on the Condition of the Colored People in Ohio," 1840, and *The Philanthropist*, July 14 and 21, 1840.

[30] These facts are taken from A. D. Barber's "Report on the Condition of the Colored People in Ohio" and from other articles contributed to *The Philanthropist* in July, 1840.

[31] In this case I have taken the statements of Negroes who were employed in this capacity.

[32] *The Philanthropist*, July 14 and 24, 1840; and May 26, 1841.

[33] Hickok, "The Negro in Ohio," 89.

[34] *The Philanthropist*, July 14 and 21, 1840.

[35] *The Philanthropist*, July 21, 1840.

[36] *The Cincinnati Daily Gazette*, September 14, 1841.

[37] *The Philanthropist*, July 21, 1840.

[38] *Ibid.*

[39] *The Cincinnati Daily Gazette*, September 14, 1841.

[40] A detailed account of these clashes is given in *The Cincinnati Daily Gazette*, September 14, 1841.

[41] *The Cincinnati Daily Gazette*, September, 1841.

[42] A very interesting account of this riot is given in Howe's "Historical Collections of Ohio," pages 226–228.

[43] It was discovered that not a few of the mob came from Kentucky. About eleven o'clock on Saturday night a bonfire was lighted on that side of the river and loud shouts were sent up as if triumph had been achieved. "In some cases," says a reporter, "the directors were boys who suggested the point of attack, put the vote, declared the result and lead the way." — Cin. Daily Gaz., Sept. 14, 1841.

[44] Hickok, "The Negro in Ohio," 90 et seq.

[45] Laws of Ohio, XL, 81.

[46] *Ibid.*, LIII, 118.

[47] The Convention Debates.

[48] Special Report of the United States Commissioner of Education, 1871, page 372.

[49] Laws of Ohio.

[50] *Ibid.*, LIII, 118.

[51] *The New York Tribune,* February.19, 1855.

[52] Lyell, "A Second Visit to the United States of North America," II, 295, 296.

[53] *The Weekly Herald and Philanthropist,* June 26, 1844, August 6, 1844, and January 1, 1845.

[54] The Cincinnati Directory of 1860.

[55] Foote, "The Schools of Cincinnati," 92.

[56] *The Weekly Herald and Philanthropist,* August 23, 1844.

[57] Special Report of the United States Commissioner of Education, 372.

[58] Simmons, "Men of Mark," 490.

[59] A white slaveholder, a graduate of Amherst, taught in this school. See *Weekly Herald and Philanthropist,* June 26, 1844.

[60] These facts were obtained from oral statements of Negroes who were living in Cincinnati at this time; from M. R. Delany's "The Condition of the Colored People in the United States"; from A. D. Barber's "Report on the Condition of the Colored People in Ohio," 1840; and from various Cincinnati Directories.

[61] Delany, "The Condition of the Colored People in the United States," 92.

[62] The Cincinnati Directory for 1860.

[63] For the leading facts concerning the life of Robert Gordon I have depended on the statements of his children and acquaintances and on the various directories and documents giving evidence concerning the business men of Cincinnati.

The Providence Negro Community, 1820–1842

Julian Rammelkamp

Gradual abolition of chattel slavery was secured by law in Rhode Island in 1784. Forty years later only four elderly slaves remained in Providence — vestiges of an age destroyed in the fiery crucible of Revolutionary idealism.[1] But the destruction of legal bondage had in Providence as elsewhere, succeeded only in creating a free Negro population still living in the deep shadows of slaveday ignorance, poverty, and dependence. Utterly devoid of economic opportunity and social self-respect, the Providence Negro eked out a precarious existence as a servant or as a manual laborer at work disdained by the white man. Scattered in the homes of white people and oppressed by the weight of white prejudice, the Negro possessed no community structure or institutions which could provide him with opportunity, recreation, or self-expression.

In 1820, however, a self-emancipation movement was set in motion when the African Union Meeting House, the first all-Negro church in Providence, was opened on Meeting Street. Twenty years later, on the eve of the Dorr War, there existed in the city a thriving, self-respecting colored community possessed of churches, schools, and fraternal societies, a community wherein a Negro not only could breathe an atmosphere of freedom, but also could exert a common pressure of protest against a white world denying him the fruits of civilization.

The pre-Dorr War history of the Negroes of Providence parallels contemporaneous Negro movements occurring in such other cities as Boston, New York, and Philadelphia. A free Negro movement was coming to life everywhere in the Northeast. For a number of years the Providence stirrings were independent of those taking place elsewhere, and, because of a smaller population, the Providence movement developed more slowly than, for example, New York's. But presently, the burgeoning societies in each of these cities, through various fraternal, religious, and political organizations, coalesced into a general movement, thereby imparting new confidence and strength to the local communities. In 1829, William Lloyd Garrison settled in Boston and began his agitation for the cause of the free Negro as well

Julian Rammelkamp, "The Providence Negro Community, 1820–1842," *Rhode Island History* VII (January 1948), 20–33. Reprinted with permission of The Rhode Island Historical Society.

as the slave. Situated so near Providence, Garrison soon exerted strong influence within the budding local society, firing it with increased self-consciousness and enthusiasm. These two extramural stimulants were supplemented by the presence in Providence of a strong humanitarian spirit which long had animated certain white groups, particularly the Quakers. In 1833, at the behest of Garrison, this spirit was crystallized into a militant anti-slavery society, which became a staunch supporter of Negro welfare. Perhaps most significant of all the forces generating the energy behind the Negro's struggle towards self-respect, however, was the growing movement of democratization which pervaded all regions and elements in the United States after 1820 — a movement which in Rhode Island erupted into the Dorr War and helped to raise the lot of all submerged classes. The creation of a Providence colored community between 1820 and 1842 was simply a small manifestation of a development national in scope.

The Negro population of Providence exhibited a number of peculiar characteristics which at the outset were to shape its course. Though in New England its size was second only to Boston's, fewer than one thousand lived in the town in 1820. Moreover, its rate of increase was negligible, as only thirteen hundred called Providence home in 1840. A second characteristic was the homogeneity of its origins. Most Negroes were descendants of slaves brought to Rhode Island in the colonial period. Thus, names prominent in white society, such as Brown, Fenner, Hazard, Congdon, and Eldridge also appear frequently as Negro surnames. Apparently because Boston in New England was the magnet attracting the escaping Southern slave, comparatively few fugitives settled in Providence. In 1860 only three hundred of a total of fifteen hundred were Southern born. A third vital peculiarity was the distribution of the population within the town. In 1820 a majority lived as servants in white homes. Nucleii for a separate community growth, however, existed on Meeting Street east of the Providence River, the Spring Street area west of the river, the Olney Street-Gaspee Street district, and along the waterfront near Fox Point.[2]

The small and scattered characteristic of the population was at first, of course, a deterrent factor in the growth of a community. But within a few years, as economic opportunities and wealth permitted more and more colored people to migrate to districts inhabited by their own kind, stability in population and similarity of origin proved to be beneficial. Gains in social organization, economic wealth and opportunity, education, and social consciousness were not continually jeopardized by an influx of illiterate, impecunious fugitives; unlike other cities, social integration assumed the character of steady and sure progress after the earliest years. Moreover, the Providence Negro's energies were directed primarily at the problems of his own self-improvement; precious strength was not wasted on Abolitionist agitation.

Needless to say, the growth of a colored community was based upon a gradually rising curve of economic wealth and opportunity. In 1820 almost all Negroes were servants or laborers; the aristocrats of the Negro world were the few barbers, carpenters, and blacksmiths. A group of transient Negro sailors lived on the waterfront. Colored folk thus were continuing in the humble pursuits they had followed as slaves. After 1820 a slow amelioration of this oppressed condition took place. Though unable to find employment in the rising textile industries, colored men took up the occupation of draymen, carting raw cotton from the docks to the mills. The older arts of cooking and farming became more specialized as grocers, bakers, and confectioners began plying their trades in the rapidly growing city. In the 1830's trades which required a small outlay of capital began to appear. Laborers like Enoch Freeman, who established the first Negro shoe repair shop, invested tiny savings in self-owned businesses. Freeman operated on a shoestring in more than one sense, for "he could hardly take care of himself by his trade." William Brown, however, bought Freeman's equipment and in a few years was doing a business which "promised to be a great success."[3] In this precarious manner many shops and trades had sprung up by 1841, including groceries, confectioneries, shoe repair shops, and two second-hand clothing stores.[4]

In time, a few Negroes succeeded in amassing enough wealth to invest in property. One of them was Eleanor Eldridge, who had saved enough from work as a laundress, whitewasher, and nurse to purchase two house lots. By 1840 her holdings were valued at $4,000. George McCarthy, operator of a refreshment stand, advertised in 1835 his willingness to sell several lots on Meeting Street on which stood substantial dwellings. "All the above property," he announced, "is free from encumbrances."[5] Altogether, the Negro population already was possessed of $10,000 worth of property in 1822. By 1830 colored persons owned about $18,000, and in 1839 estimates ran from $35,000 to $50,000. By this time a few other individuals possessed a sufficiency of wealth to deserve notice. The wealthiest of the newcomers were James Hazard, clothier, worth $2,700, and Edward Barnes, grocer, who owned $2,900.[6]

The rising scale of wealth gradually permitted more and more Negro families to live separately from the whites, and the colored settlements within the town grew and took on more of the ways of a maturing society. By 1830 half the population lived in their own homes. Nine years later the proportion had increased to two-thirds.[7]

Nevertheless, it should be said that the growing scale of wealth did not include everyone. One-third remained near-slaves in white homes, and of the others, many were "engaged in what are called menial employments, [in which they] do such things as white people are unwilling to do. . . . Some live very comfortable and happy, but the larger part are much straightened in their circumstances, and many live miserably."[8] Notwithstanding, the economic gains registered between 1820 and 1842, though they benefited only a minority in a material sense, provided the economic foundations on which was built a community which spread its benefits far beyond the comparative few who possessed wealth.

The first outward manifestation of the rise of a Negro community took place in the sphere of religion. Because "the slavish and gross state of ignorance of the people of colour, has of late years excited the commiseration of those who profess [themselves] . . . the active friends of humanity," a group of white philanthropists decided in 1819 to help the Negro members of their churches form a religious society of their own.[9] They requested a number of what they considered to be pious and upstanding colored men to meet with them at the First Baptist Church. "After solemn prayer for divine direction," plans were laid, and a committee of twelve Negroes was designated to solicit interest and funds from the colored population. The Quaker humanitarian, Moses Brown, donated land on Meeting Street for the erection of a meeting house and the colored people, poor as they were, contributed eight hundred dollars. In June, 1820, the church was opened officially with a gala celebration.[10]

Perhaps one of the reasons the whites had interested themselves in the formation of a colored church was that not a "congregation in town . . . desired their attendance."[11] In every white church Negroes were "obliged to sit in a certain part of the gallery separated from the whites."[12] This accounts for the small number of church-going Negroes before 1820, and also for the rapid exodus of all but a few elderly servants from white balconies when the Union Meeting was organized.[13]

The whites who engineered the establishment of the African Union Meeting vainly hoped the Negroes could "be induced to forego their own opinions on religious matters . . . [but they] were soon disappointed, for the same causes which produced sects and dissonant creeds throughout Christendom, operated to divide and subdivide the colored people of Providence."[14] However, it was not unitl 1835, when a fiery Negro evangelist, Rev. J. W. Lewis, conducted several lively revivals in the Union Meeting House, that religious unity was destroyed. The exhortations of Rev. Lewis resulted in the secession of those who favored religion in strong doses; and a Free Will Baptist Church, the only colored one in New England, was formed. It became the largest of the Negro religious groups. In 1840 it built its own meeting house on Pond Street.[15]

Two national colored religious organizations appeared next in Providence. The African Methodist Episcopal Zion Church in 1837 and the African Methodist Episcopal Church a year later established institutions in the city. Permanent religious links with the national Negro world were thus forged. The fourth and smallest of the Providence churches founded prior to the Dorr War was Christ Church, an Episcopal body. Christ Church was chiefly notable for its young pastor, Alexander Crummell, an educated, spirited leader who later became famous in Liberia and Philadelphia as a wise and an inspiring minister of the gospel.[16]

In twenty years four churches, basic elements of society in that day, had been spawned, offering colored men and women opportunities for self-expression and leadership, solace and entertainment never before possessed. As a result, though in 1820 only one-twelfth of the population could be induced to join white churches "because they said they were opposed to churches and sitting in pigeon holes," one-sixth were members of colored churches in 1839 and many more attended frequently.[17]

In this period, too, the Providence Negro created educational opportunities where none had existed before. Prior to 1820 colored children could rely upon only well-intentioned but sporadic efforts of Quakers and other whites for the rudiments of knowledge, and it was not until the African Union Meeting was conceived that a permanent school was established. The Meeting House, built to accommodate a classroom, opened in 1819. Even this school operated under difficulties. The greatest problem was securing a teacher; colored ones were hard to find, and whites considered it a disgrace to teach Negroes. One white teacher who was hired threatened severe punishment to any of his charges who had the temerity to greet him in public. Consequently, the school was closed much of the time.[18]

At last, as a result of humanitarian pressure and a Negro petition, a public school for colored children was established in a Meeting Street building which once housed Brown University. In 1837 a second Negro school was opened on Pond Street. Tender white feelings prevented matriculation of Negroes in white schools until after the Civil War. However, because public schools for colored children were larger than those for white children, they were allocated more funds.[19]

Unfortunately, the teachers, always white, were paid less than their colleagues teaching white pupils. This fact, in addition to prejudice, resulted in the employment of instructors of low caliber. By 1840 colored attendance had dropped so sharply, because of frequent punishment, that the Pond Street school was closed. An investigation found that "an unhappy prejudice of the colored people against [the schoolmaster], although generally unfounded, . . . goes to destroy his usefulness."[20]

The growing community was not satisfied with this situation, nor with the lack of public provision for education beyond the common level. Colored pastors taught night classes for adults, and in 1836 the Rev. J. W. Lewis founded the New England Union Academy. With one assistant Lewis taught history, geography, botany, grammar, single and double entry bookkeeping, natural philosophy, and astronomy. Tuition was three dollars a quarter.[21]

Illiteracy, which in 1820 had been well-nigh universal, as a result of these efforts had dropped by 1841 to fifty per cent. The taste of this once forbidden fruit gave to the community young men who supplied the Negroes with intelligent and aggressive leadership. Men like Alexander Crummell, educated in a Massachusetts theological seminary, Jeremiah Asher, an educated Baptist minister, and William Brown, educated in Providence public and private schools, were symbols of a new age.[22]

The churches founded after 1820 provided the meeting centers for all sorts of religious and secular societies as well as platforms from which rising leaders of the colored race could organize and exhort their followers. Two fraternal groups, however, antedated the dynamic Negro movement. In 1799 the colored Masons of Boston issued to nine Providence Master Masons a warrant authorizing them to form Hiram Lodge Number Three. This was the second oldest Negro chapter in masonic history. A second lodge was formed in 1826. High sounding titles and responsibilities of office alleviated the menial drudgery of daily living. The other early fraternal group doubtless stemmed from the colored unit which fought so valiantly in the Revolution. The African Greys, a smartly uniformed outfit, headed the parade which marched through the streets of Providence in celebration of the opening of the African Union Meeting House. On that occasion their commander was "dressed up to represent an African chief, having on a red pointed cap and carried an elephant's tusk in his hand. . . . The other officers [were] carrying emblems, decked with lemons and oranges, represent[ing] the fruits of Africa." The Quaker philanthropists who aided in the founding of the church refused to allow the company to enter the new edifice until it had stacked its guns in the church yard.[23]

The most popular society grew out of the nation-wide temperance movement of the day. At a mass meeting in 1832, the Negroes organized the Providence Temperance Society. Forty charter members took the pledge to use liquor for medicinal purposes only. In the event that members transgressed, the constitution provided "they shall be conversed with and shewn the errors of their ways; if they do not reform . . . they shall be expelled from this society. . . ."[24] The society moved into high gear when the Rev. Mr. Lewis came to town, expanding to a membership of two hundred. The grandiose Reverend then set about making Providence the capital of a New England temperance movement, calling a convention in 1836.[25]

Other groups formed after 1820 were dedicated to endeavors more practical. Two mutual aid societies, designed to provide financial assistance in seasons of emergency, were founded in the late 1820's. Dues were twenty-five cents a month. These earliest attempts at mutual insurance were significant of a growing community consciousness and self-reliance. Traces of a literary and debating society on the eve of the Dorr War marked the faint beginnings of a cultural development, indeed an indication of growth.[26]

The idea implanted by slavery, that Negroes were inferior beings, clung to the whites long after the abolition of that institution. Colored people long were hedged in by discriminatory public laws and oppressed by acts of private prejudice. From the viewpoint of citizenship, the most galling was the explicit denial of an already dubious right of suffrage in 1822. Rhode Island thus joined Connecticut in being the only New England states to disfranchise Negroes as such.[27]

Not content with legal proscription, lower class whites often amused themselves by tormenting Negroes. "It was a common thing for colored people to be disturbed on the street . . . On the north side of Market Square . . . were generally found . . . a row of [white] men stretched along the doorways of the stores, . . . knocking off [colored] men's hats, pulling off [colored] ladies' shawls. . . The corner bore the name of 'Scamps' Corner.' "[28]

On very few occasions did Negroes become so embittered as to strike back. In the settlement known as "Hardscrabble," located north of the town, a race riot broke out in 1826, and in 1830 a violent riot broke out in that "sink of moral corruption" around Olney Street, a disturbance which was not quelled for three days and then only by the state militia.[29]

Like his brothers in all northern cities who faced similar circumstances, the

Providence Negro had the alternatives of flight, submission, or aggressive protest. Having become conscious of his lot after 1820, the Negro more and more emphatically rejected submission. At first flight seemed preferable. Following the "Hardscrabble" riot, a large group emigrated to Liberia. Since, however, Providence was as much home to the Negro as to the white, the Negro community turned from flight to protest. After 1830 a series of meetings, prompted by Garrison, were held to protest against the Liberian project and its sponsoring organization, the American Colonization Society. A new note of defiance was voiced in a resolution drawn up in 1832, which asserted that though ". . . we are truly sensible that we are in this country a degraded and ignorant people; . . . our ignorance and degradation are not to be attributed to the inferiority of our natural abilities, but to the oppressive treatment we have experienced from the whites in general. . . . We will not leave our homes, nor the graves of our fathers, and this boasted land of liberty and Christian philanthropy."[30]

The American Colonization Society posed such a grave threat to free Negroes throughout the North with its plans to encourage emigration that it was the catalytic agent producing the free Negro Convention movement which met first at Philadelphia in 1830 to map a nationwide protest. To it, as delegates from Providence, went George Willis and Alfred Niger, Garrison's collaborator. The local movement now became a part of a national protest, infusing the Providence community with new strength.[31]

Interestingly enough, with the exception of a group of militant fugitives, the abolition of Southern slavery probably was of only secondary importance to Providence Negroes. Rhode Island born, and with the memory of their own legal bondage fast fading, local Negroes were preoccupied with their own problems. Evidence of this attitude exists chiefly for the period subsequent to the Dorr War and one example must suffice. Upon receiving enfranchisement in 1843, because their benefactors in Rhode Island were Whigs, Negroes became Whigs, in spite of the fact that the Garrisonians labeled the national Whig Party as pro-slavery. In 1848, Providence colored men decided to vote for the Whig Zachary Taylor for President, slave-holder though he was.[32]

This is not to say that the Providence Negro was indifferent to the plight of his Southern brother. Anti-slavery papers were "patronized with great avidity by the blacks," particularly *Freedom's Journal* and Garrison's *Liberator*.[33] The meetings of the local white anti-slavery group were attended by Negroes, and when Garrison founded the New England Anti-Slavery Society several Providence leaders became members.[34]

The events leading to and resulting from the Dorr War were the clearest evidence that a colored community had been created in Providence. A majority of the whites, whether of the Landholder or Suffragist parties, continued to oppose enfranchisement of Negroes. Consequently, if the Dorr War had not occurred to divide white society into two factions, colored enfranchisement might have been long delayed. But though white men of all classes remained unaware of its existence, the agitation over broadening the franchise soon brought to light evidence that a self-reliant colored community had grown up in their midst, a community which demanded political equality in recognition of its growth. At first the Landholder aristocrats chose to ignore the colored demand, and in their proposed constitution of 1841 they not only denied the Negro the vote, but also denied completely the loudly proclaimed principle of political equality voiced by the Dorrites. A majority of the Dorrites, too, did not believe in their own principles to the extent of abolishing racial inequality at the polls. A strong anti-slavery minority threw the Suffragist convention into an uproar in the autumn of 1841 by proposing to strike the word "white" from an otherwise manhood suffrage clause in the Dorrite constitution, but the motion was defeated by a large majority.[35]

The colored community itself demanded its rights before the Suffrage convention. A committee of six, led by the Rev. Alexander Crummell, presented a petition which not only called upon the delegates to stand by their principles, but announced in clear tones that the Negro community could no longer be ignored. "It is evident," said the petition, "that, repelled and disfranchised as we have been, we have, nevertheless been enabled to possess ourselves of the means and advantages of religion, intelligence, and property. . . . Is a justification of our disfranchisement sought in our want of Christian character? We point to our churches as refutation. In our want of intelligence? We refer not merely to the schools supported by the state, but to the private schools . . . taught by competent teachers of our own people. Is our industry questioned? This day, were there no complexionable hindrance, we could present a more than proportionate number of our people, who might immediately, according to [present] . . . qualifications, become voters." The petition ended with a warning which the Dorrites might well have heeded. "It is the warrant of history . . . that thus striking off from us the . . . precious birthright of freemen, . . . the poisoned chalice may be returned to the lips of those who departed from their principles."[36]

To placate anti-slavery dissidents and perhaps to calm uneasy consciences, the Suffragists thereupon provided for an eventual plebiscite to determine whether the people of the state desired to eliminate "white" from the franchise clause. But the concession was too little and too late. Abolitionists sent such orators as Frederick Douglass throughout Rhode Island in a vain attempt to defeat the Suffragist constitution.[37]

The Dorr War broke out in the spring of 1842. As part of their preparations to destroy the Dorrite government, the aristocrats proceeded to grant tacit recognition to the colored community by endowing it with the public responsibility of helping to keep law and order in the city while Landholders sallied forth to do battle. Colored men were enlisted in units to patrol the streets.[38]

After the rebellion was crushed, the aristocrats, realizing that substantial concessions must be made to prevent a recurrence of violence, presented a third constitution. They rewarded their ally, the colored community, by at last abolishing the color line at the polls; but they effectively prevented many foreign born whites, who had been Dorrite adherents, from voting by demanding a high property qualification for aliens. Colored men for long after amply rewarded their benefactors by consistently voting Whig.[39]

Victims of their own prejudice, the Dorrites — in other respects the truly democratic party — fulminated against the Negroes' friendship for the Landholders, sneering that the colored people were "their dependents, their laborers, their coachmen, and their domestics."[40] But coachmen and servants did not motivate the Negro-Landholder alliance; it was independent shoemaker William Brown, preacher Alexander Crummell, store proprietor James Hazard, and teacher Ransom Parker who led their fellows into the aristocratic camp. The Suffragists refused to recognize the existence of a Negro community in Providence, a community no longer composed of obsequious outcasts, but of persons now thoroughly awake to the wrongs which white society had heaped upon it. Fundamentally, though for reasons of expediency, the Landholders recognized, as the Suffragists did not, Rev. Crummell's assertion to the Suffrage Convention, that "we have long, and with but little aid, been working our way up to respectability and confidence."[41]

Notes

[1] E. M. Snow, *Census of the City of Providence, taken in July, 1855* (Providence, 1856) p. 72.

[2] Snow, *Op. Cit.*, p. 73–74; E. M. Snow, Director, *Census of the City of Providence, 1860.*

[3] William Brown, *The Life of William J. Brown of Providence, R.I.*, (Providence, 1883) p. 107–108.

[4] Brown, *Op. Cit.*, p. 19, 33; *The Providence Directory*, 1824, 1830, 1840, 1841; W. D. Johnston, "Slavery in Rhode Island, 1755–1776," *R. I. Historical Society Publications*, vol. 2, July, 1894, p. 129.

[5] *The Liberator*, (Boston) May 4–Aug. 29, 1835.

[6] Eleanor McDougall, *Memoirs of Elleanor Eldridge*, (Providence, 1842) p. 8–13, 70–84; Brown, *Op. Cit.*, p. 85–86, 110, 173; *Providence Directory*, 1841; *List of Persons Taxed in the City Tax*, 1824, 1830, 1840; *Liberator*. Oct. 18, 1839.

[7] C. G. Woodson, *Free Negro Heads of Families in 1830*, (Washington, 1925) p. 153–154; Brown, *Op. Cit.*, p. 33, 113; *Liberator*, Oct. 18, 1839.

[8] *Liberator*, Oct. 18, 1839.

[9] *A Short History of the African Union Meeting and School-House, Erected in Providence, (R.I.)*, (Providence, 1821) p. 3.

[10] *Ibid.*, p. 4–7.

[11] W. McDonald, *History of Methodism in Providence, Rhode Island*, (Boston, 1868) p. 53.

[12] J. S. Buckingham, *America: Historical, Statistic, and Descriptive*, (London, 1841) v. 3, p. 491.

[13] *Liberator*, Oct. 18, 1839; Brown, *Op. Cit.*, p. 83; McDonald, *Op. Cit.*, p. 65; H. M. King, *Historical Catalogue of the Members of the First Baptist Church in Providence, Rhode Island*, (Providence, 1908).

[14] W. R. Staples, *Annals: The Town of Providence from its First Settlement to the Organization of the City Government in June, 1832*, (Providence, 1832) p. 489–490.

¹⁵ *Ibid.*, p. 641; Brown, *Op. Cit.*, p. 135; *Inventory of the Churches of Rhode Island: Baptists*, (Providence, 1941) p. 166.

¹⁶ Staples, *Op. Cit.*, p. 641; J. J. Moore, *History of the A.M.E. Zion Church, in America*, (York, Pa., 1884) p. 56; *MSS. Documents of Christ Church* (Colored) Providence, R.I., Historical Society; Benjamin Brawley, *Early Negro American Writers*, (Chapel Hill, 1935) p. 299.

¹⁷ Brown, *Op. Cit.*, p. 46; *Liberator*, Oct. 18, 1839.

¹⁸ McDonald, *Op. Cit.*, p. 54; Brown, *Op. Cit.*, p. 40–44. *African Union Meeting*, p. 9.

¹⁹ G. W. Williams, *History of the Negro Race in America*, (New York, 1883) v. 2, p. 178; T. B. Stockwell, *A History of Public Education in Providence, R.I.*, (Providence, 1876) p. 196, 211; *Records and Documents, Relating to the History and Condition of Public Schools of the Various Towns: Providence*, (Providence, 1849) p. 59; *The Charter and Ordinances of the City of Providence*, (Providence, 1845) p. 54–59.

²⁰ Charles Carroll, *Public Education in Rhode Island*, (Providence, 1918) p. 157; *Reports and Documents*, p. 54–59.

²¹ Brown, *Op. Cit.*, p. 126; *Liberator*, Apr. 2, 1836.

²² *Liberator*, Oct. 18, 1839; Brawley, *Op. Cit.*, p. 299; Jeremiah Asher, *An Autobiography*, (Philadelphia, 1862) p. 61–62.

²³ Brown, *Op. Cit.*, p. 83; W. H. Grimshaw, *Official History of Freemasonry among the Colored People of North America*, (New York, 1903) p. 122; W. H. Upton, *Legitimacy of the Masonry Existing among the Negroes of America*, (Cambridge, Mass., 1907) p. 106.

²⁴ *Liberator*, Oct. 13, 1832.

²⁵ *Ibid.*, Oct. 27, 1832; Apr. 30–May 7, 1836.

²⁶ Brown, *Op. Cit.*, p. 51–55, 81–33.

²⁷ J. T. Adams, "Disenfranchisement of Negroes in New England," *American Historical Review*, v. 30, p. 544–546.

²⁸ Brown, *Op. Cit.*, p. 124–125.

²⁹ *Literary Cadet and Saturday Evening Bulletin*, (Providence) Nov. 25, 1826; *The Genius of Universal Emancipation*, (Washington and Baltimore) v. 2, p. 78; Brown, *Op. Cit.*, p. 89; Staples, *Op. Cit.*, p. 397–399.

³⁰ W. L. Garrison, *Thoughts on African Colonization*, (Boston, 1832) Part 2, p. 44–45; *African Repository*, American Colonization Society Reports, v. 29, p. 86–89.

³¹ J. W. Campbell, "The Early Negro Convention Movement," *Negro American Academy, Occasional Papers*, (Washington, 1904) No. 9, p. 5, 32.

³² Brown, *Op. Cit.*, p. 159, 167–169.

³³ *Literary Cadet*, Nov. 24, 1827.

³⁴ *Freedom's Journal*, (New York) Apr. 11, 1827; *Liberator*, Jan. 5, 1833, May 14–Aug. 25, 1836; *Annual Reports of the Executive Committee of the American Anti-Slavery Society*, (New York) v. 6. The New England Anti-Slavery Society later became the American Anti-Slavery Society.

³⁵ A. M. Mowry, *The Dorr War*, (Providence, 1901) p. 326, 350; *Providence Journal*, Oct. 25, 1841.

³⁶ *Burke's Congressional Report*, Rpt. No. 546, House of Reps., 28th Congress, First Session, P. 111–113.

³⁷ William Goodell, *The Rights and Wrongs of Rhode Island*, (Whitesborough, N.Y., 1842) p. 5; Mowry, *Op. Cit.*, p. 98–99; Frederick Douglass, *Life and Times of Frederick Douglass*, (Boston, 1893) p. 272–275.

³⁸ *The New Age* (Providence) Nov. 14, 1842; Brown, *Op. Cit.*, p. 173.

³⁹ Mowry, *Op. Cit.*, p. 370.

⁴⁰ Goodell, *Op. Cit.*, p. 6.

⁴¹ *Burke's Report*, p. 111–113.

The Negro Vote in Old New York

Dixon Ryan Fox

The attachment of the colored citizen to the Republican party is usually explained by reference to the memory of Lincoln, Stevens, Grant and Sumner; but in New York, at least, the freedman learned to vote against St. Tammany before most of those apostles of his "rights" were born, and the jealous hatred of poor mechanics helps far more than reconstruction policies to account for the attitude of New York Democrats towards Negro suffrage.

The appearance of the Negro in the Hudson River region is no novelty of recent years. The Dutch brought the *swarten* to the colony before Manhattan houses were a decade old;[1] when the English made Fort Amsterdam Fort James, the encouragement of the slave trade with New York became an object of solicitude in London.[2] The demand for "negears" was larger and more steady here than in other colonies of the same latitude,[3] yet slaves were not massed in large plantations but scattered by twos and threes as household servants among the well-to-do, chiefly in the houses of the aristocracy.[4] They were treated with a careful kindliness, and in return they developed an affection for the master that no shock of fortune could disturb.[5]

What was the partizan connection of New York slave owners? The Federalist party was the party of the aristocracy, especially in large communities,[6] the party of the wealth won by a century of trade. Since slaves in this colony were a luxury rather than an investment in agriculture, we should expect to find them belonging largely to members of this party; the records show such to have been the case.[7]

A great historian has truly remarked: "That New York is not a slave state like South Carolina is due to climate and not to the superior humanity of the founders."[8] Slavery for them did not pay. The Federalist masters preferred to see their Negroes free, and led the movement in New York state for their betterment. Governor John Jay organized the Society for Promoting the Manumission of Slaves and became its first president in 1785;[9] he was succeeded by Alexander Hamilton.[10] It was Rufus King who had moved "that there shall be neither slavery nor involuntary servitude in any of the states described in the resolve of Congress of 23rd of April, 1784," dealing with the Northwest Ordinance.[11] General Schuyler was found, when the time came, voting for emancipation of the Negroes of the state.[12] Next to Jay in his importance in the constituent convention at White Plains in 1776 was Gouver-

Dixon Ryan Fox, "The Negro Vote in Old New York," *Political Science Quarterly* XXXII (June 1917), 252–275. Reprinted with permission of *Political Science Quarterly*.

neur Morris, who made most earnest efforts for some scheme of gradual emancipation.[13] Party editors from Noah Webster[14] to William L. Stone[15] took up the cause with much enthusiasm. Certainly the leaders of the party might lay a claim to the black man's loyalty, and the party followed their leaders on this question. They finally enacted a well-calculated scheme of gradual emancipation which prevented the distress of any sudden readjustment.[16] The measure was opposed by the party of the small tradesman and the mechanic, for reasons of economic jealousy as we shall see. The workman did not like to see the Negro change his butler's coat for cap and jeans, and his salver for pick and shovel. It was a Federalist legislature and a Federalist governor who enacted the law of 1799, by almost a straight party vote of sixty-eight to twenty-three.[17] The Negroes had been reared in Federalist households; their cause had been advocated by distinguished Federalists, and now under the auspices of that party, freedom was provided. When they reached the estate of citizens, their political attachment could be easily foretold.

In numbers they were not to be neglected. New York had been the most important slave state in the North, and continued to have more Negroes than any other state in that section.[18] In New York city the proportion of Negroes to whites at the beginning of the nineteenth century was several times larger than now.[19] As soon as any slave was freed he became a voter, on the same terms as a white man, namely, if he paid taxes to the state, if he owned a freehold of the value of twenty pounds, or if he rented a tenement of the yearly fee of forty shillings.[20] In the eighteenth century manumission had not been uncommon, and it became more general after 1800. The erstwhile slave became in politics a client of his former master. To say that Jay or Hamilton in urging manumission had been largely moved by the hope of adding to the Federalist vote would be not only ungenerous but absurd. Yet it was only natural that in his voting, as well as in his talk and dress, the Negro should follow the example of his former master. In Brooklyn, for example, five of the thirteen Federalist candidates in 1810 were men who had set free their slaves, while there was but one such among their opponents.[21] The credit for the first manumission under the new law in this community goes to John Doughty, who served his generation as town clerk from 1796 to 1830,[22] who registered the birth of every child of slave parents after 1799, and in whose ceremonious presence almost every manumitted slave was given his certificate of liberty.[23] Is it to be expected that the freedmen who came into Albany from Rensselaerwyck where they had been so kindly treated,[24] or those who came from the great house of General Schuyler where so many had been granted freedom,[25] would vote against "the lord"?[26]

On this question the political philosophers of Tammany Hall had entertained but little doubt; they soon saw their forebodings realized. When in 1808 the colored voters in a meeting held in New York city voiced unanimous approval of the "old party," Republicans prepared a campaign song beginning "Federalists with blacks unite."[27] In 1809 a Negro orator drew applause from a large audience when, after picturing the sad conditions under Jefferson, he exclaimed, "How important then, that we, my countrymen, should unite our efforts with those of our Federal friends in endeavoring to bring about this desirable change, so all-important to commerce, to our own best interests, and the prosperity and glory of our country."[28] Republican inspectors at the polls, to minimize the danger of this co-operation, presumed as slaves all black men who could not prove their freedom by sufficient evidence. The Federalists denounced this practice,[29] and organized among the Negroes a chapter of their partizan fraternity, the Washington Benevolent Society.[30] In 1811 a Republican legislature drew up a drastic law as to the suffrage of the blacks,[31] which passed in spite of the objections of the Federalist Council of Revision.[32]

The election of 1813 in the midst of "Mr. Madison's war" was closely contested; for some time the returns for members of assembly were in doubt.[33] The result was long remembered. Eight years afterward in the constitutional convention, General Root, speaking for the limitation on the franchise for men of color, recalled that "the votes of three hundred Negroes in the city of New York, in 1813, decided the election in favor of the Federal party, and also decided the political character of the legislature of this state."[34] Not the number of the Negroes who were qualified made them formidable, but the strategic strength of their location. At the next election, however, the Federalist majority was overturned, and it is not surprising to find soon presented before the reformed legislature a more severe measure to limit the political influence of the Negro in New York city. This not only provided for the elaborate registration of every freedman, but obliged him always to bring full copies of such registration to the officers of election.[35] Yet these laws were made effective with much difficulty; in spite of all precautions, "Negro ballots" had to be accepted. When Clinton brought to his standard the majority of Federalists he gained the colored men as well.[36] Therefore in 1821 the Republicans were in no mood to trifle with this question.

The convention of 1821 has been called with somewhat pompous phraseology "a dominant emancipating agent in American democracy."[37] That one of its major purposes was to extend the suffrage to new classes was realized by friend and foe alike. "This is one of the crying evils for which we were sent here to provide a remedy," said Mr. Ross, of the committee to which this subject was referred.[38] Old qualifications of property, the remnant of the English practice of colonial days, were to be swept away, and it was known that the question of Negro suffrage would be an important subject of debate. The members of the convention were chosen on party grounds, and a large majority of them were Democrats.[39] The convention was conducted on party principles; the chairmen of all committees were appointed by the president, ex-Governor Tompkins, from his own supporters. These gentlemen differed sharply with the Federalist minority on the extension of the suffrage to poor white men, and to Negroes also. The committee in charge proposed, not to continue a twenty-pound qualification for the Negro, while giving the indigent white the vote, but actually to take away the privilege that the Negro already had.

At the opening of the debate, Mr. Ross laid down the doctrine of the Democracy: "They are a peculiar people, incapable, in my judgment, of exercising that privilege with any sort of discretion, prudence, or independence." Probably the last-named quality gave him most concern, for later he complained that the black vote was a controlled vote. A petition in behalf of Negro voters "now on your table, in all probability had been instigated by gentlemen of a different colour who expect to control their votes."[40] For others the test of contribution to the state might be sufficient, but not so for the colored men.[41] There were reasons enough why the franchise should be denied the Negro altogether, said Colonel Young, a leading Democrat from Saratoga County; and if reasons did not prove sufficient, one could easily fall back on prejudice. The Negro should be entirely shut out.[42] Jacob Radcliff, who now represented the Tammany Society, "considered the privilege of exclusion to be derived, not from the distinction of color — but resorted to as a rule of designation between those who understand the worth of the privilege, and those who are degraded, dependent, and unfit to exercise it."[43] Here was a scholastic refinement that would have graced a medieval disputation. As to the Negro voter having by the exercise of the franchise for forty years and more acquired a *vested* right to such exercise, as was maintained by Abraham Van Vechten, a leader of the Albany Federalists, it was answered that the sovereign people in convention could do anything.[44]

Again and again the complaint was heard that the Negro lacked independence, that he was amenable to other influences than argument. The contention, significantly enough, came from one party only.[45] The Democrats had every reason to subscribe to the opinion that the Negroes, born in slavery, and accustomed to take orders, would now vote according to the dictates of their employers.[46] To extend to blacks the same provisions as were contemplated for whites would, as Mr. Radcliff well observed, be attended with most serious results. It would let loose two thousand five hundred Negro voters in the city of New York, and a small part of these might determine the result in such close state elections as, for example, that of 1801.[47] General Root declared himself an abolitionist as to slavery[48] — for now, as later, we find opinion upon slavery and upon the suffrage bearing small relation — but he was aware of the dangerous importance of the Negro vote. He said:

At present the number of blacks who are voters is so small, that if they were scattered all over the state, there would not be much danger to be apprehended, but if we may judge of the future by the past, I should suppose that there was some cause for alarm, when a few hundred Negroes of the city of New York, following the train of those who ride in their coaches, and whose shoes and boots they had so often blacked, shall go to the polls of the election and change the political condition of the whole state. A change in the representation of that city may cause a change in your assembly, by giving a majority to a particular party, which would vary your council of appointment, who make the highest officers of your government. Thus would the whole state be controlled by a few hundred of this species of population in the city of New York.[49]

The Federalist members did not content themselves with silence. The committee had scarcely presented their report, in which there appeared no provision for any Negro vote, when Peter Augustus Jay, an able father's able son, arose to ask an explanation why, while extending the privilege of the franchise to some men, "they deny it to others who actually possess it." Though he abhorred slavery, he was not, he said, what was called an abolitionist; yet he would not stand by and hear it said that this denial was made "because all who were not white ought to be excluded from political rights, because such persons were incapable of exercising them discreetly, and because they were peculiarly liable to be influenced and corrupted."[50] Mr. Van Vechten had not understood that the convention was expected "except by some of the citizens of New York to disfranchise anybody." Why should the Negro voters be attacked? "Have they done anything to forfeit the right of suffrage? This has not been shown."[51] Dr. Clarke, a Federalist from Delaware County, desired to learn why Negro soldiers should not vote as well as whites; there had been nothing but applause for their service as state troops in the War of 1812. The fact that they were not liable to militia duty had made their volunteering in that crisis all the more occasion for respect and gratitude.[52] General Van Rensselaer thought any man of either race should vote, provided he had property and paid taxes.[53]

Mr. Jay moved that the word "white" be struck out of the committee's proposed amendment. After due debate the matter was referred to a select committee,[54] which finally proposed:

That no male citizen, other than white, shall be subject to taxation, or entitled to vote at any election, unless in addition to the qualifications of age and residence, last above mentioned, he shall be seised and possessed in his own right of a freehold estate of the value of two hundred and fifty dollars, over and above all debts and incumbrances charged thereon, and shall have been, within the next year preceding the election, assessed, and shall have actually paid a tax to the state or county.[55]

Judge Jonas Platt, who had been the Federalist candidate for governor in 1810, moved to strike out the words, "other than white." The qualification of two hundred and fifty dollars freehold he thought might be applied to white and black alike; if poor Negroes were to be excluded, then he would have the same exclusion for poor white men. He declared:

I am not disposed, sir, to turn knight-errant in favour of the men of color. But the obligations of justice are eternal and indispensable. . . . The real object is, to exclude the oppressed and degraded sons of Africa, and, in my humble judgment, it would better comport with the dignity of this Convention to speak out, and to pronounce the sentence of perpetual degradation on Negroes and their posterity forever, than to establish a test, which we know they cannot comply with, and which we do not require of others.[56]

No man was more opposed to running after the *ignis fatuus* of universal suffrage than Chancellor Kent, but he could see no proper reason for discrimination against the Negro.[57] Rufus King believed that "universal suffrage was perilous to us and to the country" and yet took this same position.[58] But the majority were not moved by Federalist oratory. The qualification of two hundred and fifty dollars passed into the fundamental law to remain until 1870.[59]

The difference regarding Negro suffrage between the opposing parties was not fortuitous; their contemporaries noticed the alignment. The careful Hammond writes:

It is somewhat curious that General Root, Colonel Young, Mr. Livingston, Mr. Briggs, &c., who were most anxious to abolish the property qualification and extend the right of suffrage to all white men, were equally zealous to exclude black citizens from the right to exercise the elective franchise; while those who most strenuously contended for retaining the freehold qualification as respected white citizens, were very solicitous to prevent an exclusion of the blacks from an equal participation with the whites. Of this last description of members, Chancellor Kent, Mr. Van Rensselaer, Mr. Jay, Mr. Van Vechten and Judge Platt were the most prominent.[60]

We have seen that the Negro had been a Federalist.[61] As soon as an ambitious freedman gained the prescribed amount of property — and we shall see that this group grew — he would now hesitate still less in choosing between the two parties. We are not to understand that the Negro was a lover of strong government in the abstract, or that he admired the British Constitution or suspected Jacobinical innovation; his Federalism was in his feeling. As long as the party lasted under the old designation, he voted faithfully for its candidates; and we have traced, it is hoped sufficiently, the considerations that commanded his allegiance.

The Federalist party as an organization was in 1821 already passing into history, but the feud between Van Buren's "Bucktails"[62] and all others was kept up. When in 1826 the few restrictions on white suffrage which had survived five years before were swept away, it was a Democratic legislature which retained the qualification for the blacks.[63] This fact was probably not lost upon the colored voter; and despite the hope and expectation of the convention of 1821, his tribe increased in thrift,[64] so that his political importance was not lost. In the decade after 1830, in three contests for governor, in New York city, always of such critical importance, the fifth ward — where the Negroes were most largely settled — was carried against Tammany, apparently by Negro influence.[65] The same result was brought about here in at least three municipal elections, and likewise in the eighth ward, next to the fifth in Negro population, in 1834, 1837 and 1838.[66] The sachems had little reason to look with complacency upon the slowly growing Negro influence. In Brooklyn, the fourth, ninth and seventh wards, where the Negroes were most numerous, yield corroborative evidence.[67] In Albany, a little later, it was probably Negroes in the first and tenth wards who swelled the Whig majorities.[68]

When the people of New York voted that a convention for the revision of the constitution should be held in 1846, no gift of prophecy was needed to foretell that Negro suffrage would again furnish a theme of bitter controversy. The movement to take away the privilege altogether was begun before the delegates were chosen. A pamphleteer[69] who declared himself "a steady supporter of the principles and regular nominations of the Democratic party" urged the complete exclusion of all men of color from the right to vote. "Some of our people, from false notions of benevolence, or political hypocrisy, deny the natural inferiority of the black race," but as for himself he would maintain that their political proscription was in no way inconsistent with good Democratic doctrine:

In the country, where there are but few Negroes, the danger of encouraging them to remain in the State, invite others from adjacent States and fugitive slaves to join them, and interfere in our political affairs, through the aid of a fanatical party of whites, is not so apparent as in our great cities where they are already numerous.

This broad distinction founded on geography we shall later put to test. On the other hand, the Whigs, in a mass meeting in New York city, October 28, 1845, presided over by the venerable Federalist, Philip Hone,[70] resolved that one of the first reasons for holding a convention was that "the inestimable Right of Suffrage is not secured equally to all citizens, but is clogged as to a part with a proscriptive and anomalous Property Qualification."[71]

Horace Greeley, publishing an address from colored men who asked the return of equal suffrage, endorsed their claim that manhood alone must be the test for the elective franchise,[72] and later printed this demand at the head of seven reforms that must be struggled for.[73] He bewailed "the Colorphobia which prevails so extensively in the ranks of our modern 'Democracy',"[74] and declared that the "body of the People are divided into two great parties, one of which is generally favorable, and the other notoriously hostile to the extension of the Right of Suffrage to every peaceable, orderly citizen, without regard to the color of his skin or the amount of his property." He urged the Birneyites, the members of the small and struggling group of abolitionists, to name no candidates for the convention, but to vote for Whigs, who, however they might differ with these enthusiasts as to the proper way to deal with slavery, were one with them upon the poorest Negro's right to vote.[75] As to the candidates the colored voters would themselves prefer, he, of course, had little doubt. He knew they would recall that it was the Democrats of 1821 who had excluded them, when "every Federalist in the Convention strenuously opposed the proscription."[76] And the Negro voter seemed to understand. "The Democratic party of this City," wrote one of them, "with the loud profession of the largest liberty, is the first and the only one to announce its determination to go for the curtailment of Human Freedom."[77]

It must not be considered that this was but a passing crotchet of Greeley's. The other most important Whig editor in the state was Thurlow Weed, who attempted to lead no forlorn hopes. For universal suffrage in the abstract he had no approval;[78] that was one thing in which he would if necessary stand alone. He did not care to jeopardize the union of the party and of the nation[79] by stirring up trouble in the South, and he made no secret of his hatred for the fanatical zeal of northern abolitionists.[80] Indeed, in after years Greeley charged him with a "poor white" prejudice against the black.[81] Yet at the very outset of this contest he had written, "Above all, let that class of our fellow-citizens, whose intellectual capacities are measured under our present Constitution by *property*, be relieved from the stigma under which they rest, and be placed on the footing where they belong — that of men."[82] Seward, the other member of that famous firm, likewise favored equal suffrage.[83] And despite the opposition of a few, the majority of Whigs seem to have stood behind the trusted leaders.[84]

There was as little doubt as to the policy of the Democrats. The *Journal of Commerce,* the *Argus* and the *Evening Post* had no word to say for the extension of the franchise. Bryant, who in his vagarious days of Equal Rights had brought upon his own head round condemnation for countenancing abolition, who had pointed out with all Cassandra's certainty the danger which followed in the train of the "domestic institution," and had stood among the staunchest in support of Adams in his fight for freedom of petition, now wrote with care to establish the doctrine that civil freedom and suffrage presented two quite different questions. The Negro as a voter was the Negro as a peril.[85] Bennett, who in spite of claims of independence was at heart a Tammany man, complained in the *Herald* of "the detestable cry of Negro suffrage raised as a rallying cry for the election of delegates to the Convention;"[86] the *Globe* expressed a similar sentiment;[87] and the *Morning News* attributed all the Whigs' zeal to an appetite for votes.[88] This view is doubtless exaggerated; yet the hope of party gain certainly performed its part.

The election of the delegates to the convention of 1846, as a quarter of a century before, was made a party question, and again the Democrats were represented by the large majority.[89] In the course of time the matter of the franchise was presented and a long debate was begun.[90] There was no doubt as to how the parties stood. The committee report, presented by its chairman, ex-Governor Bouck, recommended suffrage for white men only;[91] if the convention should desire, it might offer unrestricted colored suffrage as a separate option. If this report were adopted by the delegates, the proposition of the black man's complete exclusion, as the majority of Democrats in 1821 had wished, would go before the people with the prestige of the approval of the convention. No provision was here made for the continuation of the existing limitation of two hundred and fifty dollars, but the minority report called for equal suffrage. Mr. Bruce, a Whig from Madison County, moved to strike out the word "white," and the contest was begun. J. Leslie Russell, of St. Lawrence, took up the challenge:

For one, he knew . . . that nine-tenths of the people in St. Lawrence county — abolitionists and all — were opposed to the admission of the Negroes to the right of suffrage. . . . He agreed in this perfectly with his constituents. This was the only issue in St. Lawrence at the Convention election. He was interrogated on this subject, and informed them expressly that he should vote against suffrage to the Negro.[92]

He was answered by Mr. Strong, a Whig member from Monroe, who declared himself no abolitionist, but who knew this question would never be finally settled until right should be done all classes of the citizens of the state.[93] Mr. Kirkland from Oneida wanted at least to save the Negro what he had.[94] But Mr. Kennedy, a Democrat from New York city, declared that a holding of real property or any other kind was no fit test for the franchise; in any change only character and manhood should be considered; but

the females of mature age, of our own race, were entitled to a preference, when we were prepared to make such an extension. [A gentleman had] remarked that delicacy should prevent females from uniting in the exercise of political power, but what sort of delicacy was that which . . . would squander it upon those whom nature had marked as a distinct race; and who were merely an excrescence upon our society! . . . Nature revolted at the proposal.

He claimed that the freedmen in New York were more degraded than the like class in the South. He had statistics to prove Negroes far more vicious than whites.[95]

Federal Dana, Mr. Bruce's colleague, said if the Negro were but given decent opportunities in life like the suffrage, he would not be so vicious. Mr. Young, a Wyoming Whig, contended that colored people were as intelligent as immigrants from foreign countries and as much entitled to the elective franchise. He regretted that statistics of the good portion of those other groups had not been furnished also. Mr. Rhoades, of Onondaga, scouted a so-called democracy that would deprive men of rights simply on the ground of a difference in complexion. Mr. Waterbury, of Delaware, reverted to the case of women. "The wives and children of all our white citizens were protected in their rights and privileges by husbands and brothers. Where do you find anyone to stand up for the colored man? — Not one." But Mr. Hunt, from Tammany Hall, would listen to no such talk. "His doctrine and that of his constituents, in relation to the right of suffrage, was briefly this: We want no masters and least of all no Negro masters, to reign over us."

It was Mr. Hunt who introduced a new note in the debate. In 1821 the franchise question had been settled without reference or citation beyond the plain facts of social prudence and the experience of this world. But a new day of religious enthusiasm had come since then, and the simple words of scripture were frequently taken as the unfailing guide of life.[96] In the view of most men, "common sense, reason and reflection pronounced a solemn amen to every doctrine taught in that fearful and precious book" and it was held "that all the truth to which reason ever assented had been first taught by revelation."[97]

Mr. Hunt appealed to Leviticus: "The Jews were forbidden to yoke animals of different kinds together; and if it were wrong to unite the cow and the ass in the same yoke, would it be right to unite the Caucasian and the Negro race in the same government?"[98] In some way equal suffrage was considered to imply social equality as well. Mr. Perkins, of St. Lawrence, said he should not enter the controversy further than to say that if there were any verity in scripture, mankind were at Babel divided into separate classes, "that it was the fiat of the Almighty that they should remain separate nations — that he put his mark on these creatures, that it might be known that it was a violation of the law of God to commingle our blood with them in marriage." — "Does the gentleman find that in the Bible?" asked Mr. Dana. — "Yes," was the reply; "not in those words, however." Mr. Waterbury wished to know, "If they were thus separated at Babel, how came they to go through the ark with the rest?"[99] Pausing for a moment's comment on the limitations of the gentleman from Delaware in the field of sacred chronology, the debate went forward. Mr. Dana remembered nothing in the account of Babel that properly could be cited against the right of the colored man to vote. "And before he could be convinced of that, he must have chapter and verse." Mr. Harrison, of Richmond, offered specific reference to Ham and Canaan: "Cursed be Canaan; a servant of servants shall he be to his brethren."[100] Yet Mr. Dana recalled that Noah was at this time intoxicated, and that at any rate this had no bearing upon political rights. Mr. Perkins "laid it down as the economy of Providence that there should be separate races and grades of beings on earth." The great offense that had brought on the flood had been the commingling of races. He maintained his exegesis that the female progeny of Cain, lately damned with a black mark, had as partners to this indiscretion occasioned that calamity.[101] Mr. Simmons, of Essex, on the other hand, attributed the deluge to God's wrath at slavery. "My Bible says so," he exclaimed; but he was interrupted by a voice, "Yours is a Whig Bible."[102]

When the vote was taken on Mr. Bruce's proposition to strike out the word "white," there were thirty-seven for and sixty-three against. Among the thirty-seven that favored equal suffrage there were two Democrats; while among the sixty-three opposed there were eight Whigs.[103] But when a member of the latter party proposed that the property qualification for the Negro be lowered from two hundred and fifty to one hundred dollars, seven of these eight were willing to make this reduction.[104] The Democrats were in the majority, however, and the Whigs had to be satisfied with a separate submission to the people of the paragraph on equal suffrage.[105]

The Democrats had won a party victory. But since 1842 at least, there had been internal strife. Because of difference about canal expenditures or the Texas annexation, or from jealousies in office-holding, there had been developing a breach within the Democratic party of the state.[106] The Conservatives, or "Hunkers," abhorred the radical "Barnburners," and were themselves despised in turn. Yet faction made no break in this alignment in the convention. Bouck, the foremost Hunker, was no more against the Negro voter than was Michael Hoffman, the

Barnburners' champion.[107] It was as straight a party question as one often finds. The charge that the country districts, ignorant of the true nature of the Negro, would unite in his behalf,[108] could not be sustained. Six counties were divided in their delegation — Albany, Greene, Wayne, Dutchess, Onondaga and Schoharie, and in every one the Whig members voted on the one side and the Democrats, if present, on the other. Acquaintance with the black man seemed to count for little. In St. Lawrence, where there were thirty-seven Negroes,[109] it had been "the only issue" and the delegates had been instructed to exclude them altogether. At the election in the autumn their position was maintained in that county by a vote of nearly two to one. Neighboring Franklin county gave equal suffrage a majority of seven hundred and thirty-two.[110] Essex county had forty Negroes; the adjacent Warren, with a population somewhat less, had thirty-five. Essex went for equality; Warren, by nearly the same majority, against.[111] Livingston, with about the same proportion of colored population as Steuben, next to it in the south, went in favor, and Steuben against.[112] The same was true of Oneida and Herkimer, Cortland and Tioga, and other pairs of counties in the different sections of the state. Yet when one looks at the political complexion of these counties the inference is plain. Whig counties followed the direction of their leaders, and Democratic counties did the same. When Washington gave its vote in favor, Greeley wrote, "This Washington is called a *Federal* county, while the party which has polled ninety-nine hundredths of its vote *against* Equal Rights vaunts itself *Democratic.*"[113]

Nor did abolitionism play a considerable part in the opinion on Negro suffrage. St. Lawrence abolitionists, if Mr. Russell is to be credited, were emphatically against all concession in the franchise. Men who did not follow Birney, like Mr. Strong and Dr. Backus,[114] were in favor of equality. It has been said that there was a connection between equal-suffrage sentiment and that which produced the Free-Soil party in 1848.[115] Yet in the convention no man was more steadily opposed to Negro suffrage than Samuel J. Tilden,[116] who became a pillar of that party;[117] and in the test of the ballot box such an hypothesis fails utterly. In 1848 seven counties voted for Van Buren, but only one of these had desired equal suffrage, and the county which by far surpassed all others in affection for Free Soil was none other than St. Lawrence.[118] The ward in New York city most favorable to equal suffrage was the fifteenth, always Whig,[119] which in 1844 had given Birney but twelve votes out of three thousand, and which in 1848 gave Van Buren a lower fraction of its votes than almost any other ward.[120] The sixth, which gave the largest vote against the Negro, was the very citadel of Tammany. Horace Greeley, long afterward at a public meeting, recalled that election: "Twenty-five years ago, I stood at the poll of the nineteenth ward of this city all one rainy, chilly November day, peddling ballots for Equal Suffrage. I got many Whigs to take them, but not one Democrat."[121] In this recollection he no doubt was right. It was a party matter in which personalities or the fortunes of slavery in southern states or in the territories had but little bearing.

The traditional alliance between the well-to-do and the Negroes was maintained. This of itself would pique the fear of Tammany and sharpen its attack, but this was not all. The Democratic party in the cities was the party of the little man, the day worker and the mill-hand. The laborers of the forties certainly prized the luxury of feeling themselves better than the Negro; on his subordination hung their pride. And then there was the economic danger of too much encouragement. In Tammany Hall it had been resolved that suffrage for the Negro was "fraught with incalculable evil and mischief, both in a social and political point of view,"[122] but this organization had reasons, based on work and wages, to fear the Negro's rise. It had likewise laid down the doctrine "that the inevitable result of the success of abolitionism would be to create a pinching competition between the labor of the Negro and that of the white man. Thus the aspiration of the blacks for suffrage met with the "steady and determined opposition of Tammany Hall."[123] Reason was supported by race prejudice in the heart of the mechanic. It was in the sixth and fourteenth wards of New York city that the anti-Negro vote was strongest, and here were found the largest number of immigrant citizens.[124] The connection of these facts was plain, and it was accepted as a large factor in the explanation of the outcome.[125]

Though the average Negro did not think of the connection, there was doubtless, now and then, a leader to whom these things were clear. Allied by long tradition to the Federalist Whig party, he accepted its direction with docility. As to the charge that the Whigs were low-hearted opportunists on the slavery issue he made no extensive inquiry. In feeling more concern about his own improvement than about the labor system beyond the Mississippi, he presented no exception to the custom of mankind. The Wilmot Proviso was interesting in its way, but Texas was a long way off. Since the leaders of the Free-Soil party had been Democrats, he felt no strong enthusiasm to march behind their banner. In the abolitionists he no doubt felt an interest, but there was little use in casting votes for them.[126] When the Whigs made their transition to the Republican party he of course followed, but he had no hunger for third parties. "For the last five or six years before I left New York," testified a witness in far-away Iowa, "their votes were deposited sometimes for the third-party candidate, but most generally for the old Whig party."[127] They were Whigs because their fathers had been Federalists. If there had never been a Negro south of the Potomac, still the Negro in New York would never have voted the Democratic ticket.

Notes

[1] Mrs. S. Van Rensselaer, History of the City of New York in the Seventeenth Century, N.Y., 1909, vol. i, pp. 191–195.

[2] Instructions to Governors Bellomont, Hunter etc., in N.Y. Colonial Documents.

[3] H. R. Stiles, History of the City of Brooklyn, Albany, 1869, vol. i, p. 231.

[4] In the Documentary History of New York (edition of 1850), vol. iii, pp. 505–521, is a list of slave-holders in the colony in 1755. Few masters had more than five slaves. The rolls

of New York city and Albany have been lost, but we are able to form some estimate of the distribution of slaves in the "Wills on File in the Surrogate's Office," abstracts of which have been printed in the Collections of the New York Historical Society, volumes from 1900 to 1906 dealing with the years 1780 to 1800. See also Stiles, *op. cit.*, vol. ii, p. 65, and J. Munsell, Collections on the History of Albany, vol. i, p. 60, vol. ii, pp. 49, 382.

⁵ C. F. Hoffman, The Pioneers of New York (delivered before St. Nicholas Society), N.Y., 1848, pp. 30–33; T. E. V. Smith, The City of New York in the Year of Washington's Inauguration, N.Y., 1889, p. 122. For legal status of slaves see E. V. Morgan, "Slavery in New York," Papers of the American Historical Association, vol. v, pp. 337–380.

⁶ A. C. McLoughlin, The Confederation and the Constitution, N.Y., 1905, pp. 290–291. C. A. Beard, Economic Interpretation of the Jeffersonian Democracy, N.Y., 1915, *passim*. On the New York aristocracy, see T. Roosevelt, Gouverneur Morris, Boston, 1892, pp. 17 *et seq.*

⁷ E. g., "Wills" as cited, liber xxxix, p. 127; xli, pp. 48, 128, 141; xlii, p. 191; N.Y. Doc. Hist., vol. iii, pp. 510, 512, 514, 519, for well-known Federalist names.

⁸ George Bancroft, History of the United States (edition 1883), vol. i, p. 513.

⁹ Wm. Jay, Life of John Jay, N.Y., 1833, vol. i, pp. 229–235; vol. ii, p. 406. It was Jay's custom to purchase slaves of promise that he might, after due instruction, set them free. G. Pellew, John Jay, p. 294. See also Correspondence of John Jay, N.Y., 1893, vol. iv, p. 320.

¹⁰ For Hamilton on slavery see "A Full Vindication," in Works (edited by J. C. Hamilton), N.Y., 1851, vol. ii, p. 9, and vol. vi, p. 298. See also F. G. Mather, "Slavery in the Colony and State of New York," in *Magazine of American History*, vol. ix, p. 408.

¹¹ The Life and Correspondence of Rufus King (edited by C. R. King), N.Y., 1900, vol. i, pp. 39, 268–292. On King's later stand against slavery see J. Q. Adams, Memoirs, Philadelphia, 1877, vol. vi, p. 467.

¹² N.Y. Assembly Journal, 1799, pp. 47, 49, 77.

¹³ Jared Sparks, Life of Gouverneur Morris, Boston, 1841, vol. i, p. 125. See also his speeches in the Federal Convention of 1787, The Records of the Federal Convention (edited by Max Farrand), New Haven, 1911, vol. ii, pp. 221, 415, 417, 574. See also A. J. Northrup, "Slavery in New York," in N.Y. *State Library Bulletin*, History, no. 4, 1900.

¹⁴ See his Effects of Slavery on Morals and Industry (pamphlet), Hartford, 1793; see also Frederick Hudson, Journalism in the United States, N.Y., 1873, p. 192.

¹⁵ W. L. Stone, Jr., Life and Writings of William Leete Stone (bound with W. L. Stone, Life of Red Jacket, 1866), pp. 41–42.

¹⁶ After July 4, 1799, no man or woman was to be born a slave; C. Z. Lincoln, Constitutional History of New York, Rochester, 1906, vol. i, p. 658; also comment in J. H. Dougherty, Legal and Judicial History of New York, N.Y., 1911, vol. ii, p. 94. Those who set free their slaves had to guarantee that their freedmen would not become public charges.

¹⁷ See on the principle of general emancipation, N.Y. Assembly Journal, 1799, p. 77. Comparing the names of the minority with those who voted for Addison and Haight, the candidates of the opposition for members of the Council of Appointment (*cf.* J. D. Hammond, History of Political Parties in the State of New York, N.Y., 1842, vol. i, p. 122), we see that of those who objected to the measure all but three were Republicans.

¹⁸ U.S. Census of 1790; Census of 1820, supplement, p. 1.

¹⁹ See table in Mary H. Ovington, Half a Man, N.Y., 1911, p. 10; and *Analectic Magazine*, vol. xiii (1819), p. 279.

²⁰ Constitution of 1777, article vii, in U.S. House Documents, vol. xci, part 1, pp. 2630–2631. The New York pound was the equivalent of $2.50.

²¹ Compare the ticket printed in the *N.Y. Herald*, April 7, 1810, with the list of manumissions, 1797 to 1825, as printed in the Corporation Manual of the City of Brooklyn, 1864, pp. 153–165. Jacob Hicks, the Quaker, was the single Republican nominee who had held slaves.

²² Corporation Manual of the City of Brooklyn, 1864, pp. 167–179.

²³ T. F. DeVoe, in *Historical Magazine*, Second Series, vol. ii, p. 342. E. A. Doty, "The

Doughty Family on Long Island," in the N.Y. Genealogical and Biographical Record, vol. xliii, p. 321; H. R. Stiles, *op. cit.,* vol. ii, p. 65.

[24] M. Van Rensselaer, Annals of the Van Rensselaers, Albany, 1888, p. 170.

[25] G. W. Schuyler, Colonial New York, N.Y., 1885, vol. ii, p. 497.

[26] Had the promising movements toward gradual emancipation by state action in the South in the early part of the nineteenth century succeeded, no doubt the same conditions would have followed there.

[27] From a broadside quoted in T. E. V. Smith, Political Parties and their Places of Meeting in New York City (pamphlet), N.Y., 1893, p. 10.

[28] Joseph Sydney, An Oration Commemorative of the Abolition of the Slave Trade in the United States (delivered before the Wilberforce Philanthropic Association), N.Y., 1809, a pamphlet in the N.Y. Historical Society Collection.

[29] *N. Y. Commercial Advertiser,* April 26, 1809. See resolutions, Federalist meeting, *ibid.,* May 22, also *N.Y. Spectator,* April 29, 1809. The practice was defended the following year by the Republican *N.Y. Advertiser,* April 26, 1810.

[30] *Analectic Magazine,* vol. xiii (1819), p. 287.

[31] J. D. Hammond, Political History, vol. i, p. 296.

[32] See objections stated in *N.Y. Spectator,* May 8, 1811. The N.Y. *Evening Post* called it an "Act to prevent people of colour from voting at the next election;" see issues of April 16, 22, 1811. The official caption was "An Act to prevent frauds at election and slaves from voting;" Laws of New York, Revision of 1813, vol. ii, p. 253. See N.Y. Assembly Journal, 1811, pp. 251, 310 etc., and N.Y. Senate Journal, 1811, pp. 143, 163.

[33] Hammond, vol. i, p. 357.

[34] Carter, Stone and Gould, Reports of the Proceedings and Debates of the Convention of 1821 etc., Albany, 1821, p. 212. In 1813 there was a bill providing for a very strict superintendence of the colored voters, which passed the senate only. The six senators who voted against it were Federalists; N.Y. Senate Journal, 1813, p. 120.

[35] See N.Y. Assembly Journal, 1814–1815, pp. 469 *et seq.,* and N.Y. Senate Journal, 1814–1815, p. 326. At a large Negro meeting in New York city thanks were voted to the Federalist Judges Kent and Platt for their spirited opposition in the Council of Revision, the Republicans were berated, and continued support was promised to those "whose opinions appear more consonant to our own." *N.Y. Spectator,* April 19, 1815. This matter was made an issue in the next campaign and was the subject of the longest of the resolutions of a Federalist meeting; see *N.Y. Commercial Advertiser,* April 11, 1816.

[36] "Extracts from the minutes of the Electors of the People of Colour of the 5th Ward at a Meeting to Express Congratulations to his Excellency. Resolve[d] that we the People of Colour present Our humble Congratulations to his Excellency's Veneration of Being Reelected By our utmost Endeavors as our Chief Commander and Governor of the State of New York;" N.Y., June 15, 1820, DeWitt Clinton MSS., Columbia University.

[37] F. N. Thorpe, Constitutional History of the American People, Chicago, 1901, vol. ii, p. 354. *Cf.* E. Olbrich, The Development of Sentiment on Negro Suffrage to 1860, University of Wisconsin, 1912, p. 38.

[38] Carter, Stone and Gould, Debates etc., pp. 180, 193. The report of the debates on Negro suffrage is quoted extensively in C. Z. Lincoln, Constitutional History of New York, vol. i, pp. 661–668, and in the admirable monograph of E. Olbrich, pp. 30–39. But neither of these authors has given his attention to the connection between the arguments and the partizan allegiance of the members. The same is true of Dr. H. L. Young's dissertation on The New York Constitutional Convention of 1821, which may be consulted in manuscript in the library of Yale University.

[39] J. D. Hammond, Political History, vol. ii, p. 2. Judge Hammond from this date uses the designation "Democratic" to describe the old Republican party.

[40] Debates, pp. 180, 181.

[41] The suffrage was extended by this constitution to all male residents of proper age who

paid taxes (or were exempt by law), who did militia duty (or were exempt), or who worked at call upon the highways (or paid an equivalent), except Negroes, for whom, as we shall see, special provision was made.

[42] Debates, pp. 190–191. Colonel Young criticized the argument for suffrage from natural right when Dr. Clarke quoted the Declaration of Independence. It was a question of expediency. Democratic doctrine was beginning to be modified in statement.

[43] Debates, p. 190.

[44] *Ibid.*, p. 193; see Hammond, vol. ii, pp. 3 etc., on Van Vechten's importance in the party.

[45] One Federalist opposed his colleagues — Chief Justice Ambrose Spencer, who, however, classed the improvident mechanic with the Negro. With him it was not a matter of race; *ibid.*, p. 377.   .

[46] *Ibid.*, p. 195.

[47] *Ibid.*, pp. 198, 199 (Livingston).

[48] D. S. Alexander, Political History of New York State, N.Y., 1906, vol. i, p. 229.

[49] Debates, pp. 185, 186.

[50] Debates, p. 180 (Ross), and p. 183 (Jay).

[51] *Ibid.*, pp. 193, 195.

[52] *Ibid.*, p. 187.

[53] *Ibid.*, p. 182.

[54] *Cf.* Olbrich, *op. cit.*, p. 36. Ex-Governor Tompkins, who presided, contrary to parliamentary usage appointed as nine of the thirteen members men who had voted against the Jay motion; Debates, p. 289.

[55] Debates, p. 329.

[56] *Ibid.*, pp. 374, 375. Two hundred and fifty dollars had been the sum qualifying for the vote for governor, lieutenant-governor and senators. It was now extended in the Negro's case to that for member of assembly.

[57] *Ibid.*, pp. 190, 191, 221, 377.

[58] *Ibid.*, pp. 191, 287. King, though elected with the help of Democratic votes, was still a Federalist.

[59] The qualification was removed only with the passage of the Fifteenth Amendment to the Constitution of the United States. The New York Democrats protested bitterly against this amendment.

[60] Political History, vol. ii, p. 21.

[61] "The Negroes, with scarcely an exception, adhered to the Federalists. Their number in the city of New York was very great, and parties in that city were so evenly divided, that it was often sufficient to hold the balance between them, at times, too, when the vote of New York, in the legislature, not unfrequently decided the majority of that body;" Life of Martin Van Buren, a campaign pamphlet, published in Philadelphia in 1844 (in N.Y. Public Library), p. 6.

[62] The bucktail was the badge of the Tammany Society.

[63] The six senators (out of twenty-eight) who voted for equal suffrage were all anti-Tammany men; N.Y. Senate Journal, 1825, p. 147. For names *cf.* Hammond, vol. i, pp. 235, 237; vol. ii, pp. 139, 175, 193; and Alexander, vol. i, p. 156.

[64] See the testimony of W. E. Shannon, formerly of New York, in the Report of the Debates in the Convention of California etc., 1849, Washington, 1850, p. 143. Much was accomplished in New York city by the Phoenix Societies; see Minutes and Proceedings of the Third Annual Convention for the Improvement of Free People of Color etc. (pamphlet), N.Y., 1833, pp. 36–40; F. Bancroft, Life of Seward, vol. i, p. 139; C. C. Andrews, History of the New York African Free Schools etc., N.Y., 1830.

[65] E. Williams, New York Annual Register, 1835, p. 52; *ibid.*, 1840, p. 224; N.Y. *Evening*

Post, Nov. 26, 1836; Census of N.Y. State, in O. C. Holley, New York State Register, p. 109.

⁶⁶ Williams, 1834, p. 279; *ibid.,* 1837, p. 348; *ibid.,* 1840, p. 224; Holley, *loc. cit.*

⁶⁷ *Cf.* N.Y. *Evening Post,* Nov. 4, 1836; Williams, 1836, p. 95; *ibid.,* 1840, p. 222; Holley, 1843, p. 82; *ibid.,* 1846, p. 107.

⁶⁸ *Cf.* J. Munsell, Annals of Albany, Albany, 1870, vol. ii, pp. 361–362; Holley, 1846, p. 107; *ibid.,* 1843, p. 69; *ibid.,*1845, p. 69; *N.Y. Tribune,* Nov. 4, 1846.

⁶⁹ H. P. Hastings, An Essay on Constitutional Reform, N.Y., 1846, in N.Y. Public Library.

⁷⁰ To see how important a part Hone played in carrying this measure through, consult report in N.Y. *Evening Post,* Oct. 29, 1845; yet Hone had no sympathy with abolitionism. See Diary of Philip Hone, N.Y., 1889, vol. i, p. 79. (The full manuscript is in the N.Y. Historical Society Collections.)

⁷¹ *N.Y. Tribune,* October 30, 1845. It must be said that this was not the unanimous opinion of those attending. Col. Webb, of the *Courier and Enquirer,* who had written very gingerly about the Texas question and was anxious that the party in New York should commit itself to no principle distasteful to the southern Whigs, was able at a subsequent smaller meeting to have all such resolutions stricken out.

⁷² *N.Y. Tribune* January 23, 1846. The address itself is interesting; apparently in the hope of proselyting among Democrats its authors recalled general statements of D. D. Tompkins and Silas Wright about slavery and the rights of man.

⁷³ *Ibid.,* March 23, 1846.

⁷⁴ *Ibid.,* Feb. 12.

⁷⁵ *N.Y. Tribune,* Feb. 17. It seems that the inference as to a connection between these sentiments was unwarranted.

⁷⁶ *Ibid.,* March 23.

⁷⁷ *Ibid.,* April 28.

⁷⁸ Life of Thurlow Weed (Autobiography), Boston, 1884, pp. 89–90. For his later revision of opinion, see *ibid.* (Memoir), p. 561.

⁷⁹ *Cf.* W. E. Dodd, Expansion and Conflict, N.Y., 1915, p. 171.

⁸⁰ *Albany Evening Journal,* Nov. 30, 1860; also Autobiography, p. 98.

⁸¹ Horace Greeley, Recollections of a Busy Life, N.Y., 1873, p. 313. This reference to Weed's humble origin was no less ungenerous than unfair. See Weed's Memoir, p. 297.

⁸² *Albany Evening Journal,* Oct. 30, 1845.

⁸³ See his Reply to the Colored Citizens of Albany, Works, N.Y., 1853–1854, vol. iii, pp. 437–438.

⁸⁴ N.Y. *Evening Post,* Oct. 6, 1845. See Greeley's comment on the Webb faction, "so utterly out of place in our party;" *N.Y. Tribune,* April 1, 1846. After the election the Young Men's General County Committee of the Whigs tried to read Webb out of the party.

⁸⁵ Parke Godwin, A Biography of William Cullen Bryant, N.Y., 1883, vol. i, pp. 327–331, and N.Y. *Evening Post,* April 21, 1836.

⁸⁶ He "was a recognized member of the Tammany party;" Memoirs of James Gordon Bennett and his Times, N.Y., 1855, p. 80. He was not complimentary to the Negro, "on whom education, and every other means of moral enlightenment have been tried in vain;" *N.Y. Herald,* March 17, 1846.

⁸⁷ Quoted in *N.Y. Tribune,* Feb. 12, 1846.

⁸⁸ March 24, 1846. See Frederic Hudson, Journalism in the United States, pp. 576, 667.

⁸⁹ Hammond, *op. cit.,* vol. iii, p. 605.

⁹⁰ Croswell and Sutton, Debates and Proceedings in the New York State Convention etc., Albany, 1846, pp. 246, 775, 782 etc. See also C. Z. Lincoln, Constitutional History, vol. ii, pp. 118–123 and E. Olbrich, *op. cit.,* pp. 72–78.

⁹¹ No. 51 in Documents of the Convention of the State of New York, 1846, vol. i.

[92] Debates, p. 777. Mr. Russell, like the majority of the voters of St. Lawrence County, was an ardent Democrat. He was in the complete confidence of his fellow-citizen of Canton, Governor Wright, who had taken a deep interest in his career; R. H. Gillett, Life and Times of Silas Wright, N. Y., 1874, vol. ii, p. 1727; J. D. Hammond, Life of Silas Wright, Syracuse, 1849, p. 730; and Russell to A. C. Flagg, Flagg MSS., N.Y. Public Library. We may infer that Wright's opinions were similar to Russell's.

[93] Debates, p. 777.

[94] *Ibid.*, p. 778. It may be said here that no Democrat spoke for the extension of the franchise, and no Whig against it, except Mr. Kirkland and Mr. Stow, who were content with a restricted suffrage, and Mr. Harrison, who stood with the Tammany men in the desire to shut out the Negro altogether.

[95] Debates, pp. 782–786, for this and the speeches in the next paragraph.

[96] W. Walker, History of the Congregational Churches in the United States, N.Y., 1894, p. 320; R. E. Thompson, History of the Presbyterian Churches in the United States, N.Y., 1895, pp. 129–149.

[97] David Nelson, The Cause and Cure of Infidelity, N.Y., 1841, p. 351. This was one of the most popular and influential of the volumes issued by the American Tract Society.

[98] Debates, p. 786.

[99] Debates, p. 789.

[100] *Ibid.*, p. 790.

[101] *Ibid.*, p. 796.

[102] *Ibid.*

[103] *Ibid.*, p. 788. The party affiliation of each member of the convention may be learned from the list published in the *N.Y. Tribune*, May 5, 1846.

[104] Debates, p. 790.

[105] The proposition was heavily defeated at the polls, especially in New York city.

[106] J. S. Jenkins, Lives of the Governors of New York State, Auburn, 1851, p. 705; D. S. Alexander, *op. cit.*, vol. ii, pp. 56–76.

[107] J. S. Hammond, Political History, vol. iii, pp. 314, 387. In the partial list published in the *N.Y. Herald*, May 1, 1846, the Hunkers and Barnburners among the Democrats are differentiated. No relation to the vote on suffrage is observable.

[108] H. P. Hastings, *loc. cit.*

[109] Census of the State of New York, 1845, in O. L. Holley, New York State Register, 1846, p. 115.

[110] Table in *N.Y. Tribune*, Nov. 19, 1846.

[111] Holley, *op. cit.*, pp. 104, 119.

[112] *Ibid.*, pp. 108, 117.

[113] *N.Y. Tribune*, Nov. 14, 1847.

[114] Thurlow Weed, Autobiography, p. 98.

[115] E. Olbrich, Negro Suffrage before 1860 etc., p. 77.

[116] At least as indicated by his votes; Debates, pp. 788, 790, 791.

[117] John Bigelow, The Life of Samuel J. Tilden, N.Y., 1908, vol. 1, p. 119. Tilden wrote much of the address called "The Corner Stone of the Free Soil Party."

[118] See returns of election of 1846 in *N.Y. Tribune*, Nov. 14, 1846, and those of 1848 in Whig Almanac, N.Y., 1849, p. 54.

[119] Table in N.Y. *Evening Post*, Nov. 7, 1846, and election tables in E. Williams, New York Annual Register, 1832–1840.

[120] Whig Almanac, *loc. cit.*

[121] In a speech at a meeting of welcome after his southern journey of 1871; Mr. Greeley's Record on the Question of Amnesty and Reconstruction (pamphlet), N.Y., 1872, p. 221. As

to exactly where he stood, Mr. Greeley's memory must have been at fault, as there was in 1846 no nineteenth ward.

[122] Report of meeting, N.Y. *Evening Post,* Oct. 31, 1846.

[123] *Ibid.,* Oct. 31, 1845.

[124] Greeley claimed this question brought out extra thousands of Tammany votes; *N.Y. Tribune,* Nov. 7, 1846.

[125] *N.Y. Tribune,* Nov. 8. Yet Greeley was a steady opponent of nativism.

[126] Compare Birney's total vote in New York city in 1844 with the Negroes' voting strength; Constitutional Debates, 1846, p. 790, and Holley, *op. cit.,* 1845, p. 85.

[127] Mr. Clarke in the Debates of the Constitutional Convention of the State of Iowa, 1857, Davenport, 1857, vol. ii, p. 671. Mr. Clarke had left New York in 1831; *ibid.,* vol. i, p. 4 (biographical table).

The Negro in Gold Rush California

Rudolph M. Lapp

When Marshall discovered gold on the South Fork of the American River, he initiated a change in the lives of tens of thousands of people of many races and nationalities. The Negroes of the United States, slave and free, were not exempt from this change. Even the Negroes of the West Indies and Latin America were caught up in the sweep of the Gold Rush. The literature of this period frequently mentions the slave and "persons of color," but too often they are merely noted as "someone's cook" or as a member of a passing party of immigrants. Some of the "mug books" of California's history refer to Negroes who "struck it rich," and other books report the fact of slave miners in the gold fields. There are places in the Mother Lode country that bear the name "Negro" or "Nigger" indicating that Negroes were present, but specific accounts of Negroes in California during the Gold Rush are not numerous. The most ambitious book attempting to show the role of the Negro in early California is marred by "mug book" deficiencies.[1]

From the first days of the conquest by the Americans, Negroes could be found in California,[2] but after the discovery of gold was reported in the Eastern states, their number rapidly grew. By 1850, there were nearly a thousand in the state;[3] by 1852, over two thousand;[4] and by 1860, over four thousand[5] — or slightly more than one per cent of the total population. After 1860, the Negro population of the state increased slowly; in 1870 it was a little more than four thousand,[6] and this slow rate of growth continued until the beginning of World War I.

The Negro came to California by all the major routes to the gold fields. There are many references to slave owners taking their slaves to California by the most common route, the overland route, and there are references to many wagon trains which included free Negroes in their complements.[7] Still we cannot say with absolute certainty that most Negroes came overland to California because there are also references to Southerners bringing large numbers of their slaves to San Francisco by the Panama route.[8]

These slaves, destined for employment as miners in the valleys of the Mother Lode, worked as cooks, barbers, and servants for their masters and employers while enroute; and there is even one mention of a Negro who served as an overland guide. One forty-niner noted that a Virginia group, camped near him on the trail one night,

Rudolph M. Lapp, "The Negro in Gold Rush California," *Journal of Negro History* XLIX (April 1964), 81–98. Permission granted by the Association for the Study of Negro Life and History.

included a Negro guide who attracted his attention because of his musical ability.[9] Many Negroes who came to California came as slaves without any hope of obtaining their freedom, but it is clear that many free Negroes came to California during this period; future research may reveal that more free Negroes than slaves made the long journey West.

The long overland journey was a grueling experience for all travelers, but the sufferings of the Negro may have been greater than those of the white man because of his subordinate status. One account illustrates this possibility. Two men of an Alabama company had a quarrel and later, when one of them was away, the second took out his anger on the slave of the other. Fortunately, the men in the company protected the Negro from further harm.[10] It is extremely unlikely that this was a unique occurrence. The presence of the Negro had a special meaning for some gold-seekers. One diarist noted that after leaving the artifacts of civilization his one reminder of his religion was the daily manifestations of faith quietly performed by a slave attached to the company.[11] In another case, the evenings of the company were brightened by the singing of a group of Negroes.[12]

When the Panama route to the gold fields transformed the Isthmus into a boom area, a great number of Jamaican Negroes thronged Panama; most of them hoped to find work on the portages. These Negroes had known slavery in the relatively recent past: the British Emancipation Act had ended slavery in Jamaica in 1838; Colombia abolished it in the Isthmus in 1852. These newly freed men were involved in frequent open clashes with the American immigrants regardless of their color. Attempts were made by these local Negroes to persuade American slaves to escape while they were still on the Isthmus. Some American Negroes were kidnapped for ransom by gangs that thought this might be a lucrative business. There were those who remained in the Isthmus to go into the hotel business.[13] However, the average experience of the Negro crossing the Isthmus was perhaps that of the average white man. The case of James Williams, a fugitive slave, who virtually hitch-hiked a good part of the way to California and included the Isthmus in his itinerary is unusual.[14]

The belief that most California Negroes of this period were slaves gains little support from the manuscript census. The county enumerations show that most Negroes came from Northern states and from those Upper South states that had immense free Negro populations. States like South Carolina, Georgia, Alabama, and Mississippi contributed only a very small part of the Negroes who participated in the Gold Rush;[15] Thus, there is the probability that many of the Negroes who arrived in California were free men. Many others undoubtedly came with the prospect of freedom. Slavery in the old South had long shown signs of deep decay as an economic institution, and many slave owners saw a last chance for income by permitting trusted slaves to go to the gold fields to earn their freedom.

Borthwick noted the presence in northern California of Negroes who had been given their freedom to go to the mines and of others who still were nominally slaves but who were working to buy their freedom. Daniel Woods noted that an old Negro belonging to the president of his company was promised his "freedom papers."

Thomas Gilman, a Tennessee planter, promised his slave "Thomas Gilman" his freedom with money earned in the mines. "Thomas Gilman" had to pay several times before he got his freedom. Some Negroes hoped to earn enough in California to buy their mates back in the slave states. One such person was the Negro manager of the Frisbie Hotel in Sonoma whose wife was still a slave in Virginia.[16]

The census also reflects certain other trends. Negroes from the Southern states were more numerous than Northern Negroes in the Mother Lode counties, throughout the decade, whereas in San Francisco, in 1860, the Northern Negroes outnumbered the slave-state Negroes.

San Francisco and Sacramento counties, because of their large cities, contained almost one-third of the state's Negro population. By 1860 San Francisco's Negro population of 1,176 was the largest; 468 Negroes lived in Sacramento. Most Negro San Franciscans of the 1860's lived in the first, second, and fourth wards, a roughly triangular area bounded by the Bay and by Washington and Larkin streets.[17] The rest of the colored population was scattered throughout the state in widely varying numbers: there were eighty-seven Negroes in Los Angeles County and four Negroes in Klamath County.[18] In some cities, such as Stockton, Grass Valley, Nevada City, and Marysville there were enough Negroes to establish churches of their own and to carry on a separate community life.

In the early days of the Gold Rush, the overwhelming majority of the Negro population was involved in mining. In El Dorado County, in 1850, eighty-six of 123 occupationally defined Negro men were classified as miners. In that same year, fifty-two of sixty-two Negroes in Tuolomne County were miners. This pattern of occupations was true of the other mining counties.[19] It was also in these counties that the Negroes from the Southern states were a majority. This reinforces the impression that these colored miners were predominantly under the supervision of gold seeking masters or under obligation to gain their freedom in this occupation.

It has been noted that on occasion, when masters were gaining little gold from the hills of the Sierra or arrived in California a bit short of cash that they would hire out their slaves in menial occupations to gain some revenue.[20]

Those Negroes in the mining counties who were not employed as miners were employed in various service occupations or as laborers, or quite often, as cooks. The manuscript census shows that there were great numbers of Negro cooks, many of whom were employed in restaurants or hotels or generally in the food dispensing business.

In San Francisco, in 1860, 463 Negroes of both sexes were occupationally classified, not including about 40 transient Negro seamen. Almost 20 per cent of the 463 Negroes were cooks. The remaining 80 per cent included waiters, stewards, porters, barbers, and sewing women as well as mechanics, businessmen, and many common laborers.[21]

In Sacramento, in 1860, of the 151 occupationally classified Negroes, over thirty per cent were laborers, over twenty-five per cent were cooks, and the remaining forty-five per cent included stewards, porters, and barbers as well as skilled artisans and businessmen. For some reason, best explained by the individual differences between census takers, the Sacramento census reported eleven Negro prostitutes, and the San Francisco census reported only one.[22]

In the mining counties, in 1860, mining remained the chief occupation among Negroes, but it had decreased in importance; Negro artisans, cooks, and barbers had begun to establish their places in the community.[23]

Despite the unsettled character of the decade of the Gold Rush, organized life began to take shape for the Negro as it did for other Californians. Schools of a rudimentary character, churches and family life began to develop. The over 130 Negro families in San Francisco comprised more than half of San Francisco's Negro population, and in Sacramento there were at least sixty Negro families. There was a marked tendency for Negro families to live within a definite area in a city; for instance, the Second Ward was the residential area for Negro families in San Francisco.[24] In the mining counties, the small Negro populations were composed of unmarried men.

By 1860, the colored population had made its contribution to the native-born population; there were several hundred California-born Negro children. San Francisco, alone, had accounted for 84, Sacramento had 51, and Eldorado and Tuolomne counties had 24 and 25, respectively.[25]

The manuscript census occasionally lists a mixed marriage; careful examination of these listings gives the historian some insight into the racial attitudes of the period. In these marriages the Negro husband-white wife combination occurred as frequently as the white husband-Negro wife. In most cases, the white spouse was originally from a country in Europe or from the British Isles. White spouses who were Americans were usually of Southern origin. These mixed marriages were most often found in the mining counties, and very few are noted in the San Francisco or in Sacramento census, which strongly suggests that these couples sought a degree of isolation.[26] Their geographical location in the census sometimes does hint that the couples in these marriages sought, or at least found themselves in the neighborhood of, Chinese miners where public opinion was least likely to disturb them. The fact that prejudice had not affected the Chinese can be deduced from the fact that the census reported Chinese servants in Negro households in San Francisco.[27]

California was often described in those years as a land where every man stood on his own individual merits and where a man's former social class or his origin was of no matter. While this is a highly idealized image of the egalitarian atmosphere of the state in the Gold Rush Era, there was a degree of truth in it. It was certainly true for most of the relations between white men of Anglo-Saxon origin, and there is some evidence that the democratic conditions of pioneer life in California during the Gold Rush also affected Negro-white relations.

The English traveler and gold seeker, J. D. Borthwick, touched on the basic ingredient in this pioneer democracy when he wrote, "The almighty dollar exerted a still more powerful influence than in the old states, for it overcame all pre-existing false notions of dignity." Borthwick observed this, particularly in the matter of white men serving food to Negroes and permitting them to lose their money along-side of white men at the gambling tables in the mining towns.[28] In Marysville, a saloon called the "Round Tent," advertised in the local directory that it welcomed customers, "with no regard to distinction of color."[29] One Mississippian noted with distaste in his journal that free Negroes in the gold fields were quite insolent.[30] Goldsborough Bruff recorded an incident where three white men and a Negro named Andy went off together on a spree involving the collective seduction of an Indian woman. Andy was associated with a party in which he was prospector, hunter, baker, and cook.[31] A less successful attempt at rape in Stockton by three Negro men resulted in a public lashing. In the South these men would have been hanged or lynched. On the other hand, their getting off with their lives may have been a local variety of race prejudice. The woman involved was Chilean.[32]

Bishop Kip also noted the effect of mining life on the position of the Negro. In his *Sketches,* he wrote that "A Negro cook is one of the most independent men alive. Being a rather scarce article, he can act pretty much as he pleases . . . and he is allowed to enter into certain familiarities, which would ensure him a cowhiding in almost any other part of the globe."[33] One senses this independence again in the Stoutenburgh (Calif.) Negro laundryman who told his customers when they called for their clean garments to go and pick them out themselves.[34]

In the urban areas of California something similar was taking place. In his column of city items, the editor of the *Daily Alta California* made the following observation: "What a change has California wrought in the organization and feel-ings of society. We were very much amused yesterday at seeing a gentleman of the colored persuasion, decked in a full suit of broadcloth, and sporting a gold watch and chain, standing on the square having his boots blacked by a good-looking white man."[35]

This item is probably best explained by the observation made by Borthwick that a great many recently arrived Frenchmen went into the bootblacking business to save up a stake for the expenses of heading for the mining country.[36] Many Frenchmen of this period were refugees of the ill-fated 1848 revolution and were likely to be quite free of race prejudice.

Many Southerners were undoubtedly displeased by the freedom which the Negro enjoyed in California. One Southerner decided to take his slave back to the South because, as he put it, he was "getting drunk and doing as he pleased," while associating with free Negroes. The slave, incidentally, refused to go and the result was a street brawl between master and slave creating a scene that would have been most unlikely 3000 miles east and south of the Mason-Dixon line.[37]

In San Francisco, tolerance toward the Negro had been quite general from the earliest days of the Gold Rush period. Daniel B. Woods preached in the open air to an audience that contained Negroes.[38] The same mingling of peoples took place in what was called Washerwoman's Bay in 1851 — a small lake between the city and the Presidio. As the *Daily Alta* put it, "Women of every clime and color are kneeling down along the bank engaged in the pious work of washing."[39] As time went on Mexicans and Negroes began to meet socially. During the pre-Christmas season of 1854, they organized a masquerade ball which took place on Kearny Street. Unfortunately, the notice does not reveal the actual sponsors, and it is only reported because the police had to break up a fight during the festivities and make some arrests.[40]

The churches of the Negro grew slowly during this period. The denomination-ally affiliated California Negro was either a member of the African Methodist Episcopal Church or the Baptist Church. By the early 1850's, Negro communities had established two A.M.E. churches and one Baptist church in San Francisco and one A.M.E. church in Sacramento. By the end of the decade the Negro Baptists had established churches in Stockton, in Marysville, and in Sacramento; and Negro A.M.E. churches could be found in Stockton, in Marysville, and in Grass Valley. The congregations of these churches were never very large. The largest were those of the San Francisco Baptist Church and of the two A.M.E. churches of San Francisco, and they were the centers of organized Negro life in the state.[41] They provided much of the leadership for civil-rights activities and through them Negro children obtained their first educational opportunities.

A number of the ministers were well-educated and came to the West with experience in church work. They were tireless in their efforts to establish churches in areas throughout the state wherever Negroes were numerous enough to provide congregations.

Little is known of the work of the white denominations among the Negro population before the Civil War. The Unitarian minister Thomas Starr King is known to have been friendly to them and to have facilitated the purchase of his church building by the A.M.E. Zion church when his congregation moved into larger quarters during the Civil War period.[42] But it is not known whether Unitari-ans invited Negroes to their church before his arrival. The Methodist Episcopal Church was perhaps the only denomination to do mission work among Negroes, and this effort yielded extremely modest results and then only after the Civil War.[43] White efforts in this direction were not likely to be too successful because of the strong desire of the Free Negro to have independent churches. This sentiment was based on a movement that had its beginnings before the turn of the century. It had its roots in the Free Negro's revolt against second-class status in religion.

The first schools for Negro children were the work of the churches. Classes were conducted in the church itself or in the basement, but the Negro community was always working for the time when it could build a separate school. Records of Negro attendance in California schools are unsatisfactory for the period before the Civil War, because it was not until 1874 that Negro children were integrated into the California public school system.[44] However, by 1860 there were close to 200 students enrolled in the state's schools, and, if San Francisco records are a guide, the average daily attendance of Negro students was only slightly less than that of white students.[45]

Public school systems, even before 1874, were gradually assuming some of the financial responsibilities for Negro education and were even building separate schools for colored children in answer to the petition of Negro communities.[46] In the work of promoting schools and in then gaining public support for them, Massachusetts-born Rev. J. B. Sanderson was a central figure. He sought out teachers for these schools, and he maintained a steady pressure on local school boards to build schools for Negro children. His reputation as a teacher was so well-known among California Negro parents that they wanted to have their children enrolled in any school in which they knew he was teaching.[47]

The legal position of the Negro in California is the background for one of the most interesting developments in the pre-Civil War period. The 1849 constitution had outlawed slavery with little debate over that question. The pro-slavery element presented the arguments already made famous in the debates over the Wilmot Proviso. However, its position had little support because a great many Southerners at the convention who cared little for the slave but even less for slavery joined forces with the others to make California a free state.[48] Hopes of eventually bringing slavery to the West, however, did not die there. When the southern counties of the state organized movements to separate from the rest of the state because of economic discrimination, pro-slavery elements had hopes that this might be slavery's wedge to establish itself on the West Coast.[49] And, when the elections in 1854 seemed to favor the pro-Southern element in state politics, the Southern planter-class journal, *DeBow's Review,* greeted it with elation. The *Review* reported a statement from a Richmond, Virginia, paper as follows: "Happily, the result of the recent election is not altogether disastrous to the South . . . The unseen but active issues between these factions is, whether the southern portions of California shall be organized into a separate state with a constitution recognizing and establishing slavery . . . Southern California is peculiarly propitious to negro labor."[50]

Many Southern planters were undoubtedly stimulated by the glowing reports of California's agricultural possibilities that appeared in innumerable issues of *DeBow's Review.* At one time in the 1850's the state legislature was presented with a *Memorial* from a large group of Southern planters asking for special permission to come to California to cultivate its soil.[51] This was never granted. One Virginia-born California legislator seriously suggested that, since poison oak was such a serious problem in the state, slaves should be considered for work in agriculture.[52]

While slavery never took root in California through agriculture, it lingered as a legal problem because the anti-slavery constitution failed to provide for the problem created by the presence of those slaves brought before the constitution was adopted (not to mention those brought afterwards). This left each case to be decided by local judicial sentiment as it came up. It would be hard to say how many cases gave the Negro freedom and how many returned him to slavery. There were well-publicized cases that resulted in both kinds of decisions. Cornelius Cole recalled that most of the legal talent of Sacramento favored the slave-owner and that he and Judge Crocker seemed to be the only friends of the Negro.[53] However, throughout the state and in San Francisco there were friends of the Negro in the legal profession and in politics. Outstanding in their friendliness to the Negro were Colonel E. D. Baker, a Republican lawyer, and David Broderick, Democratic political leader.

While state law did not protect slavery, neither did it free the slave. Negroes who wished to gain their freedom in California had to hope for a favorable interpretation of the law. Judges in the state who ruled unfavorably for the Negro cited the National Fugitive Slave law and in some cases used language that anticipated the Dred Scott Decision.[54]

California, in fact, passed its own fugitive slave law in 1852.[55] This was done to counteract the interpretation of some judges that the federal Fugitive Slave Law did not apply to masters who tried to force the return of their slaves to the South.[56] It must be remembered that the federal law was designed to catch runaway slaves, and it was obviously extremely unlikely that the Underground Railroad was transporting runaway Negroes to California in the 1850's.

The fugitive slave issue kept the Negro community in a constant state of uncertainty, but this particular anxiety ended with the fantastic Archy Lee case. Archy Lee was brought to California in 1857 by C. V. Stovall, who claimed to be a transient in order to retain his possession of the slave. When Stovall took employment, free Negroes correctly advised Archy that the white man had lost legal claim to him. Archy tried to win his freedom and Stovall fought the case to the state supreme court where the pro-Southern judges handed down the amazing decision that Archy was within his rights but, since this was the first case of its kind, Stovall would be permitted to return Archy to slavery. The resulting uproar in the state was tremendous, with ridicule being heaped on the state supreme court from even its friends. What followed reads like fiction and is too detailed for elaboration here. Suffice it to say that Archy, enroute home to the South with his owner, had to go through San Francisco, and there the most elaborate preparations were made to free him. After a series of dramatic events, Archy and his master came before a federal official in San Francisco who freed him. After this decision, with the immense amount of support that the white community gave Archy, California Negroes felt less terrified about the Fugitive Slave Law.[57]

In 1857 the state legislature considered a bill to restrict free Negro immigration to California.[58] This was not the first attempt of this sort. Burnett, Wozencraft, and others at the Constitutional Convention tried to exclude Negroes. This failed in 1849,[59] but legislators, with prejudices based on Eastern conditioning, proposed exclusion again. The proposal became a bill that resulted in some interesting debate and maneuvering. The dilemma that faced the legislators, who listened to arguments that lacked reality in California, is well demonstrated by the remarks of DeLong, a mining county legislator. He said, ". . . it has become a stinking thing . . . I do not want to vote against a bill of this nature; but I cannot tolerate this proposition at all. I believe that a negro is a human being. I believe that under the operations of this bill, negroes coming into this State may be made slaves for life."[60] The bill was defeated by a vote of 30 to 32 in the same session that it was proposed.[61]

The most interesting and illuminating campaign conducted by California

Negroes in this period was that involving the Right of Testimony. While the Fugitive Slave Act and the exclusion bills drew their protests and indignation, nothing mobilized their concerted statewide actions more thoroughly than their demand for the right of testimony in cases involving white persons. The persistence of the California Negro in this campaign reflects a number of elements peculiar to California in this period. First, the turbulence of society in California at this time placed life and property in constant jeopardy. Second, the Negro population had accumulated more wealth in a shorter period of time in California than anywhere else in the nation. And, third, Negro leadership was well-organized, well-educated, articulate, and possessed a great deal of unity, especially on this question. There is evidence that some of the leaders had had organizational experience in the Eastern states. Some of them were Oberlin graduates. J. B. Sanderson, already noted for his efforts in organizing schools for his people, had worked in the Abolitionist Movement with Federick Douglass in the Eastern states in the early 1840's.[62]

The movement began in 1852 through the organization of the Franchise League. This was prompted by a court case involving the murder of a Negro barber by a white man and the rejection of a Negro witness's testimony.[63] The Franchise League organized a petition campaign to change the law in regard to Negro testimony in court, and this petition was presented to the state legislature; only one legislator voted to receive this petition.[64]

The Franchise League, which had been primarily a San Francisco organization, proceeded to lay the groundwork for a statewide organization of California Negroes. This led to three "Colored Citizens Conventions," held in 1855, in 1856, and in 1857; the first two were held in Sacramento, and the last was held in San Francisco. From the first, these gatherings determined to devote themselves to the one problem of the Right of Testimony. A temperance resolution offered at the 1855 gathering by a minister was rejected as irrelevant to the purposes of the convention. Not declared irrelevant was a financial progress report of the Negro in California which announced that in six years Negroes in California had accumulated wealth totaling $2,375,000. It is clear from this that the Negro felt a need for legal defense of his growing assets as important as the legal rights to guarantee full citizenship.

There were 49 delegates to this convention, representing 10 counties, with the largest delegations coming from San Francisco and Sacramento.[65] The convention received friendly letters from several newspapers.[66] It concluded with the decision to intensify the petition campaign among white Californians.

During the following year, petitions were presented to the state legislature from San Francisco, Sacramento, and El Dorado counties by their elected representatives. Even a San Francisco County grand jury report recommended a change in the testimony laws. All these petitions were referred to the Judiciary Committee where they apparently died.[67]

In the winter of 1856, the second "Colored Convention" met again. Now there were 61 delegates representing 17 counties. This meeting seems to have been the best-reported and most fully recorded, and one can gain a fuller idea of the senti-

ments expressed. With pride one delegate reported that Negroes in his country had
$300,000 in mining claims. He went on to say,

> . . . we are showing our white fellow citizens that we have some natural
> abilities. . . . We intend to disprove the allegation that we are naturally inferior
> to them.[68]

Another delegate, in a shrewd as well as eloquent appeal to white sensibilities,
exclaimed,

> Why have we convened together? Because the law, relating to our testimony
> in the courts, is but a shadow. It affords no protection to our families or our
> property. I may see the assassin plunge the dagger to the vitals of my neighbor . . .
> I may overhear the robber or incendiary plotting the injury or utter ruin of my
> fellow-citizen . . . The robbery may follow, the conflagration may do its work, and
> the author of the evil may go unpunished because only a colored man saw the act
> or heard the plot. Under these circumstances who are not really injured and lose
> by the law? . . . Is it not evident that the white citizen is an equal sufferer with
> us? When will the people of this state learn that justice to the colored man is justice
> to themselves?[69]

This kind of argument was apparently not without its effect. Five hundred
white citizens, in San Francisco alone, petitioned the legislature to change the law.[70]
The following year saw white petitions supporting this issue presented to the legislature from seven counties.[71]

The depth of feeling at this convention is further illustrated by a debate over
a general resolution involving the free Negroes' feelings towards the United States.
A resolution had included the sentiment that Negroes would under all conditions
come to the military aid of the country. A number of the more militant delegates
rose to take exception, one of them saying,

> I would hail the advent of a foreign army upon our shores, if that army
> provided liberty to me and my people in bondage." Another said, "I love the land
> of my birth and hail its progress in the right; but the laws that sustain her slave
> pens and her prisons, her auction blocks, and the selling of human beings . . . I
> hate them.[72]

How the delegates actually felt about these remarks remains obscured in the
confused resolutions that followed. Perhaps this was deliberate because there were
those who felt that these remarks clouded the main purpose of the convention and

would not further the Negro cause. While the press did report this convention,[73] apparently these remarks only appeared in the convention proceedings.

At the 1857 convention, 55 delegates came representing 17 counties. The previous year had produced more petitions, more favorable comments in the press. But still no change was made in the law.[74] It must have been a rather discouraged group that met. The Dred Scott decision had been handed down that year and the delegates resolved against it.[75] There was talk in the air of a mass migration to British Columbia or to Mexico.[76] The gathering resolved to continue the Right of Testimony petition campaign,[77] but what actually happened in the next few years is rather obscure. In the early 1860's some of the San Francisco merchants wanted the Chinese to have the right of testimony but, as one contemporary noted,

The question is too much mixed up with that relating to Negroes to be settled on its own merits. It would scarcely do to allow the Chinese coolie to testify against a white man and to refuse the same privilege to an intelligent Negro.[78]

Under the impact of the Civil War, the effort to change the testimony laws finally became a bill, but it was defeated in 1862.[79] Not until 1863, after the Emancipation Proclamation, was the California Negro granted the legal right to testify in cases where white men were defendants.[80]

Research suggests that selective processes were at work that brought a larger group of energetic and educated Negroes to California during the Gold Rush than might have been found in the Negro populations of the East and the South. Even allowing for the supposed docility of the slave, owners would have been inclined to bring their brighter slaves to the new and unpredictable conditions of the West. Those slaves who used this opportunity to gain their freedom by purchase or otherwise were obviously persons of spirit and energy, and a large number of the free Negroes were persons of ability and daring who saw in California a new land that held great promise for the Negro race.

Notes

[1] Delilah Beasley, *Negro Trail Blazers of California* (Los Angeles, 1919).

[2] Alcalde Walter Colton had a San Domingan mulatto cook who came to California with the Fremont party. Walter Colton, *Three Years in California* (Stanford, 1949), 235.

[3] Compendium, *Ninth Census* (Washington, 1872), 29.

[4] Governor Bigler's Message and Report of the Secretary of Census of 1852 (published by state printers).

[5] Compendium, 29.

⁶ *Ibid.*

⁷ Not definitive, but based on an examination of several dozen accounts.

⁸ From accounts cited in Lucille Eaves, *A History of California Labor Legislation* (Berkeley, 1910) 90,91.

⁹ Ralph Bieber (ed.), "Diary of a Journey from Missouri to California," in 1849, *Missouri Historical Review* XXIII (1928), 35.

¹⁰ Richard Dillon (ed.), *The Gila Trail* (Norman, 1960), 83.

¹¹ *Ibid,* 56.

¹² Diary, MHR, 35.

¹³ Sarah Bixby-Smith, *Adobe Days* (Cedar Rapids, 1926 Rev.) 52; Amelia R. Neville, *The Fantastic City* (Boston, 1932), 29; John E. Minter, *The Chagres* (New York, 1948), 250–1; Elizabeth Martin (ed.); "The Hulbert Walker Letters," *California Historical Society Quarterly* XXXVI (1957) 142; *Panama Herald,* April 28, 1851; footnote, George Tinkham, *California Men and Events* (Stockton, 1915), 134.

¹⁴ James Williams, *Life and Adventures of James Williams* (San Francisco, 1873), 24–29.

¹⁵ Ms. Returns, Population Schedules, Seventh Census, El Dorado, Sacramento and Tuolomne Counties; Eighth Census, El Dorado, Sacramento, Tuolomne and San Francisco Counties. (Microfilm, Bancroft Library).

¹⁶ J. D. Borthwick, *Three Years in California* (Oakland, 1948), 134; Daniel B. Woods, *Sixteen Months at the Gold Diggings* (New York, 1851), 155; Edna Bryan Buckbee, *Saga of Old Tuolomne* (New York, 1935), 308; James Lynch, *With Stevenson in California* (Oakland, 1954), 33.

¹⁷ *Compendium,* 29; William P. Humphreys, *Atlas of the City and County of San Francisco* (Philadelphia, 1876), 7.

¹⁸ *Compendium,* 29.

¹⁹ *Ibid,* Ms. Returns, Seventh Census, El Dorado and Tuolomne Counties.

²⁰ Eaves, *A History,* 99; Ralph Friedman, "They Came as Bonded," *Fortnight,* Oct. 1955, 39; "To California through Texas and Mexico," *C.H.S.Q.* XVIII (1939), 244.

²¹ *Ibid,* Ms. Returns, Eighth Census, San Francisco County.

²² *Ibid,* Ms. Returns, Eighth Census, San Francisco County and Sacramento County.

²³ *Ibid,* Ms. Returns, Eighth Census, El Dorado and Tuolomne Counties.

²⁴ *Ibid,* Ms. Returns, Eighth Census, San Francisco and Sacramento Counties; Humphrey's Atlas, 7.

²⁵ *Ibid,* El Dorado, Tuolomne, Sacramento and San Francisco Counties.

²⁶ From research that I have done in the census of Southern rural counties in the course of other investigations, I believe that these couples were most likely the common-law combinations that one occasionally detects in the ante-bellum enumerations.

²⁷ *Ibid,* Passim.

²⁸ Borthwick, *Three Years,* 135.

²⁹ Cited in "The Beginnings of Marysville," *C.H.S.Q.* XIV (1935), 216.

³⁰ Howard Mitcham (ed.), "A Mississippian in the Gold Fields," *C.H.S.Q.* XXXV (1956), 215.

³¹ G. W. Read and R. Gaines (eds.), Gold Rush, *The Journals of J. Goldsborough Bruff,* 2 vols., (New York, 1944) 894.

³² Bayard Taylor, *El Dorado* (New York, 1949), 76.

³³ Leonard Kip, *California Sketches with Recollections of the Gold Mines* (Los Angeles, 1946), 51.

³⁴ Gerstaecker, Friederick, *California Gold Mines* (Oakland, 1946), 89.

³⁵ *Daily Alta California,* Feb. 1, 1851, 2.

³⁶ Borthwick, *Three Years,* 38.

[37] *Daily Alta,* Feb. 16, 1850.

[38] Woods, *Sixteen Months,* 65.

[39] *Daily Alta,* Feb. 14, 1851, 2.

[40] Dorothy Huggins, compiler, *Continuation of the Annals of San Francisco* (San Francisco, 1939), 26–7.

[41] *Minutes of a Baptist Convention* (San Francisco, 1860), 22; *Proceedings of the California Baptist State Convention* (San Francisco, 1867) 11. *Minutes of the Third Anniversary of the San Francisco Baptist Association* (San Francisco, 1853), 36. See Sue Bailey Thurman, *Pioneers of Negro Origin in California* (San Francisco, 1952) 23–36, for most of the material on the A.M.E. churches. For more fragmentary material, see John Frederick Morse, *The First History of Sacramento City* (Sacramento, 1945), 111, 115 and *Journal* of the African Methodist Episcopal Convention (San Francisco, 1863), 28, 29.

[42] Thurman, *Pioneers,* 30.

[43] Lionel U. Ridout, "The Church, The Chinese and the Negroes in California 1849–1893," *Historical Magazine of the Protestant Episcopal Church* XXVIII (June 1959), 132.

[44] Henry G. Langley, *San Francisco Directory* (San Francisco, 1858), 374; Thurman, *Pioneers,* 37–41.

[45] Report of the Superintendent of Common Schools, *San Francisco Municipal Reports* 1859–60 (San Francisco, 1860), 64.

[46] Thurman, *Pioneers,* 38–40.

[47] *Ibid,* 37–42.

[48] *Report of the Debates in the Convention of California* (Washington, 1850), 43–4.

[49] Eaves, 91–4.

[50] *DeBow's Review* XVII (1854), 613.

[51] *Eaves,* 92.

[52] *Ibid,* 91.

[53] *Memoirs of Cornelius Cole* (New York, 1908), 94.

[54] *Ibid,* 96.

[55] *Statutes of California,* 1852, 77.

[56] *Eaves,* 94–5.

[57] There are several versions of this story. The best concise one is *Eaves,* 99–103.

[58] *Journal of the Assembly,* Eighth Session (Sacramento, 1857), 811.

[59] *Report of Debates,* 49–50.

[60] Carl Wheat (ed.), "Journals of Charles E. DeLong, 1854–1863," *C.H.S.Q.* IX (1930), footnote, 87.

[61] *Journal,* 824.

[62] Carter Woodson, *The Mind of the Negro as Revealed in His Letters* 1800–1860 (Wash., D.C., 1926), 350; 384–5.

[63] Beasley, *Negro Trail Blazers,* 54.

[64] *Journal of the Assembly,* Third Session, 395.

[65] *Pacific Appeal,* April 12, 1862, 2; *Sacramento Daily Union,* Nov. 21, Nov. 23, 1855.

[66] *Daily Union,* Nov. 21, 1855.

[67] *Journal of the Senate,* Seventh Session, 488, 496, 559; *Sacramento Union,* Dec. 10, 1856, Letter to the Editor.

[68] *Proceedings* of the Second Annual Convention of the Colored Citizens of the State of California (San Francisco, 1856), 8.

[69] *Ibid,* 9.

[70] Beasley, 56.

[71] *Journal of the Senate,* Eighth Session, 285, 294, 337.

[72] *Proceedings,* 14, 15.

[73] *Daily Alta,* Dec. 12, 1856; *Sacramento Union,* Dec. 11, 1856.

[74] *Pacific Appeal,* April 12, 1862, 2.

[75] *Ibid.*

[76] *Beasley,* 78; Mifflin Wistar Gibbs, *Shadow and Light* (Washington, 1902), 59; *Eaves,* 103.

[77] *Appeal,* April 12, 1862.

[78] John H. Kemble (ed.), "Andrew Wilson's Jottings on Civil War California," *C.H.S.Q.* XXXII (1953), 308.

[79] Journal of the Assembly, Thirteenth Session, 670.

[80] *Statutes of California,* 1863, 69.

The Rise of
Negro Society

Robert Austin Warner

A century ago in Connecticut the "big wheel" was the church. At the ordina-
tion of a Negro minister in the Second African Society in Philadelphia in 1841, the
Rev. Thomas Brainerd presented the prevailing Congregational conception of the
place of the church in society. Besides the clear Calvinistic objective of saving
mankind by affording "encouragement in consciousness of sin" and by providing
"the correct creed," the church was considered as serving other important functions.
First, it "brought the practical learning of the schools to the people," primarily by
providing educated ministers. Second, it "stimulated friendships among the best of
society." Third, it tended to raise the "rude and degraded" to "neatness and good
order" by well-regulated meetings. Fourth, it endeavored to advance industry,
economy, moderation, and temperance. Finally, it pretended to enforce all the laws
and customs by the moral surveillance of "the eye of God."[1]

Brainerd's conception of the ideal church as an extraordinarily important
agency was as nearly a fact in Connecticut society as anywhere. Originally the
Congregational church had been the social and civil unit in the colony and state,
and its established customs persisted, though growth of the population and schism
in many churches, as well as the coming of other sects, brought complications. The
standards and customs enforced became those of the group and class dominant in
the particular church, but the importance and social effectiveness of the religious
institution were little diminished. To belong to a church remained important and,
also, it may be added, it mattered to what church one belonged.

In New Haven in the early nineteenth century, the Negroes were scattered
among the white churches. Most of them, like their masters, were Congregational-
ists and Episcopalians; but many had been attracted to the Baptist and Methodist
sects. In the larger congregations they were lost among the mass of whites and often
overlooked by the ministers as individuals and spiritual beings. More important,
caste custom so separated them socially from the rest of the congregation that they
were isolated from the beneficent social pressures and influences.

People are induced to assume self-discipline by the grant of recognition and
social approval, but the color line cut sharply across this mechanism. True social

From Robert Austin Warner, *New Haven Negroes* (New Haven, Conn.: Yale University
Press, 1940), pp. 78–94. Copyright © 1940 by Yale University Press. Reprinted with permission of Yale University Press.

mingling of whites and blacks was taboo, and, worse than that, independent, well-dressed, self-respecting, educated Negroes were not approved, not "expected" by white opinion, and no conforming black opinion yet existed. Therefore, the radical abolitionists, who were willing that Negroes should become merged in the general population, offered them recognition and approval in their efforts to adopt the cultural rules of general American society. They assisted them to build their own institutions favorable to that adoption and aroused a race consciousness that protected from the general white hostility. They gave the Negroes what they most needed, a church of their own.

Some time before 1820 Simeon Jocelyn, white middle-class member of the Center Congregational Church, of which the Rev. Nathaniel Taylor was the pastor, was moved by Christian benevolence to assist the Negroes. He held regular Sunday services with some of them, in spite of white opposition, and in 1824, having obtained a meetinghouse on Temple Street, his group formed the "African Ecclesiastical Society."[2] Of the officers, the clerk was Prince Duplex, the grandfather-to-be of the first Negro physician in New Haven, Dr. Creed; and the treasurer was Bias Stanley, to whom many Negro youths were to be indebted for aid in their education. On the society's committee were Scipio Augustus, representative to national conventions, and the well-known William Lanson. The first year, congregations of a hundred or more were meeting in the thirty-by-forty-foot unplastered church, with Jocelyn officiating. In 1826 the African Improvement Society, mentioned earlier, was formed under Leonard Bacon's direction to assist them.[3]

On August 25, 1829, in the Center Church, the Western Association of New Haven County formally recognized the "United African Society" as a Congregational church. Four men and seventeen women satisfactorily passed an examination, made a profession of faith, and entered into covenant, becoming thereby Congregational members in communion, quite possibly "among the elect of God." A few of these who had experienced grace were transfers from the white churches, but almost half had been, as the *Religious Intelligencer* expressed it, "gathered from the world, as fruits of a revival" the previous winter.[4] The Rev. Theodore S. Wright, colored, of New York was present at the ceremonies and addressed the gathering of several hundred Negroes "with much propriety and feeling."[5] After the transactions creating the first[6] Negro Congregational church were completed, the presbytery of pastors proceeded to ordain the Rev. Simeon S. Jocelyn as an evangelist, and the Rev. Mr. Merwin fittingly preached from the text: "Not by might, nor by power, but by my spirit, saith the Lord of hosts."

For the whites, Jocelyn had provided a benevolent project, and the religious press thereafter kept sympathetic track of its "Progress in grace";[7] for the Negroes, he had provided an institution to measure up to the Rev. Thomas Brainerd's conception. A description of the church's activities was published by the African Improvement Society just before 1830 when the Connecticut common schools were at their worst and neglected by both the legislature and public opinion. There were, besides the church, a Sabbath school, a day school, an evening school for adults, and a temperance society. An ell costing $300 had been added to the church building to house the educational activities. For no salary but the meager offerings Jocelyn was preaching three fourths of the Sabbaths and carrying all the pastoral work; and the Rev. Henry Lines substituted the other Sundays. There were two Sabbath services, two evening meetings during the week, and a monthly "concert," all "well-attended." The Sunday School, in which were eighty scholars, was taught, according to the account, by "ardent" young people, and the Bible classes principally by students from the Yale Theological Seminary, which, perhaps, was the explanation of their popularity with the young ladies and of their neglect by the young men.

Sunday schools were then rather new, having been adopted generally in Connecticut only during the preceding decade. The sponsoring organization, the Connecticut Sunday School Union, was undenominational, including Baptists and Methodists, and revealed the contemporary preference for social ideals rather than theological. The basis of the ideals was the family with its mores of strict religious upbringing; the doctrine was elaborated by Horace Bushnell in his theory of "Christian nurture."[8] Although in the Sunday schools the lessons and methods of learning them appeared elementary and negligible — conning Bible verses by rote for all but the more mature — the results possibly went deeper. At Temple Street, as the church was usually called, the teaching by the well-brought-up and the well-born may possibly have been influential in emphasizing for the Negroes many Connecticut mores and folkways, and it may have subjected them to some slight intellectual, and to considerable moral and social discipline and encouragement.

The day school taught by Miss Duplex, daughter of the deacon, was intended to provide the educational opportunities from which caste excluded Negroes. The Improvement Society took the initiative and managed to obtain half the expenses from the school fund, since the members had exerted pressure to get Negroes their due share of this public money. Jocelyn and his assistants persistently sought out the children and persuaded their parents to send them to school regularly. Also, shocked by the discovery that many adults were unable to read the Bible, the abolitionists established an evening school, held twice a week through the three winter months. In 1829 the teacher reported that punctuality and concentration among the twenty who attended, "most of them females," were excellent and the interest so great that the pupils themselves had paid all but a dollar and a half of the expenses.[9] All this was before the work of Horace Mann and Henry Barnard. Unfortunately, the night school was ahead of its time, and soon disappeared.

The church itself remained the center of the Negro social development in New Haven. The Rev. Simeon Jocelyn moved to New York in 1834, but the lay members maintained the society with the aid of various white ministers, and — a sign of a new stage — the next effective pastors were Negroes.

In New Haven during the 'thirties there was an aggressive growth of Negro race consciousness. Abolitionism and white benevolent aid were one of the causes, but another was the antagonism which antislavery and "African improvement" agitation aroused. The new Negro leaders were raised under a double influence of encouragement and opposition. Those who became the first Negro pastors of the Temple Street Church, for example, had obtained the education requisite for the Congregational ministry against opposition, but with abolitionist aid. James W. C. Pennington, an escaped slave, was refused admission to the seminary at Yale but was permitted to obtain his preparation by sitting with the classes though not participating. Working under these limitations, unable even to take a book from the library, he persevered, and during the same time officiated in the African Church. In 1838 he was given a license to preach,[10] and left for a Hartford pastorate, beginning a distinguished career which eventually brought him an honorary degree from Heidelberg University. The next pastor of the church, Amos Gerry Beman, who had left Middletown because he had been threatened with violence while receiving private tutoring from a Wesleyan student,[11] had received his training at Oneida Institute, which had been founded and was supported by abolitionists.[12] Although, under the abolitionist influence, restrictions were being removed and new schools opened, almost every improvement was won by a battle, which naturally left scars upon the personalities of the colored scholars, the future leaders of their race. In New Haven the attempted establishment of a Negro "college" demonstrated, as Jocelyn acutely observed, that white people were offended by the implication that colored people were entitled to literature, and to Latin, the prerogatives of aristocracy.[13] On the other side, however, the public opposition gave the colored group there the strong stimulus of resentment. During the controversy over the college one Afro-American wrote a violent protest which the newspaper ridiculed by printing with all its errors in words and spelling.[14] Another, Bias Stanley, who had been one of the agents to collect funds for the college, was more literate and his protest could not be laughed down. His attitude showed clearly how far Negro race pride had developed in New Haven. Replying to the charge that the college tended to amalgamation, he wrote condemning race mixture:

I did not favor the academy because I thought it would connect us any more with you, — I would to God that the white population did not connect themselves with the colored population any more than the colored population do with the white; we should then stand a distinct nation; more than twenty to one, to what we now do.

This "race man" was an original member and a lifelong pillar of the African Congregational Church.

With the rise of Negro race consciousness and the development of leaders in New Haven, other denominations followed the example and founded separate churches. Four Negro churches whose earlier origins were obscure became permanently established during the 'forties, and one more was founded in the next decade.

The Methodist church in 1818 was composed of thirty-six white and thirty-five colored members,[15] but the organization of a separate Negro church was not the direct product of a schism. The initiative came from New York, where for some time James Varick's Zion church had been more or less independent of the white church. Reverend William H. Bishop visited New Haven and found support in setting up a separate congregation. Through the efforts of two energetic women, by 1841 the group was in possession of its own building.[16] It is interesting to note that one of these founders, Mrs. Eliza Ann Galpin, the daughter of Jeremiah Paine, was employed with the family of Theodore Dwight Woolsey,[17] a charter member of the African Improvement Society. The church had grown to eighty communicants in 1848,[18] the largest of the sect in New England, and has been, through various vicissitudes,[19] in continuous existence to the present day.

The Bethel branch of the Methodist Episcopal Church dates from almost as early[20] as the Zion. The New Haven church was the result of the devotion of a layman, Deacon John R. Cannon, who, like Mrs. Galpin, worked in service. For more than ten years the small congregation met in Lyman's barn out on the road to the poorhouse.[21] Then they assembled here and there for some years, finally becoming established in a heavily mortgaged frame church.

The third Negro Methodist organization in New Haven, the Union Church, was founded later, in 1852, located on Webster Street on a site from which it did not move until 1940. All three Methodist denominations suffered from changing leadership, having had a succession of short-term ministers sent in accordance with episcopal policy; all were small and poor during this early period; yet all showed the vitality required for continued existence.

The Baptist church,[22] which started in the early 'forties, struggled with economic difficulties. After the colored members of the first and second Baptist churches formed a separate church called the third, they built a meetinghouse, thereby overestimating their financial strength. Within two years it was advertised to be sold for the mortgage, and despite the self-sacrifice of Deacon Harris and others, it was sold at auction four years later. The church continued with short-term pastors, meeting in halls, homes, and a schoolhouse. Another building was lost by debt in the early 'sixties, but the pastor then was able and aggressive, and willing to stay. The Rev. Leonard A. Black, who served without a fixed salary and contributed of his own property, stimulated offerings, and even went to England to raise $600 to build again. After an eight-year pastorate, he left the church in a strong and thriving condition, but under the financial supervision of white trustees,[23] who were presumably large contributors.

The fourth separate Negro church which began in the early 'forties was St. Luke's Episcopal. The parish records, which are still in existence, give the intimate story. The rumor is that Alexander Crummel started the movement for separating the colored members from Trinity Parish about 1842.[24] He was then studying for the ministry in New Haven, and he consented to lecture to the colored Episcopalians once a week. The rector, Rev. Harry Croswell, approved the plan, gave Crummel specific license, and lent the use of a room which was the property of the parish.

Two years later St. Luke's was organized, meeting in that same Gregson Street Lecture Room. The parish was formed June 7, 1844, also with the approbation of the rector and vestry of Trinity Church. The first clerk was Peter Vogelsang, a minor national leader, and the first treasurer was Alexander Dubois, great uncle of W. E. B. DuBois, the eminent Negro leader and author. Henry Merriman, janitor, and Richard Green, shoemaker, were warden and vestryman, respectively. The diocese of Connecticut, meeting in New Haven four days later, admitted the parish to union with the church.

The financial history of St. Luke's and Temple Street, although their members were better trained and more economically secure than others, shows the difficulties they overcame. Peter Vogelsang reported at the end of the first year on the state of St. Luke's parish affairs. Each of the twenty-seven forming members had pledged a certain sum annually to the society fund, the total to amount to $162. Almost a third was uncollected, but expenses had been kept so low that $38 was in the treasury. The mother church continued to permit the free use of a meeting place, and students training for the ministry afforded cheap services as lay readers, so that within eight years the church saved $433. When the Negro Baptist Church was up for auction, Henry Merriman bid on it and bought it for $1,000. Five hundred dollars were paid in cash and the rest procured by mortgage. To the $433 of savings Rev. Harry Croswell of the white church had added the considerable gift of $30, and the other $37 was raised by vigorous efforts, through subscriptions, penny collections, and by the Ladies Sewing Circle. Then some used Sabbath-school books were bought for thirty-one cents, total cost, and a donated bookcase was carted to the church for twenty-five cents. Yet even these light financial burdens were so great that when all details of installation were complete and repairs made, the vestryman passed a heartfelt vote of congratulation to God.

The ministers had to endure financial sacrifice. The first rector at St. Luke's was white, but in 1856 the church obtained an able Negro, the Rev. James T. Holly, who stayed for five years. His promised annual salary was to be $150, and although supposedly covered by the pew rent, it fell each year $30 to $70 in arrears. In 1860, $139.25 remained unpaid on three years' salary, and the next year he resigned to emigrate as a missionary to Haiti. In his time, however, the church was relatively strong financially. During the depression of 1858, his extraordinary efforts, which included the preparation of a "History and Appeal of St. Luke's Church," raised $335.50 in cash and $13.50 in groceries for the repair of the church. Six hundred dollars had been needed, and some years later, when the members were struggling along under a less-trained minister, more carpenter work had to be done. Gifts by whites continued; for example, in 1857 Mr. John B. Kirby presented gas fixtures and by "his personal intercession" obtained the lowest rate on gas. In all financial crises the solution was "an appeal to the benevolent."

Meanwhile, during the period of growth of other churches, the Temple Street Church was the wealthiest and largest institution. In contrast with the $150 salary promised Holly two decades later, the Rev. Mr. Beman in 1839 was to receive $400 annually. Although the members of the congregation managed to raise most of it, they gradually got behind and had to seek white aid. In 1844, when the decayed condition of the original building necessitated a new one, two thirds of the money raised came from the white people upon appeal by the leading Congregational pastors and laymen. The announcement in the press over the names of Leonard Bacon, Nathaniel W. Taylor, and others commended the Temple Street Church, and established the request for aid upon the plane of dignified "solicitation."

The Christian order and sobriety of their assemblies, and the high stand on the subject of temperance, taken by the leading members, are exerting a most salutary influence on that portion of our population; and the interests of all classes are advanced by their elevation and improvement.[25]

The new meetinghouse, which was of brick, cost $2,500, and the society was left with a heavy mortgage which so burdened its members that in 1849, with foreclosure threatened and Beman's salary over a year in arrears, they again sought assistance. The minister remained unpaid, but the church was saved, primarily by white John G. North, who reached deep into his own pocket. This time the white benefactors stipulated that the building be in the hands of trustees, a majority of whom should be white, and exacted a promise that the society keep out of debt. After four years the congregation was still unable to maintain its minister, and he asked permission to resign. The Congregational council refused the resignation and raised enough money by public appeal to pay the salary due and to ensure $200 annually for the pastor's support.[26] However, financial troubles continued. At one time the distinguished sponsors hoped that this church would not be confused with others whose too frequent begging had weakened public confidence and respect. For economic reasons, even the Temple Street Church remained dependent upon white philanthropy, which was naturally touched with paternalism. If the members were protected from the indignity of begging pennies from door to door, they were not yet free, independent. The institution was still a "benevolent project."

Records of most of the churches, financial or otherwise, do not exist, for the reason that none were consistently kept. The officials did not command the requisite skill and knowledge, and the institutions suffered from consequent losses, peculations, and cankering mistrust of leaders. Pennies were even scarcer in other churches than in St. Luke's and Temple Street, and only by self-sacrificing efforts were those that were needed raised. Through the misunderstandings, quarrels, and suspicion, only the stubborn devotion of small, indomitable groups kept these institutions going. The overwhelming impression from the many details of these histories is of a folk movement with many little leaders striving against ignorance of letters, of mathematics, and of the forms of doing things; and against poverty, fatigue, and the lack of time, so that they might have churches in which they could share without the discrimination of caste. The inspiration came probably from the impulse given by the efforts of the abolitionists. The maintenance and the continuance of these institutions were often dependent upon white aid. Yet the development of separate Negro churches in New Haven, once started, must be primarily ascribed to the Negroes themselves and to their growing consciousness of race.

Another institution which was originated in New Haven by Jocelyn and which expanded into a race movement was the Temperance Society. It was formed in the Temple Street Church in 1830 and antedated by a month even the one in Richard Allen's church in Philadelphia.[27] Within a year it boasted forty members, and during the next decade its influence spread. A state society was organized in 1836, and at the third annual meeting in 1840, Temple Street Church members predominated among the delegates, although one New Haven delegate was Richard Green, soon to be a founding member of St. Luke's Episcopal Church. Henry Foster of Hartford was the president, A. C. Luca of Temple Street a vice-president, and Amos Beman, the new pastor, was corresponding secretary and general agent. In 1842, the Connecticut society united with those of New York, New Jersey, and Massachusetts to form the States' Delavan Union Temperance Society of Colored People, which held several imposing annual meetings. Three thousand people attended the one in 1845, which was gay with banners, badges, and bands of music. The Rev. Amos Beman addressed the meeting. About the same time the Temple Street Church determined to deny membership to those refusing to promise total abstinence. The peak in New Haven was reached with 190 names on the pledge in Temple Street, and with another society formed by a Negro Methodist church. Beman was reëlected president of the state organization, and members of his congregation were conspicuous in other offices.

The temperance movement provided not only prestige but amusement, in the form of ritual, slogans, signed pledges, and desperate oaths. If these practices added more to its appeal than to its validity, they nevertheless showed that it was linked in spirit at least with the fraternal movement. Much more important, temperance advanced race organization and unity. If some of the meetings were purely sociable — with cold water — where the members displayed such talents as a good voice, a fine presence, or a ready wit in conversation, at other "serious" ones they "engaged in discussion," listened to speakers, elected officers, and passed resolutions. All this trained colored people in organization and race consciousness.

Temperance, like the church, brought together the able and ambitious Negroes for the good of society, and stimulated interest and confidence in the future of their race. Temperance meetings eventually became centers of agitation for social and political rights for the race. At meetings in Connecticut resolutions were discussed and passed in favor of emancipation and the antislavery movement, of education for Negro children, of the newspaper, the *Colored American,* and of the action of the Massachusetts Abolition Society in opening an employment office for colored job hunters.[28] And, as will be mentioned later, temperance organizations also urged the advance of Negroes to citizenship and civil equality.

The church remained the primary influence in Negro society; and in New Haven, the descendant of Simeon Jocelyn's institution remained preëminent. Congregationalism had prestige, and Temple Street was the foremost Negro church. Since at the beginning it had been somewhat nonsectarian in character, most of the leading families had joined; and it tended to remain the most aristocratic. An impressive proportion of the barbers, the waiters at Yale, and the shoemakers were members. The standards of industry, sobriety, education, and family morality were the highest of the Negro community. It was "exclusive," inasmuch as these "visible signs of election" were required for membership. The ambitious and able of other religious backgrounds were attracted, especially when, as newcomers to town, they found there the group in colored society to which they aspired or to which they were accustomed. For example, James Brooks, painter, came up from the South and became a member, as did Thaddeus Newton, shoemaker. Good Connecticut mores and folkways were to be found at the Temple Street Church, and the influence filtered down to all the Negroes in New Haven.

Likewise, the Temple Street Church best exemplified the germinant social forces among the Negroes during the 'forties and 'fifties. It remained associated with the militant abolitionism in which it had had its origin, but it also tended toward Negro race consciousness and Negro independence. Amos Gerry Beman, the first long-term Negro pastor in Temple Street, was a man of dignity and importance. In character and performance, he might well be considered an embodiment of the Negro spirit of the age in which he lived and worked. He was a child of the times.[29] The son of a minister, L. C. Beman of Middletown, who knew Garrison,[30] and subscribed to the *Liberator,* he served his apprenticeship in his father's church and in the temperance movement. The Bemans, father and son, started the Middletown Society and the state organization[31] before Amos came to New Haven, and they had attended the Boston convention for the promotion of temperance in New England.[32] Amos was acquainted with Horace Bushnell, Simeon Jocelyn, Arthur Tappan, and Gerrit Smith, as well as with Cinqué and the *Amistad* captives. Later he was to attain prominence as an abolitionist and national standing and importance among his people.

Both his ideas and activities were characteristic of the period. Self-improvement was popular, and lyceums, private libraries, and literary and debating clubs flourished. The Rev. Simeon Jocelyn had introduced to New York the Phoenix Societies which held "mental feasts" for whites and Negroes (they would be called interracial forums today); the Dorcas Societies made clothing for impecunious school children; and some Negro groups existed for the purpose of supporting race newspapers;[33] others were mutual-benefit insurance societies. In New Haven, under Beman's guidance, all these methods were utilized to evolve a social fabric in his congregation and people. There were a "Beman Benevolent Association" and a library club, "Circles of Improvement," and temperance societies. The church had practically a seven-day-a-week program, with forums on the radical subjects of that day and with protest and agitation meetings against slavery. Beman urged support of Negro newspapers and for a few months he himself published one called *Zion's Wesleyan.* And he gathered all encouraging or stimulating information about Negroes, stories of achievement or of unfair discrimination to sow seeds of emulation or of race consciousness.

Beman's doctrine was also characteristic of his time. He emphasized what he called "the great work of moral improvement." Believing progress a divine law, he asserted that the Negro people, too, could attain "virtue, intelligence, and wealth," which he termed the true measure of "the social elevation of a people." Property might be secured by industry, he said, and by economy and saving; "intelligence," since Negroes had sufficient native ability, by study; and "moral elevation" God required of all. He urged as motives personal and family comfort and respectability, pleasure in intellectual exercise, and race pride and unity in the task of destroying slavery.[34] He condemned the obstacles of indifference and selfishness, of disunion, and of lack of perseverance. It may be said against him that he was the preacher who believed in the complete efficacy of praising virtue and condemning sin; and his thinking was sometimes fumbling and confused, but he did effectively teach the conventional Connecticut morality, and he infused his teaching with the confidence and hope of the age. Himself an example, he assisted the formation of a Negro social group which encouraged and enforced high standards of self-imposed conduct.

His church vitalized a Negro upper class in New Haven. In 1851, with characteristic enthusiasm and only slight exaggeration, Beman noted that the fruit of his planting was beginning to appear. Twenty-one houses were being completed for Negroes within the city, building lots bought, and money deposited in the savings bank. The future was bright, he proclaimed, if the Negroes would only be industrious, "intelligent," honest, sober, virtuous, and prudent; if they would study and practice "the principles and spirit of the Gospel," if they could understand and would obey "the science of domestic and political economy."[35] Beman was more than a preacher. As we shall find, he was also an aggressive abolitionist; and he led his people in an active fight for citizenship.

Notes

[1] Pamphlet, *Religious Services in the Second African Church, Philadelphia.* . . . Sermon by the Rev. Thomas Brainerd. Yale Slavery Pamphlets, Vol. 78, pp. 6–8.

[2] For much of the history and historical material about this church, now the Dixwell Avenue Congregational, the author is indebted to the Rev. E. F. Goin, the present pastor. His pamphlet, prepared on the one-hundredth anniversary, the church papers, the Beman Collection in his possession, and his advice and recollections have been invaluable.

[3] Chap. ii, p. 46.

[4] *Religious Intelligencer,* August 29, 1829.

[5] *Ibid.*

[6] C. G. Woodson, *History of the Negro Church,* p. 99. One was also meeting in Middle-

town as early as 1829. A mixed or undenominational church with Congregationalism predominant was found in Boston in 1805 and was possibly a descendant of an African Society formed in 1797. See J. Daniels, *In Freedom's Birthplace*, p. 21, 21 n. The Presbyterian Church in Philadelphia, of course, was also earlier, 1807. C. G. Woodson, *Negro in Our History*, p. 156, Washington, D.C., 1931.

[7] e. g., see *African Repository* (1832), pp. 184, 192, and *Connecticut Journal*, September 6, 1831; and an announcement of an address to be given by the Rev. Simeon S. Jocelyn in *Religious Intelligencer*, February 28, 1835.

[8] J. M. Morse, *Neglected Period*, pp. 137–138.

[9] *Third Annual Report*. Afr. Imp. Soc. 1829.

[10] *Fred Douglass' Paper*, August 14, 1851.

[11] Manuscript, Beman Collection.

[12] The founder was George W. Gale, whose pastor was Charles S. Finney, the evangelist. Gerrit Smith contributed liberally to its support.

[13] *Connecticut Journal*, October 4, 1831.

[14] *Ibid.*, October 11, 1831.

[15] E. E. Atwater, editor, *History of New Haven*, p. 142.

[16] Broad Street at the corner of Morocco. See map, p. 28.

[17] Her obituary, press clipping, Beman Collection.

[18] *Minutes* of the General and the Several Annual Conferences of the African M. E. Zion's Church, 1848. Yale Slavery Pamphlets, Vol. 80.

[19] In 1842 they suffered a fire causing $500 damage, of which $350 was covered by insurance. New Haven Directory, 1860.

[20] 1841.

[21] *Minutes* of the African Methodist Episcopal New England Annual Conference, June 10–21, 1852, in New Bedford, showed only 14 in the New Haven society compared with 15 in Bridgeport; 231 in New Bedford; 81 in Boston; 120 in Providence, etc. Yale Slavery Pamphlets, Vol. 80.

[22] The material for this paragraph was derived principally from the pamphlet history of the church by the Rev. A. C. Powell. *A Souvenir of the Immanuel Baptist Church, its Pastors and its Members*. New Haven, 1895.

[23] New Haven Directory, 1870.

[24] Church Records. The account is written in by an unknown hand some years after the event. The writer may have known of what he wrote from personal experience.

[25] Beman Collection.

[26] Manuscripts and clippings, Beman Collection, and Church Records of Dixwell Avenue Congregational Church.

[27] Established May 30 at a public meeting at which a sermon was presented by the Rev. Mr. Beecher of Boston. The New Haven society in the United African Church was formed April 16. *Religious Intelligencer*, June 26, 1830.

[28] All these facts are derived from contemporary clippings preserved by Beman. Beman Collection.

[29] For a fuller, biographical account, see R. A. Warner, "Amos Gerry Beman. A Memoir on a Forgotten Leader," *Journal of Negro History*, April, 1937.

[30] W. P. and F. Garrison, *William Lloyd Garrison*, I, 341.

[31] The first meeting was in Middletown, May 11, 1836.

[32] Held May 17–19 and October 26, 1836. *Minutes* of a Convention of People of Color for the Promotion of Temperance in New England. Yale Slavery Pamphlets, Vol. 79. Providence, 1836.

[33] B. Gross, *"Freedom's Journal,"* *Journal of Negro History*, XVII, 245, 245 n.

[34] Speech in 1839 at Hartford. Clipping, Beman Collection.

[35] Clipping, Beman Collection.

Free Blacks and the Federal Government

3

The Federal Government and the Free Negro

Leon Litwack

Since the Constitution made no mention of race or color, the states and the federal government separately defined the legal status of free Negroes. Both generally agreed, however, that the Negro constituted an inferior race and that he should occupy a legal position commensurate with his degraded social and economic condition. If God had not ordained such an inferior status, public opinion at least demanded it. "The federal constitution is silent about race or colour," an English visitor observed, "but in interpreting it, American lawgivers arrive at the conclusion, that the United States are the property of whites, and that persons with a tinge of dark colour in their countenance, though born free, are not citizens. . . . There seems, in short, to be a fixed notion throughout the whole of the states, whether slave or free, that the coloured is by nature a subordinate race; and that in no circumstances, can it be considered equal to the white."[1]

While most states were circumscribing the Negro's legal position, federal authorities frequently questioned his claim to exercise the rights and privileges of American citizens. Not until 1857, however, when the Supreme Court ruled on the case of *Dred Scott* v. *Sanford,* did the federal government finally dispel all doubts concerning Negro citizenship. By then, Chief Justice Roger B. Taney could find appropriate precedents in the actions of Congress and "the conduct of the Executive Department."

Reflecting the popular conception of the United States as a white man's country, early Congressional legislation excluded Negroes from certain federal rights and privileges and sanctioned a number of territorial and state restrictions. In 1790, Congress limited naturalization to white aliens; in 1792, it organized the militia and restricted enrollment to able-bodied white male citizens; in 1810, it excluded Negroes from carrying the United States mails; in 1820, it authorized the citizens of Washington, D.C., to elect "white" city officials and to adopt a code governing free Negroes and slaves.[2] Moreover, it repeatedly approved the admission of states whose constitutions severely restricted the legal rights of free Negroes.[3] On the basis of such legislation, it would appear that Congress had resolved to treat Negroes neither as citizens nor as aliens. But consistency did not distinguish the actions of the national legislature. On at least one occasion, it recognized — perhaps inadvertently — that Negroes might qualify as citizens. Against a background of increasing foreign difficulties, including the impressment of American seamen into the British navy, the House of Representatives resolved in 1803 "to enquire into the expediency of granting protection to such American seamen citizens of the United States, as are free persons of color."[4] Protecting the rights of Negro seamen in foreign waters apparently posed no threat to white supremacy at home.

The failure of Congress to legislate in certain areas also raised doubts about the Negro's legal position. Although an early act excluded Negroes from the militia, no such legislation barred them from the Army, Navy, or Marines. In 1798, the Secretaries of War and Navy issued separate directives forbidding Negro enlistments in the Marine Corps and on naval warships. Military necessity, however, apparently negated this policy, for Negro soldiers and sailors served prominently, and often courageously, during the naval war with France (1798-1800) and the War of 1812. "I have yet to learn," Captain Oliver H. Perry wrote, "that the color of a man's skin or the cut and trimmings of the coat can affect a man's qualifications or usefulness." (Of Perry's four hundred men, an estimated one hundred were Negroes.)[5] The absence of any congressional prohibition and the subsequent enlistment of Negro troops raised at least one troublesome question in the postwar years: Could Negroes qualify for land bounties promised the veterans of the War of 1812? Attorney General William Wirt replied in 1823 that they could, although he felt "that it was not the intention of Congress to incorporate negroes and people of color with the army any more than with the militia of the United States."[6]

In an effort to clarify congressional policy regarding Negro troops, Senator John C. Calhoun moved in 1842 to exclude Negroes from the Navy, except as cooks, stewards, and servants. "It was wrong," the South Carolinian declared, "to bring those who have to sustain the honor and glory of the country down to a footing of the negro race — to be degraded by being mingled and mixed up with that inferior race." Although several northern congressmen cited the valuable military service of Negroes in the War of 1812, the Senate agreed to Calhoun's proposal, rejected an amendment which would have permitted the employment of Negro sailors "In unhealthy climates," and, for good measure, voted to exclude Negroes from the Army. The House, however, took no action on these measures.[7]

Occasional congressional lapses did not nullify the intent and impact of earlier legislation. By 1820, free Negroes could not legally exercise certain rights and privileges guaranteed to American citizens and aliens. Moreover, the adoption of these restrictions had prompted little or no debate, and no real effort was made in the ante-bellum period to change or repeal them. Although free Negroes failed to secure any alteration of legislative policy, they did succeed on several occasions in arousing the wrath of Congress by exercising one of their few remaining rights, that of petitioning the national legislature for a redress of grievances. In 1800, for example, a group of Philadelphia free Negroes, headed by the Reverend Absalom Jones, petitioned Congress to take appropriate steps to correct the evils of the African slave trade and the fugitive-slave act and to provide for the gradual abolition of slavery. Although the petition admitted the impropriety of immediate emancipation and couched its appeal in very mild terms, it threw the House of Representatives into momentary turmoil. Representative Harrison Gray Otis of Massachusetts immediately opposed referring the petition to committee, as was the normal practice, because to encourage such a measure "would have an irritating tendency, and must be mischievous to America very soon. It would teach them the art of assembling together, debating, and the like, and would soon . . . extend from one end of the Union to the other." Henry Lee of Virginia agreed; indeed, it should not even be tabled but simply returned to its authors. So improper was the petition, John Rutledge, Jr., of South Carolina added, that several states would never have ratified the Constitution had they imagined that such sentiments might be entertained as a proper subject of debate. Only one member of the House, George Thacher of Massachusetts, pressed for congressional consideration on grounds that slavery was "a cancer of immense magnitude, that would some time destroy the body politic, except as proper legislation should prevent the evil." After a two-day debate, the House voted 85 to 1 (Thacher) that those portions of the petition asking Congress "to legislate upon subjects from which the General Government is precluded by the Constitution, have a tendency to create disquiet and jealousy, and ought therefore to receive no encouragement or countenance."[8]

Free Negroes had much greater reason to be concerned with the legislative debates of 1820-21 on the admission of Missouri, for Congress now had an opportunity to clarify once and for all the matter of Negro citizenship. In November, 1820, the prospective state submitted its constitution for the necessary approval of Congress. The right of Missourians to own slave property had been conceded in the previous session, but a new issue had now been raised. The proposed constitution, written and adopted by an aggressively proslavery convention, not only sanctioned slavery but enjoined the state legislature to pass such laws as might be necessary "to prevent free negroes and mulattoes from coming to and settling in this state, under any pretext whatsoever." This had not been conceded or expected, and many found it impossible to reconcile such a clause with the guarantee of the federal constitution that "the citizens of each state shall be entitled to all privileges and immunities of citizens of the several states." If Congress agreed to such a measure, Secretary of State John Quincy Adams told a Pennsylvania representative, it would, in effect, alter the terms of the Constitution and deprive thousands of citizens of their just rights. "Already cursed by the mere color of their skin," Adams remarked, "already doomed by their complexion to drudge in the lowest offices of society, excluded by their color from all the refined enjoyments of life accessible to others, excluded from the benefits of a liberal education, from the bed, from the table, and from all the social comforts of domestic life, this barbarous article deprives them of the little remnant of right yet left them — their rights as citizens and as men."⁹

Since Congress had adopted no consistent position on Negro citizenship, Missouri's congressional defenders searched elsewhere for appropriate precedents. Why not consult the state constitutions and statutes, Senator William Smith of South Carolina urged, for these had given "a decisive character" to the legal status of free Negroes, and they demonstrated beyond a doubt that neither the North nor the South had ever regarded them as suitable members of the political community. Nearly every state barred the Negro from voting, giving evidence in court, and marrying with white persons; no state admitted him into the militia or made him a citizen by legislative act; and at least one northern state, Pennsylvania, had only recently considered prohibiting further Negro immigration. Moreover, in admitting new states, Congress had already approved racial restrictions. Indeed, the very act that had authorized Missouri to elect delegates to a constitutional convention had limited the suffrage to free white male citizens. "This is unanswerable proof," Senator Smith concluded, "of the degraded condition in which Congress consider free negroes and mulattoes ought to be placed. With this strong and peculiar example before their eyes, well might the people of Missouri conceive they had a right to provide against this evil."¹⁰

Advocates of Missouri's unqualified admission saw no inconsistency between the anti-free Negro clause and the guarantees of the federal constitution. Using the evidence accumulated by Senator Smith, they simply noted that every state had found it necessary to legislate against the free Negro. Someone, of course, might charge that all such state measures were, in fact, unconstitutional. In this regard, however, Missouri's defenders could find comfort in the remarks of the venerable Representative Charles Pinckney of South Carolina. A delegate to the Constitutional Convention in 1787, Pinckney claimed that he had been responsible for the disputed section on the privileges and immunities of citizens. Now — thirty-four years later — he explained to Congress what he had meant by this clause: "I perfectly knew that there did not then exist such a thing in the Union as a black or colored citizen, nor could I then have conceived it possible such a thing could ever have existed in it; nor notwithstanding all that is said on the subject, do I now believe one does exist in it." Turning his attention to the degraded position of the northern Negro, Pinckney charged that the free states were seeking to rid themselves of the black population "by treating them, on every occasion with the most marked contempt" and excluding them from any political privileges. Not until northerners altered their constitutions and laws and granted Negroes a full enjoyment of the rights of white citizens could they expect the southern states to recognize Negro citizenship.¹¹

Were Congress to ignore state precedents, reject Missouri's racial bar, and thus elevate the Negro to citizenship, several congressmen predicted disastrous consequences. Emancipated and fugitive slaves would inundate the free states, where they would vote and send black representatives to sit in the state and federal legislatures. Was this not "a supposition too absurd to be for a moment entertained?" Senator

John Holmes of Maine asked. "Gentlemen, with all their humanity, to be obliged to sit in this Senate by a black man, would consider their rights invaded." In the face of increasing pressure on southern free Negroes, Holmes warned his northern colleagues that every state might be well advised to retain its power to check the movements of such "a troublesome or dangerous population." Self-protection also demanded that the South be able to adopt appropriate controls, for free Negroes posed serious dangers there. "They are just enough elevated to have some sense of liberty," a Virginia representative declared, "and yet not the capacity to estimate or enjoy all its rights, if they had them — and being between two societies, above one and below the other, they are in the most dissatisfied state. They are themselves perpetual monuments of discontent, and firebrands to the other class of their own color. And if the time ever came when the flames of servile war enwrap this Union in a general blaze, perhaps we may have to look to them as the primary cause of such horrors." Under such circumstances, had not any state "a right to get rid of them"?[12]

Those who assailed Missouri's free-Negro proviso generally argued that the Constitution, unlike various state laws, made no distinctions based on color. Moreover, some states accorded their black citizens equal rights with whites. How, then, could the Negroes of New York, Massachusetts, Vermont, and New Hampshire constitutionally be prohibited from settling in Missouri? Southern critics had charged that various northern states prohibited interracial marriages, but how could this be considered discriminatory when it applied to both races? Although they defended the Negro's legal position, few northern congressmen denied the existence of strong racial prejudices in their constituencies. "Custom has made a distinction between them and other men," a New Hampshire senator remarked, "but the constitution and laws make none." Noting the fear that Negroes might be elected to public office, a Pennsylvania representative reminded the House that this had never occurred in states that acknowledged Negro citizenship and undoubtedly never would occur. "The manners and practical distinctions in private life," he asserted, "will form a barrier, in this respect, as insurmountable as if engrafted in the constitution itself; and no danger need be feared that there will be any other commixture of community than we see at present." Nevertheless, Negroes should be accorded "such rights of citizenship as our customs and habits may approve of as suitable to their condition."[13]

On March 2, 1821, Congress voted to admit Missouri on condition that the disputed free-Negro clause "shall never be construed to authorize the passage of any law, and that no law shall be passed in conformity thereto, by which any citizen, of either of the States in this Union, shall be excluded from the enjoyment of any of the privileges and immunities to which such citizen is entitled under the constitution of the United States." The Missouri legislature accepted this vague condition, and subsequent state legislation rendered it ineffective. Congress' action came as no surprise to Representative William Plumer, Jr., of New Hampshire. Two months before, he had predicted that Missouri would be admitted "with some declaratory proviso . . . which will in fact amount to nothing, but serve merely as a salve to tender consciences."[14] Determining the legal status of free Negroes remained a matter for local, state, and federal discretion.

After 1821, Congress debated Negro rights with greater regularity and intensity. As abolition sentiment and agitation increased, southern and "Doughface" congressmen seized every opportunity to demonstrate the inconsistency of northern pronouncements on equality and freedom with the treatment accorded free Negroes in the North. In the classic Webster-Hayne debate of 1830, for example, the South Carolina Senator charged that those slaves who escaped to the North found themselves treated as outcasts and assigned to "the dark and narrow lanes, and obscure recesses" of the cities. "Sir," he cried, "there does not exist on the face of the earth, a population so poor, so wretched, so vile, so loathsome, so utterly destitute of all the comforts, conveniences, and decencies of life, as the unfortunate blacks of Philadelphia, and New York, and Boston. Liberty has been to them the greatest of calamities, the heaviest of curses." How, southerners asked, could the North so glibly condemn slavery when it worked free Negroes severely in menial employments, excluded them from the polls, the juries, the churches, and the learned professions, snubbed them in social circles, and finally even barred them from entering some states? Did not northerners place the Negro in a much higher scale by their rhetoric than by their practice? "Go home, and emancipate your free Negroes," a Virginia congressman demanded. "When you do that, we will listen to you with more patience."[15]

The South made its point, found it to be a most effective one, and used it to frustrate abolitionist spokesmen for the remainder of the ante-bellum period. Southern travelers in the North buttressed the argument with their own observations. "What's the use to talk about equality when no such thing exists," a Georgian noted in Philadelphia. "A body sees that in ther churches, and theatres, and courts, and evrywhar else. Nobody here that has any respect for themselves, treats a nigger as their equal, except a few fannyticks, and they only do it to give the lie to ther own feelins, and to insult the feelins of others."[16] The security of southern society, however, required that its spokesmen in and out of Congress overlook one major fallacy in an otherwise effective indictment of northern racial hypocrisy. The northern Negro admittedly faced political, economic, and social restrictions. Nevertheless, he spoke out freely against his condition; he organized, agitated, penned editorials and pamphlets, and petitioned state and federal bodies to improve his position. Much of this agitation proved legislatively fruitless, but the northern Negro could place his grievances before the public, and few whites challenged his right to do so. Organized slave or even southern free-Negro protests, on the other hand, invited severe repression, punishment, or death.

After 1840, southern congressmen could assert that the federal government itself offered documentary proof of the advantages of slavery over freedom for Negroes. The sixth census of the United States, released in 1841, enumerated for the first time the mentally diseased and defective — or "insane and idiots," as they were then officially described — and contained the startling revelation that their prevalence among free Negroes was about eleven times higher than among slaves. In the southern states, the ratio of insane or idiotic among Negroes stood at 1 to every 1,558; in the northern states, it was 1 to every 144.5. In fact, the frequency of these afflictions among Negroes decreased from Maine to Louisiana with virtual mathematical precision. For example, it was found that in Maine every 14th Negro was either a lunatic or an idiot; in New Hampshire every 28th; in Massachusetts every 43d; in Connecticut every 184th; in New York every 257th; and in New Jersey every 297th. This was in sharp contrast with the South, where the proportion ranged from 1 in 1,229 in Virginia and 1 in 2,477 in South Carolina to 1 in 4,310 in Louisiana.[17]

Such statistics not only offered obvious moral lessons but gave official credence to popular "scientific" ideas about the peculiar suitability of Negroes for slavery. One northern observer, in a letter to a New York business journal, explained that the prevalence of insanity among local Negroes resulted from "the rigors of a northern winter, which have no influence on the temperament of the whites" but "which affect the cerebral organs of the African race." Slavery, he added, apparently helped to lessen such occurrences among southern Negroes.[18] The *Southern Literary Messenger,* however, dismissed the climatic explanation, attributed the sectional disparity to "moral causes" resulting from the condition of Negroes in the two sections, and concluded that they fared worse in those areas where slavery had been abolished. On the basis of the recent census, the journal warned its readers that the consequences of emancipation might be disastrous. "Let us . . . suppose," it remarked, "a half of a million of free negroes suddenly turned loose in Virginia, whose propensity it is, constantly to grow more vicious in a state of freedom. . . . Where should we find Penitentiaries for the thousands of felons? Where, lunatic asylums for the tens of thousands of maniacs? Would it be possible to live in a country where maniacs and felons met the traveller at every cross-road?"[19] Seizing upon the census for political profit, southern congressmen contrasted "the happy, well-fed, healthy, and moral condition of the southern slaves, with the condition of the miserable victims and degraded free blacks of the North." Such must be the case, a Mississippian declared, for "idiocy and lunacy . . . in the lower classes, had been shown by medical men to be invariably caused by vice and misery."[20]

These remarkable statistics could be used to counter foreign as well as domestic criticism of southern slavery. This was most vividly demonstrated during the diplomatic crisis over Texas. In 1844, the British government, in a communication to Secretary of State Abel Upshur, had expressed a desire to see slavery abolished in Texas and throughout the world. John C. Calhoun, Upshur's successor and a firm defender of the "peculiar institution," replied that slavery in Texas was the concern of neither the British nor the federal government, but was a local matter. Calhoun nevertheless took this opportunity to lecture the British foreign secretary on the relative merits of slavery and freedom for American Negroes, and he used the latest statistics to support his argument. The recent census, Calhoun wrote, demonstrated, on the basis of "Unquestionable sources," that "in all instances in which the States have changed the former relation between the two races, the condition of the African, instead of being improved, has become worse. They have invariably sunk into vice and pauperism, accompanied by the bodily and mental inflictions incident thereto — deafness, blindness, insanity, and idiocy — to a degree without example." In the slaveholding states, on the other hand, Negroes have shown marked improvement "in number, comfort, intelligence, and morals." Experience and recent statistical evidence had thus conclusively demonstrated that the subjection of Negroes to whites secured the peace, safety, and progress of both races, while that relation demanded by Great Britain — "under the plausible name of the abolition of slavery" — would either destroy the inferior race or reduce it to "vice and wretchedness."[21]

Calhoun's "Unquestionable sources" did not go unchallenged. Dr. Edward Jarvis, Massachusetts-born physician and specialist in mental disorders and one of the founders of the American Statistical Association, delivered the fatal blow.[22] In his first reaction to the census tables on insanity and idiocy, Jarvis agreed that slavery must have "a wonderful influence upon the development of moral faculties and the intellectual powers." Upon more careful investigation, however, he found that the errors in these returns were nearly as startling as the statistics themselves, and in January, 1844 — four months prior to Calhoun's letter — Jarvis thoroughly refuted the census findings. Contrasting the population returns with the insanity figures, he found that in many northern towns the census listed insane Negroes where no Negro population existed and that in others the figures exceeded the reported number of Negro residents. Jarvis concluded that the census contributed nothing to the statistical classification of diseases among Negroes but that, instead, it constituted "a bearer of falsehood to confuse and mislead." In the name of the nation's honor, medical science, and truth, he demanded that appropriate steps be taken to correct the census.[23] Hoping to precipitate such action, the American Statistical Association submitted to Congress a memorial which enumerated the errors found in the insanity tables.[24]

Similar objections were raised elsewhere. After carefully examining the returns, a Boston newspaper concluded that the startling prevalence of insanity among northern Negroes existed "only in the error of the census." The *The North American Review,* one of the nation's leading journals, regretted that obvious carelessness virtually invalidated the statistics on insanity. Meanwhile, northern Negroes vigorously denied the association of insanity with emancipation. "Freedom has not made us mad," a Negro leader wrote to the New York *Tribune,* "it has strengthened our minds by throwing us upon our own resources, and has bound us to American institutions with a tenacity which nothing but death can overcome." Reinforcing this sentiment, a group of prominent New York Negroes petitioned Congress to re-examine the recent census and make appropriate revisions.[25]

Against this background of growing protest, Representative John Quincy

Adams of Massachusetts took the initiative in Congress to call for a thorough investigation and revision of the 1840 census. There existed in that document, Adams declared, gross errors by which "atrocious misrepresentations had been made on a subject of deep importance." Referring to Calhoun's use of the statistics, the former President charged that the United States had nearly found itself at war with Great Britain and Mexico on the basis of those census errors. It was imperative, therefore, that the true state of facts be reported.[26] But census critics faced a formidable obstacle in the person of John C. Calhoun, whose Department of State was responsible for the findings and would have to undertake any revision. On February 26, 1844, the House directed the Secretary of State to investigate and report on the existence of alleged "gross errors" in the census, but Calhoun evaded the inquiry by finding a technical error in the resolution. Adams then called on the Secretary of State, only to be told "that where there were so many errors they balanced one another, and led to the same conclusion as if they were all correct."[27] In June, the House committee to which the memorial of the American Statistical Association had been referred reported that it could find no reason to doubt the validity of the criticism and agreed that this destroyed the utility of the findings on Negro insanity and negated any conclusions that might be based upon them. Apparently aware of the futility of securing a revision, the committee hoped that no such errors would appear in the next census.[28]

Although confronted with hostile House and Senate committee reports, Calhoun adamantly maintained his defense of the census. In response to a new House resolution of inquiry, he stated that his department had given a "full and thorough examination" to the alleged errors and that "the result would seem fully to sustain the correctness of the census." Errors could be expected in such an ambitious undertaking, Calhoun conceded, but they did not alter the conclusion that a far greater prevalence of the diseases of insanity, blindness, deafness, and muteness existed among northern Negroes. This fact "stands unimpeachable." In the face of such evidence, how could one not conclude that the emancipation of southern slaves "would be . . . to them a curse instead of a blessing"?[29]

The Census of 1840 remained unaltered, and for good reason. Its findings provided anti-abolition orators and publicists with "unquestionable" proof of the benign influence of slavery on Negroes. In fact, a Georgia congressman reportedly admitted to Jarvis that the census contained a number of errors. Nevertheless, he added, "it is too good a thing for our politicians to give up. They had prepared speeches based on it, which they could not afford to lose."[30] Although readily used by slavery apologists, the statistics on Negro insanity found little support in the North once they had been refuted. On the eve of the Civil War, a Unitarian clergyman perhaps wrote their proper epitaph: "It was the census that was insane, and not the colored people."[31]

Although northern opposition to the expansion of slavery increased considerably in the 1840's and the 1850's, the free Negro found little cause for optimism.

Most proponents of slavery restriction made it clear that their concern was not for the plight of the black man but for the welfare of the white race. When Representative David Wilmot of Pennsylvania made his historic move to exclude slavery from the territories acquired from Mexico, he carefully explained that he did not propose to interfere with southern institutions and that he possessed "no squeamish sensitiveness upon the subject of slavery, no morbid sympathy for the slave." What he wanted was free states for free white men. "I plead the cause and the rights of white freemen," he told Congress in 1847. "I would preserve to free white labor a fair country, a rich inheritance, where the sons of toil, of my own race and own color, can live without the disgrace which association with negro slavery brings upon free labor."[32]

While challenging the constitutional authority of Congress to check slavery in the territories, opponents of the Wilmot proviso also reiterated the charge that northern treatment of the Negro belied a professed humanitarianism and devotion to liberty. Few northern congressmen challenged the South on this point. Representative Henry C. Murphy of New York, for example, insisted that Congress possessed full power to legislate for the territories but agreed that his state had found it impossible for the two races to live together on equal social or political terms. Nevertheless, Murphy felt some compassion for the Negro. As long as that degraded race remained in the South, it might be happy and contented. Once Negroes entered the free states, however, they would almost certainly "be the objects of contumely and scorn." Under these circumstances, he appealed to the South to retain its Negro population; indeed, he would favor the adoption of severe laws "against any who shall bring the wretched beings to our Free States, there to taint the blood of the whites, or to destroy their own race by vicious courses."[33] Such was undoubtedly the sentiment of a large portion of the North.

During the debates on slavery expansion, another New York representative formally proposed that Congress inquire into the expediency of setting apart a portion of the public domain for the exclusive use and possession of free Negroes. The area would be separately organized, governed by Congress, and eligible for territorial status. In other words, an Ohio representative charged, the Whigs and "negro-loving" New York congressmen proposed to establish a Negro colony which could eventually send blacks to Congress. The author of the resolution replied that he had no such intention, that his plan simply called for ultimate territorial status "and nothing more." The House refused to receive the resolution, and the matter was allowed to die.[34]

If the new territories were to be reserved for whites, as envisioned by Wilmot, Congress would have to bar Negroes from the benefits of federal land policy. The Senate attempted this in 1841 when it voted to confine the privileges of the new pre-emption law to whites. In casting the sole vote against the measure, Augustus Porter of Michigan explained that no previous act had embodied such a clause and that it conflicted with the right of all persons to buy and dispose of property. Although Negroes could neither vote nor hold political office in his state, they could at least enjoy the protection of life, liberty, and property, and this most certainly included the right to hold and dispose of real estate. On reconsideration, the Senate reversed itself and deleted the restriciton from the bill. Nevertheless, an opinion from the Attorney General was required to qualify Negroes for the benefits of the act.[15]

This proved to be a momentary victory for Negro rights to the public domain. On several occasions, exclusionist sentiment prompted Congress to tack white restrictionist amendments onto land and homestead bills. In organizing the Oregon and New Mexico territories, for example, Congress agreed to limit public land grants to white settlers. "This is surely a novel proposition," Representative Joshua Giddings of Ohio protested. "Will history record this as an exhibition of the narrow, the groveling prejudices which govern the American Congress?" But Giddings' colleagues apparently argued more persuasively that granting public lands to Negroes would only encourage and prolong their co-existence with whites. "I sympathize with them deeply," an Ohio representative exclaimed, "but I have no sympathy for them in a common residence with the white race. God has ordained, and no human law can contravene the ordinance, that the two races shall be separate and distinct. . . . I will vote against any measure that has a tendency to prolong their common residence in this Confederacy, or any portion of it."[36]

Prior to 1857, the federal government still had no consistent policy governing the Negro's rights to the public lands. In fact, the Secretary of the Interior informed a New York Negro that no law barred him from settling upon the public domain or claiming pre-emption rights. But the Dred Scott decision dealt a crushing blow to the Negro's position. Shortly afterwards, the commissioner of the General Land Office announced that since Negroes were not citizens, they could not qualify for pre-emption benefits.[37] Consequently, any Negro who desired to settle on the newly opened western lands now faced not only the anti-immigration laws of various territories and states but the open hostility of the federal government as well. Ironically, Taney's decision struck a severe blow at both the proponents of Negro citizenship and free white territories.

Since no federal ruling or act specifically defined the Negro's legal status, each executive department apparently felt free to pursue its own policy. Although this invariably resulted in proscription, the Negro sometimes benefited from the existing confusion and exercised the rights of white citizens. The opinions of the Attorneys General, the passport policy of the State Department, and the exclusion of Negroes from the postal service graphically illustrate a sometimes conflicting and even chaotic federal approach.

The Attorneys General usually agreed that the Constitution did not confer citizenship on Negroes. The first such ruling, handed down by William Wirt in 1821, affected only Virginia free Negroes, but later interpretations extended its meaning. Since the acts regulating foreign and coastal trade limited the command of vessels to citizens, Wirt advised a Norfolk port official that the Negroes of his state could not legally qualify. Virginia laws barred free Negroes from voting, holding political office, testifying against a white man, enrolling in the militia, possessing weapons, raising a hand against a white man, "except in defence against a wanton assault," or marrying a white woman. Consequently, such persons could not be considered as citizens of the United States. How did this opinion affect Negro rights in other states? Inasmuch as the Attorney General's definition of citizenship included "those only who enjoyed the full and equal privileges of white citizens in the State of their residence," this would appear to qualify — at least by implication — Negroes in several northern states. Wirt did not make this clear, however, and subsequent decisions failed to substantiate the implication. In fact, Chief Justice Roger Taney construed the opinion to apply to all free Negroes.[38]

The efforts of a few southern states to control the movements of American and foreign free colored seamen embarrassed diplomatic relations with Great Britain, forced the federal government to call for the Attorney General's opinion on several occasions, and prompted at least one significant though unpublicized attempt to define the constitutional position of free Negroes. Obsessed with the fear that northern or foreign Negroes had helped to instigate a recent slave uprising, the South Carolina legislature, in 1822, provided for the imprisonment of free colored seamen while the vessels on which they were employed remained in any of the state's ports. Unless the ship captains paid the costs of confinement, the Negro seamen would be sold to recover the charges. Several other southern states adopted almost identical measures.[39] Such legislation prompted some furious protests abroad and in the North. In a direct appeal to Congress, a group of Boston petitioners charged that these regulations materially affected commerce and deprived qualified Negroes of their constitutionally guaranteed rights as citizens. Endorsing this sentiment, a House committee concluded that the acts violated the Constitution and laws of the United States and should therefore be repealed.[40]

After the British government formally denounced the application of these laws against its own seamen, the State Department called upon the Attorney General for a ruling. William Wirt advised the government in 1824 that the acts violated the Constitution, treaties, and statutes, and conflicted with "the rights of all nations in amity with the United States." No mention was made of the constitutional rights of free Negroes; instead, Wirt's opinion stressed South Carolina's interference with foreign and interstate commerce. Ignoring this ruling, the offending states continued to enforce the acts. Seven years later, Attorney General John Berrien confirmed their action and found the legislation to be a lawful exercise of state police powers. "The general right of a State to regulate persons of color within its own limits," Berrien ruled, "is one too clearly recognized by the tenth amendment to the constitution to be drawn into controversy." In this case, the state had simply moved to protect its white and colored citizens from the "moral contagion" of insurrection.[41]

Refusing to accept such an explanation, Great Britain remained adamant in protesting the detention of her free Negro seamen. Upon the receipt of another formal note in 1831, Secretary of State Edward Livingston submitted the question to Andrew Jackson's Attorney General, Roger Taney. Although never completed for publication and little publicized, the reply extended Wirt's earlier opinion, affirmed the legal inferiority of all Negroes in the United States, and clearly anticipated the decision Taney made twenty-five years later. No federal act or treaty, he advised, could prevent a state from taking appropriate steps to insure its internal security. The charge that such steps might violate the constitutional rights of Negroes could easily be dismissed, for those rights simply did not exist. The framers of the Constitution, Taney contended, had not regarded Negroes as citizens, and the present condition of that race warranted no change in their legal status. "The African race in the United States even when free," the Attorney General wrote, "are everywhere a degraded class, and exercise no political influence. The privileges they are allowed to enjoy, are accorded to them as a matter of kindness and benevolence rather than of right. . . . And where they are nominally admitted by law to the privileges of citizenship, they have no effectual power to defend them, and are permitted to be citizens by the sufferance of the white population and hold whatever rights they enjoy at their mercy." Negroes thus constituted "a separate and degraded people," and each state could grant or withhold such privileges as it deemed proper and expedient.[42]

Had Taney's opinion been published, it might have settled the question of Negro citizenship well in advance of the Dred Scott decision. But such was not the case, and the confused status of the Negro continued to confront various federal agencies. Attorney General Hugh Legare decided in 1843 that free Negroes were neither aliens nor citizens, but occupied an intermediate position. When asked whether Negroes could apply for benefits under the new pre-emption act, Legare replied that no previous law had excluded them and he saw nothing prohibitory in the new statute. The "plain meaning" of the new act was to exclude aliens and to grant pre-emption rights "to all denizens"; any foreigner who filed his intention of citizenship could thus qualify for its benefits. "Now, free people of color are not aliens," Legare advised. "They enjoy universally . . . the rights of denizens. . . . How far a political *status* may be acquired is a different question, but his *civil* status is that of a complete denizenship." This novel legal position had no discernible effect on the Negro's rights or privileges. Attorney General Caleb Cushing summarily dismissed the ruling in 1856 and charged that Legare "had . . . been carried away in argument by a generous disposition to protect . . . the claim of a free African, without admitting him to be a citizen of the United States." To qualify Negroes for pre-emption rights, Cushing advised, the federal government had either to overrule or to ignore Wirt's 1821 opinion.[43] The legal status of ante-bellum free Negroes rested there until the Dred Scott decision, which cited the opinions of both Wirt and Cushing and coupled these with other manifestations of federal racial distinctions, including the State Department's passport policy.

In citing the refusal of the Secretaries of State to grant passports to Negroes, Chief Justice Taney conveniently overlooked the fact that departmental policy had been somewhat erratic and inconclusive. Prior to 1855, several Negroes secured passports which certified that they were American citizens and were thus entitled to full diplomatic protection abroad. On the other hand, the Department rejected the application of a Philadelphia Negro in 1839 because the newly revised Pennsylvania constitution, which limited the suffrage to white males, obviously did not recognize Negroes as citizens. The decision as to whether or not a passport should be granted thus appeared to depend on the rights enjoyed by the applicant in his state of residence. In some cases, however, the intercession of an influential white person might have been even more important.[44]

Hoping to clarify departmental policy, Secretary of State James Buchanan explained in 1847 that regular passports certified that the bearer was a citizen of the United States. Consequently, it had been customary to grant free Negroes special certificates "suited to the nature of the case" instead of passports. Two years later, Secretary of State John M. Clayton insisted that no passports had been granted to Negroes and that protection abroad had been granted them only when they were in the service of United States diplomatic agents. "Our shipwrecked seamen," the New York *Evening Post* protested, "discharged servants, outraged or insulted citizens, who find themselves destitute, in foreign lands, if they are persons of color, are to be thrust from the doors of our foreign ministers and consuls, and to be denied the aid, sympathy and protection which our diplomatic functionaires were sent abroad mainly for the purpose of dispensing." Nevertheless, Clayton defended his ruling as "the settled regulation of the Department."[45]

In the decade preceding the Civil War, a growing number of Negro leaders sought passports to England, where they planned to lecture and raise money for the abolitionist cause. The State Department rejected most of these applications. Although it could not bar them from traveling abroad, the Department undoubtedly had no desire to encourage or protect the criticism of American institutions. The question of Negro citizenship, Assistant Secretary of State J. A. Thomas noted in 1856, had repeatedly arisen in both the federal and state governments. In view of the opinions of Attorneys General Wirt and Cushing and certain state judicial decisions, Negroes could not be regarded as citizens, either at home or beyond the jurisdiction of the federal government. Nevertheless, the State Department was willing to grant to qualified Negroes special forms certifying that they were free and born in the United States. If any of them should be wronged by a foreign government, "while within its jurisdiction for a legal and proper purpose," American diplomatic officials would seek to protect their rights. It remained questionable, however, whether or not attacking Negro slavery or raising money for American abolitionism constituted "a legal and proper purpose."[46]

Following the Dred Scott decision, the State Department relied on Taney's ruling as proper and sufficient grounds for rejecting Negro passport applicants. Secretary of State Lewis Cass, however, refused to admit that any change had taken place but insisted that the court decision merely confirmed previous policy. "A passport being a certificate of citizenship," he wrote, "has never since the foundation of the Government, been granted to persons of color. No change in this respect has taken place in consequence of the decision of the Dred Scott case."[47] Several newspapers thereupon enumerated, for Cass's edification, those passports which had been granted to free Negroes, including one issued as late as 1854 to a Massachusetts "colored citizen." "The record is so clearly against the Secretary and the Administration," the Boston *Daily Bee* concluded, "that it would have been far more decent and respectable in them to have acknowledged the truth, that *they have changed the policy and practice of the government,* and resolved that colored men shall not be recognized in any manner as citizens of the United States, and that they have determined to degrade and oppress colored men in every possible mode."[48]

Correcting the Secretary of State's historical oversights might help to set the record straight, but it could not alter the effect of the Dred Scott decision. The State Department now had a settled and legally defensible positon. "My only hope, now," a rejected Negro applicant declared, "is to go to some foreign country, and through the assistance of friends, claim its protection, or else, through their assistance, get permission to travel as an American outlaw! How much farther this nation intends to sink in infamy, God only knows."[49] Some states, however, moved to soften the blow and afford protection to their own Negro inhabitants. The Massachusetts legislature, for example, protested that Taney's decision had "virtually denationalized" the state's Negro citizens, and it authorized its own secretary of state to grant passports to any citizen of the Commonwealth, "whatever his color may be."[50] The impact of the Civil War and a new administration made any further state action unnecessary. In 1861, Secretary of State William H. Seward, at the request of Senator Charles Sumner of Massachusetts, granted a passport to a Boston Negro, "Robert Morris, Jr., a citizen of the United States."[51]

Although the absence of any pertinent statute prompted the State Department to formulate its own racial policy, the Post Office Department simply enforced an earlier congressional act which it had helped to conceive. In a confidential letter to the chairman of a Senate committee, Postmaster General Gideon Granger explained in 1802 that there existed objections to Negro mail carriers "of a nature too delicate to engraft into a report which may become public, yet too important to be omitted or passed over without full consideration." Such Negroes constituted a peril to the nation's security, for employment in the postal service afforded them an opportunity to co-ordinate insurrectionary activities, mix with other people, and acquire subversive information and ideas. Indeed, in time they might even learn "that a man's rights do not depend on his color" and transmit such ideas to their brethren. Congress had to act against such a possibility. "Every thing which tends to increase their knowledge of natural rights," Granger warned, "of men and things, or that affords them an opportunity of associating, acquiring, and communicating sentiments, and of establishing a chain or line of intelligence" might excite alarm.[52]

The Postmaster General's warning aroused sufficient alarm to spur legislative action. In 1810, Congress ruled that "no other than a free white person shall be employed in conveying the mail" and provided fines for any offending mail contractors.[53] There might conceivably arise, however, occasions which would justify the use of Negroes for some of the physical labor associated with handling the mails. While instructing his deputies to adhere strictly to the regulations, Postmaster General John McLean thus ruled in 1828 that Negro labor might be utilized to carry mailbags from stagecoaches into post offices, providing a responsible white person carefully supervised the operation.[54]

The restriction remained in effect and went virtually unchallenged during the remainder of the ante-bellum period. Not until 1862 did Congress consider its repeal. In that year the Senate agreed to Charles Sumner's bill to revoke the bar on Negro mail carriers. Never before, a Boston newspaper recollected, had any bill concerning the Negro, either directly or indirectly, secured the necessary Senate approval without debate. "What a good time is coming, when the African race will no longer be a bone of contention in our legislative halls!" But such optimism was premature. The House agreed to table the bill after Schuyler Colfax, Republican chairman of the post office committee, objected to it on the grounds that no repeal petitions had been received, no public demand existed for such action, that it would qualify blacks, Indians, and Chinese as mail contractors and postal officers, and that the Postmaster General had not recommended its passage and did not regard it as being in "the best interest of the Department."[55]

Where Congress had explicitly proscribed the rights of Negroes, as in the postal service, no confusion existed. Elsewhere, the individual departments made their own decisions. By 1857, after some fumbling and hesitation, the executive and legislative branches appeared to have worked out a generally consistent position. That it conformed to public prejudices should not be surprising, for no political party could afford to compromise on this issue. Moreover, the supreme judicial body of the United States now moved to translate federal and state policy and public sentiment into a legal language which would permanently define the constitutional status of American Negroes.

In the Dred Scott decision, Negro citizenship and the Missouri Compromise shared a similar fate. Chief Justice Taney found both to be incompatible with the Constitution. If there existed any doubts concerning the legal status of Negroes, these could finally be dispelled. "This confusion is now at an end," one northern Negrophobe wrote, "and the Supreme Court . . . has defined the relations, and fixed the *status* of the subordinate race *forever* — for that decision is in accord with the natural relations of the races, and therefore can never perish. It is based on historical and existing facts, which are indisputable, and it is a necessary, indeed unavoidable inference, from these facts."[56]

Early in the decision, the Chief Justice confronted the crucial problem of Negro citizenship. Can the descendants of Negro slaves, he asked, be admitted into the political community created by the Constitution and thus be entitled to the rights, privileges, and immunities guaranteed to American citizens? Seeking an answer to this question, Taney reviewed the historical status of the Negro population. For more than a century prior to the Constitutional Convention of 1787, he declared,

Negroes had "been regarded as beings of an inferior order, and altogether unfit to associate with the white race, either in social or political relations; and so far inferior, that they had no rights which the white man was bound to respect."[57] This constituted at the time a thoroughly "fixed and universal" opinion in the Western world, "an axiom in morals as well as in politics"; men in every class and position, public and private, acted according to it and colonial legislation confirmed it. Under these circumstances, one could hardly suppose that the framers of the Constitution would agree to grant rights and privileges to Negroes that were denied them in the states. Had they done so, "they would have deserved and received universal rebuke and reprobation." The delegates to Philadelphia understood the state of public opinion in relation to the Negro and acted accordingly. Obviously, then, Negroes were "not intended to be included, and formed no part of the people who framed and adopted" the Declaration of Independence and the Constitution.[58]

Only because the climate and economy rendered slave labor unprofitable, Taney asserted, did the northern states decide to abolish the institution. But this did not, he insisted, alter in any way previously existing racial prejudices. Indeed, state legislation demonstrated conclusively that no moral revolution had occurred. For example, Rhode Island and Massachusetts prohibited interracial marriages; Connecticut forbade Negroes from entering the state to be educated unless civil authorities consented; and New Hampshire limited enrollment in the militia to white citizens. If further evidence were needed, Taney could cite the opinon of Chancellor James Kent of New York that in no portion of the country except Maine did the Negro exercise civil and political rights on an equal basis with whites. Was this not substantial proof that Negroes occupied an inferior status in society, one that was hardly commensurate with citizenship and its attendant rights and privileges?[59]

State and federal citizenship must not be confused, Taney warned, for while a state can legally naturalize its own residents and accord them any rights it deems proper, it has no power to secure to them the privileges and immunities of United States citizens. Only Congress, authorized by the Constitution to establish a uniform rule of naturalization, can exercise such a power. Moreover, no state may, by its own action, introduce into that political community created by the Constitution any new members or any persons "who were not intended to be embraced in this new political family, which the Constitution brought into existence, but were intended to be excluded from it." That this applied to Negroes was abundantly clear to the Chief Justice. Not only had Congress restricted naturalization to "free white persons," but subsequent state and federal legislation and "the conduct of the Executive Department" confirmed his conclusion that Negroes "are not included, and were not intended to be included, under the word 'citizens' in the Constitution, and can therefore claim none of the rights and privileges which that instrument provides for and secures to citizens of the United States."[60]

Two justices joined Taney in his opinion on Negro citizenship, four avoided the issue, and two others — John McLean and Benjamin R. Curtis — wrote vigorous dissents. Curtis contended that the right to confer citizenship rested with the states and that the federal government could only specify the manner in which an alien's disabilities might be removed. Free, native-born citizens of each state were thus citizens of the United States. Moreover, Curtis denied that Negroes played no part in the political community at the time of the Constitutional Convention. In at least five states, they could exercise suffrage on equal terms with whites. The framers of the Articles of Confederation must have known this, for they rejected a move by South Carolina to restrict the privileges and immunities clause to white persons. Thus Negroes, Curtis concluded, had not only helped to make up the political community which established the Constitution but in certain states had undoubtedly voted on the question of ratification. In view of these facts, they quite clearly qualified as citizens of the United States.[61]

Although many northern political leaders and newspaper editors assailed Taney's decision, they indicated much more concern about its repudiation of the Missouri Compromise than about the constitutional rights of Negroes. After all, the Chief Justice had told the Republican party that the major plank of its political platform — resistance to the further expansion of slavery — was unconstitutional. Few Republicans, on the other hand, had ever defended the rights of free Negroes. Had the Chief Justice confined his argument to the question of Negro citizenship, he might have gone virtually unchallenged, for it merely confirmed existing state and federal practices sanctioned by both major political parties. "Now my opinion," Abraham Lincoln observed, "is that the different states have the power to make a negro a citizen under the Constitution of the United States if they choose. The Dred Scott decision decides that they have not that power. If the State of Illinois had that power, I should be opposed to the exercise of it. That is all I have to say about it."[62] Lincoln's colleague, Senator Lyman Trumbull of Illinois, was even more explicit. What prompted him to repudiate the Dred Scott decision, he told the Senate, was its attempt to limit congressional powers over slavery in the territories. As for Negro citizenship, he could by no means agree to the doctrine that the Constitution required the states to place blacks and whites on an equal footing.[63]

Meanwhile, abolitionists and Negro leaders bitterly condemned Taney's decision. One Negro protest rally called it "a palpably vain, arrogant assumption, unsustained by history, justice, reason or common sense." Frederick Douglass predicted that "the National Conscience" would rise to overturn the clearly objectionable and undemocratic ruling. But Robert Purvis, a Negro abolitionist, warned his people not to comfort themselves with the thought that this decision was unconstitutional and that the whites would therefore rush to their assistance. It was, he declared, "in perfect keeping with the treatment of the colored people by the American Government from the beginning to this day." Several other Negro leaders shared this sentiment; they denounced the decision but expressed no great surprise. After all, it merely confirmed "the already well known fact that under the Constitution and Government of the United States, the colored people are nothing, and can be nothing but an alien, disfranchised and degraded class."[64]

The Dred Scott decision had a brief tenure. Several northern states moved at once to condemn and nullify its ruling on Negro citizenship. The Civil War completed its ruin. On November 29, 1862, Attorney General Edward Bates advised the Secretary of the Treasury that the qualifications for citizenship did not depend on color, race, "the degradation of a people," or the legal right to vote and hold office. "Free men of color, if born in the United States, are citizens of the United States."[65] Six years later, the Fourteenth Amendment confirmed this opinion.

Notes

[1] William Chambers, *American Slavery and Colour* (London, 1857), p. 37, and *Things as They Are in America* (London and Edinburgh, 1854), p. 354.

[2] *Appendix to the Annals of Congress,* 1 Cong., 2 sess., pp. 2205–6; 2 Cong., 1 sess., p. 1392; 11 Cong., 1 and 2 sess., p. 2569; 16 Cong., 1 sess., pp. 2600–10; *Appendix to the Congressional Debates,* 18 Cong., 2 sess., p. 91.

[3] After the admission of Maine in 1819, for example, every state that came into the Union before the end of the Civil War confined the suffrage to whites. Charles H. Wesley, "Negro Suffrage in the Period of Constitution Making, 1787–1865," *Journal of Negro History,* XXXII (1947), 154.

[4] *Journal of the House of Representatives,* 8 Cong., 1 sess., p. 224. Ten years later, however, Congress barred from employment on public or private vessels "any person or persons except citizens of the United States, *or* persons of color, natives of the United States." 2 *U.S. Stat. at Large* 809.

[5] Rayford W. Logan, "The Negro in the Quasi War, 1798–1800," *Negro History Bulletin,* XIV (1951), 128–31; Lorenzo J. Greene, "The Negro in the War of 1812 and the Civil War," *ibid.,* p. 133.

[6] *Official Opinions of the Attorneys General of the United States* (40 vols.; Washington, D.C., 1791–1948), I, 602–3. The acts under which these Negro troops were raised called only for free, able-bodied men.

[7] *Congressional Globe,* 27 Cong., 2 sess., pp. 805–7; 27 Cong., 3 sess., p. 175.

[8] *Annals of Congress,* 6 Cong., 1 sess., pp. 229–45.

[9] Charles F. Adams (ed.), *Memoirs of John Quincy Adams, Comprising Portions of His Diary from 1795–1848* (12 vols.; Philadelphia, 1875), V, 209–10.

[10] *Annals of Congress,* 16 Cong., 2 sess., pp. 57–71.

[11] *Ibid.,* pp. 1134–39.

[12] *Ibid.,* pp. 83–86, 549.

[13] *Ibid.,* pp. 48, 96, 108–9, 113, 537, 597, 601, 637–39.

[14] Everett S. Brown (ed.), *The Missouri Compromise and Presidential Politics, 1820–1825* (St. Louis, 1926), p. 21.

[15] *Congressional Debates,* 21 Cong., 1 sess., pp. 47, 201, 215; *Congressional Globe,* 30 Cong., 1 sess., pp. 602, 609–10, 612; *Appendix to the Congressional Globe,* 29 Cong., 2 sess., p. 349; 30 Cong., 1 sess., pp. 44–45, 581; 30 Cong., 2 sess., pp. 116–18; 31 Cong., 1 sess., p. 1654.

[16] [William T. Thompson], *Major Jones's Sketches of Travel* (Philadelphia, 1848), pp. 104–5. See also [William Bobo], *Glimpses of New York City* (Charleston, 1852), pp. 95–97,

125–30; A. A. Lipscomb, *North and South: Impressions of Northern Society Upon a Southerner* (Mobile, 1853), pp. 19–21; J. C. Myers, *Sketches of a Tour through the Northern and Eastern States, the Canadas & Nova Scotia* (Harrisonburg, Va., 1849), pp. 378–79, 381–82.

[17] *Compilation of the Enumeration of the Inhabitants and Statistics of the United States, as Obtained at the Department of State, from the Returns of the Sixth Census* (Washington, D.C., 1841), pp. 4–104; Albert Deutsch, "The First U.S. Census of the Insane (1840) and Its Use as Pro-Slavery Propaganda," *Bulletin of the History of Medicine*, XV (1944), 469–82; William R. Stanton, *The Leopard's Spots: Science and the American Idea of Equality, 1815–1860* (Chicago, 1960), pp. 58–59; Edward Jarvis, "Insanity among the Coloured Population of the Free States," *American Journal of the Medical Sciences*, VII (1844), 71–83.

[18] "Table of Lunacy in the United States," *Hunt's Merchants' Magazine and Commercial Review*, VIII (1843), 460–61.

[19] "Reflections on the Census of 1840," *Southern Literary Messenger*, IX (1843), 342, 344, 346–47.

[20] *Congressional Globe*, 28 Cong., 1 sess., p. 239.

[12] John C. Calhoun to Lord Richard Pakenham, April 18 and April 27, 1844, in "Proceedings of the Senate and Documents Relative to Texas," *Senate Document*, 28 Cong., 1 sess., No. 341 (1844), pp. 50–53, 65–67.

[22] Jarvis went to Louisville, Kentucky, to practice in 1837, but his antipathy to slavery prompted his return to Massachusetts six years later. He became a leading statistician, served for thirty-one years as president of the American Statistical Association, and helped to prepare the Censuses of 1850, 1860, and 1870. See William R. Leonard, "Edward Jarvis," in Allen Johnson and Dumas Malone (eds.), *Dictionary of American Biography* (22 vols.; New York, 1928–58), IX, 621–22.

[23] Stanton, *The Leopard's Spots*, pp. 58, 60; Deutsch, "The First U.S. Census of the Insane," pp. 475–76.

[24] "Errors in Sixth Census," *House Report*, 28 Cong., 1 sess., No. 580 (1844), pp. 1–9.

[25] Boston *Daily Advertiser and Patriot*, as quoted in *The Liberator*, August 18, 1843; "What Shall We Do With The Insane?" *North American Review*, LVI (1843), 172n.–73n.; James McCune Smith to the Editor, January 29, 1844, New York *Daily Tribune*, February 1, 1844; *The Liberator*, May 10 and 31, 1844.

[26] *Niles' National Register*, LXVI (May 11, 1844), 175. For a defense of Calhoun's use of the statistics, see *Brownson's Quarterly Review*, I (1844), 404–7.

[27] Adams (ed.), *Memoirs of John Quincy Adams*, XII, 22–23, 29; *Journal of the House*, 28 Cong., 1 sess., pp. 471, 877.

[28] "Errors in Sixth Census," *House Report*, 28 Cong., 1 sess., No. 580 (1844), p. 1. A Senate committee reached identical conclusions. *Senate Document*, 28 Cong., 1 sess., No. 146 (1845), pp. 1–2.

[29] John C. Calhoun to the Speaker of the House of Representatives, February 8, 1845, reprinted in *Niles' National Register*, LXVII (June 7, 1845), 218–19.

[30] Deutsch, "The First U.S. Census of the Insane," p. 478.

[11] James Freeman Clarke, "Condition of the Free Colored People of the United States," *The Christian Examiner*, LXVI, Ser. 5, IV (1859), 258.

[12] *Appendix to the Congressional Globe*, 29 Cong., 2 sess., p. 317.

[13] *Ibid.*, 30 Cong., 1 sess., pp. 579–81.

[14] *Congressional Globe*, 30 Cong., 1 sess., p. 778; *Appendix to the Congressional Globe*, 30 Cong., 1 sess., pp. 727, 730–31.

[15] *Congressional Globe*, 26 Cong., 2 sess., pp. 77, 114; *Appendix to the Congressional Globe*, 26 Cong., 2 sess., p. 27; *Official Opinions*, IV, 147–48.

[16] 9 *U.S. Stat. at Large* 497; 10 *ibid.* 308; *Congressional Globe*, 31 Cong., 1 sess., pp. 1090–93; 33 Cong., 1 sess., pp. 1057–58, 1071–73; *Frederick Douglass Paper*, March 17, 1854.

[17] *Annual Reports of the American Anti-Slavery Society . . . for the years ending May 1,*

1857, and May 1, 1858 (New York, 1859), p. 130; New York *Daily Times,* August 21, 1857.

[38] *Official Opinions,* I, 506–9; *Dred Scott* v. *Sanford,* 19 Howard 40.

[39] Charles S. Sydnor, *The Development of Southern Sectionalism, 1819–1848* (Baton Rouge, La., 1948), p. 152; Philip M. Hamer, "Great Britain, the United States and the Negro Seamen Acts, 1822–1848," *Journal of Southern History,* I (1935), 3–28.

[40] "Free Colored Seamen," *House Report,* 27 Cong., 3 sess., No. 80 (1843). A minority report upheld the acts, blamed recent southern disturbances on northern Negro seamen, pointed to racial proscription in Massachusetts, and dismissed the privileges-and-immunities clause of the Constitution as inapplicable to free Negroes. *Ibid.,* pp. 37–42.

[41] *Official Opinions,* I, 659–61; II, 426–42.

[42] Carl Brent Swisher, *Roger B. Taney* (New York, 1935), p. 154.

[43] *Official Opinions,* IV, 147–48; VII, 751–73.

[44] *The Liberator,* April 16, 1858; Barnes and Dumond (eds.), *Weld-Grimke Correspondence,* II, 792–93; Arnold Buffum to Roberts Vaux, May 16, 1834, Vaux Papers, Historical Society of Pennsylvania, Philadelphia.

[45] John Bassett Moore (ed.), *The Works of James Buchanan* (12 vols.; Philadelphia, 1908–11), VII, 236; *North Star,* July 20, August 24, 1849; *The Non-Slaveholder,* IV (1849), 191; John M. Clayton to the Editor of the Salem *Register,* as quoted in *The [10th] Annual Report of the American and Foreign Anti-Slavery Society, presented at New York, May 7, 1850. . . .* (New York, 1850), pp. 128–29.

[46] *The Liberator,* November 28, 1856; *Official Opinions,* X, 404.

[47] New York *Daily Times,* April 12, 1858.

[48] Boston *Daily Bee,* as quoted in *The Liberator,* April 16, 1858.

[49] Cleveland *Leader,* May 4, 1858.

[50] Massachusetts *Acts and Resolves,* 1857, p. 558; 1858, pp. 170–71.

[51] Charles Sumner, *Works* (15 vols.; Boston, 1870–83), V, 497–98.

[52] *American State Papers. Documents, Legislative and Executive, of the Congresses of the United States. . . .* (38 vols.; Washington, D.C., 1832–61), Class VII: Post Office, p. 27.

[53] 2 *U.S. Stat. at Large* 594. Re-enacted without change in 1825. 4 *ibid.* 104.

[54] Jay, *Miscellaneous Writings on Slavery,* p. 233; William C. Nell, *The Colored Patriots of the American Revolution, with Sketches of Several Distinguished Colored Persons: To which is added a Brief Survey of the Condition and Prospects of Colored Americans* (Boston, 1855), p. 312.

[55] *Congressional Globe,* 37 Cong., 2 sess., pp. 1260, 1390, 1626, 2231–32, 2262–63; Sumner, *Works,* VI, 385–88.

[56] J. H. Van Evrie, *The Dred Scott Decision* (New York, 1860), p. iii.

[57] *Dred Scott* v. *Sanford,* 19 Howard 403, 407.

[58] *Ibid.,* 407–10.

[59] *Ibid.,* 412–16.

[60] *Ibid.,* 404–406, 419–22.

[61] *Ibid.,* 572–82.

[62] Roy P. Basler (ed.), *The Collected Works of Abraham Lincoln* (8 vols.; New Brunswick, N.J., 1953), III, 179.

[63] *Congressional Globe,* 35 Cong., 1 sess., p. 1965.

[64] *The Liberator,* April 10, 1857, July 9, 1858; Philip S. Foner (ed.), *The Life and Writings of Frederick Douglass* (4 vols.; New York, 1950–55), II, 411.

[65] *Official Opinions,* X, 382–413.

Suggestions for Further Reading

There is no general reader on the ante-bellum free blacks. Early studies still of value include Carter G. Woodson, *The Education of the Negro Prior to 1861* (New York: Putnam, 1915), and *The History of the Negro Church* (Washington, D.C.: Associated Publishers, 1921), and E. Franklin Frazier, *The Free Negro Family in the United States* (Nashville, Tenn.: Fisk University Press, 1932).

Excellent studies of the Southern free Negroes are John Hope Franklin, *The Free Negro in North Carolina, 1790–1860* (Chapel Hill; University of North Carolina Press, 1943); Luther P. Jackson, *Free Negro Labor and Property Holding in Virginia, 1830–1860* (New York: Appleton-Century, 1942); and W. R. Hogan and E. A. Davis, eds., *William Johnson's Natchez: The Ante-Bellum Diary of a Free Negro* (Baton Rouge: Louisiana State University Press, 1951). Leon Litwack, *North of Slavery: The Negro in the Free States, 1790–1860* (Chicago: University of Chicago Press, 1961), treats the Northern free blacks. Emma Lou Thornbrough, *The Negro in Indiana* (Indianapolis: Indianapolis Historical Bureau, 1957), and Constance M. Green, *The Secret City: A History of Race Relations in the Nation's Capital* (Princeton, N.J.: Princeton University Press, 1967), include data on the free black communities in those localities prior to the Civil War.

William H. Pease and Jane H. Pease, *Black Utopia: Negro Communal Experiments in America* (Madison: Wisconsin State Historical Society, 1965) is an interesting study of this unusual phase of black life. Howard Bell, *A Survey of the Negro Convention Movement, 1830–1861* (New York, Arno, 1970) is definitive on this aspect of free Negro activity.

A Wadsworth Series:
Explorations in the Black Experience

General Editors

John H. Bracey, Jr.
Northern Illinois University

August Meier
Kent State University

Elliott Rudwick
Kent State University

Robert C. Weaver, "The Villain—Racial Covenants"; Robert C. Weaver, "The Role of the Federal Government"; Herman H. Long and Charles S. Johnson, "The Role of Real Estate Organizations"; Loren Miller, "Supreme Court Covenant Decision—An Analysis"; Herbert Hill, "Demographic Change and Racial Ghettos: The Crisis of American Cities"; Roy Reed, "Resegregation: A Problem in the Urban South"

4 The Process of Ghettoization: Internal Pressures

Arnold Rose and Caroline Rose, "The Significance of Group Identification"; W. E. B. Du Bois, "The Social Evolution of the Black South"; Allan H. Spear, "The Institutional Ghetto"; Chicago Commission on Race Relations, "The Matrix of the Black Community"; E. Franklin Frazier, "The Negro's Vested Interest in Segregation"; George A. Nesbitt, "Break Up the Black Ghetto?"; Lewis G. Watts, Howard E. Freeman, Helen M. Hughes, Robert Morris, and Thomas F. Pettigrew, "Social Attractions of the Ghetto"

5 Future Prospects

Karl E. Taeuber and Alma F. Taeuber, "Is the Negro an Immigrant Group?"; H. Paul Friesema, "Black Control of Central Cities: The Hollow Prize"

Suggestions for Further Reading

Black Matriarchy: Myth or Reality?

Introduction

1 The Frazier Thesis

E. Franklin Frazier, "The Negro Family in America"; E. Franklin Frazier, "The Matriarchate"

2 The Question of African Survivals

Melville J. Herskovits, "On West African Influences"

3 The Frazier Thesis Applied

Charles S. Johnson, "The Family in the Plantation South"; Lee Rainwater, "Crucible of Identity: The Negro Lower-Class Family"; Elliot Liebow, "Fathers without Children"

4 The Moynihan Report

Daniel P. Moynihan, "The Negro Family: The Case for National Action"; Hylan Lewis and Elizabeth Herzog, "The Family: Resources for Change"

5 New Approaches

Herbert H. Hyman and John Shelton Reed, " 'Black Matriarchy' Reconsidered: Evidence from Secondary Analysis of Sample Surveys"; Virginia Heyer Young, "Family and Childhood in a Southern Negro Community"

Suggestions for Further Reading

Black Workers and Organized Labor

Introduction

Sidney H. Kessler, "The Organization of Negroes in the Knights of Labor"; Bernard Mandel, "Samuel Gompers and the Negro Workers, 1886–1914"; Paul B. Worthman, "Black Workers and Labor Unions in Birmingham, Alabama, 1897–1904"; William M. Tuttle, Jr., "Labor Conflict and Racial Violence: The Black Worker in Chicago, 1894–1919"; Sterling D. Spero and Abram L. Harris, "The Negro Longshoreman, 1870–1930"; Sterling D. Spero and Abram L. Harris, "The Negro and the IWW"; Brailsford R. Brazeal, "The Brotherhood of Sleeping Car Porters"; Horace R. Cayton and George S. Mitchell, "Blacks and Organized Labor in the Iron and Steel Industry, 1880–1939"; Herbert R. Northrup, "Blacks in the United Automobile Workers Union"; Sumner M. Rosen, "The CIO Era, 1935–1955"; William Kornhauser, "The Negro Union Official: A Study of Sponsorship and Control"; Ray Marshall, "The Negro and the AFL-CIO"

Suggestions for Further Reading

The Black Sociologists: The First Half Century

Introduction

1 Early Pioneers

W. E. B. Du Bois, "The Study of the Negro Problems"; W. E. B. Du Bois, "The Organized Life of Negroes"; George E. Haynes, "Conditions among Negroes in the Cities"

2 In the Robert E. Park Tradition

Charles S. Johnson, "Black Housing in Chicago"; E. Franklin Frazier, "The Pathology of Race Prejudice"; E. Franklin Frazier, "La Bourgeoisie Noire"; Charles S. Johnson, "The Plantation during the Depression"; Bertram W. Doyle, "The Etiquette of Race Relations—Past, Present, and Future"; E. Franklin Frazier, "The Black Matriarchate"; Charles S. Johnson, "Patterns of Negro Segregation"; E. Franklin Frazier, "The New Negro Middle Class"

3 Black Metropolis: Sociological Masterpiece

St. Clair Drake and Horace Cayton, "The Measure of the Man"

Conflict and Competition: Studies in the Recent Black Protest Movement

Introduction

1 Nonviolent Direct Action

Joseph S. Himes, "The Functions of Racial Conflict"; August Meier, "Negro Protest Movements and Organizations"; Lewis M. Killian and Charles U. Smith, "Negro Protest Leaders in a Southern Community"; Ralph H. Hines and James E. Pierce, "Negro Leadership after the Social Crisis: An Analysis of Leadership Changes in Montgomery, Alabama"; Jack L. Walker, "The Functions of Disunity: Negro Leadership in a Southern City"; Gerald A. McWorter and Robert L. Crain, "Subcommunity Gladiatorial Competition: Civil Rights Leadership as a Competitive Process"; August Meier, "On the Role of Martin Luther King"

2 By Any Means Necessary

Inge Powell Bell, "Status Discrepancy and the Radical Rejection of Nonviolence"; Donald von Eschen, Jerome Kirk, and Maurice Pinard, "The Disintegration of the Negro Non-Violent Movement"; Allen J. Matusow, "From Civil Rights to Black Power: The Case of SNCC, 1960–1966"; Joel D. Aberbach and Jack L. Walker, "The Meanings of Black Power: A Comparison of White and Black Interpretations of a Political Slogan"; David O. Sears and T. M. Tomlinson, "Riot Ideology in Los Angeles: A Study of Negro Attitudes"; Robert Blauner, "Internal Colonialism and Ghetto Revolt"; Charles V. Hamilton, "Conflict, Race, and System-Transformation in the United States"

Suggestions for Further Reading

Rosita Jackson
2 of Dec.
1063 - Rise Of Facism